10 Steps to Confident Entertaining

1. Keep a well-stocked bar.

2. Equip your kitchen with purchases that reflect the way you like to cook and entertain.

3. Use the concept of a butler's pantry as an organizational tool to serve your entertaining needs.

4. Use an index card file for a logical, systematic approach to entertaining.

5. Make sure your invitation tells your guests everything they need to know about your party.

6. Relax. The most enjoyable parties for guest and host alike are given by a relaxed host who lets his or her own personality shine through.

7. Pay special attention to introductions, initiating conversations and guiding the party's course. Remembering something special about each guest and sharing it in a warm and personal way takes a party over the top.

8. Create a theme. Themes lend a joie de vivre to any party. Simple themes and personal touches are more meaningful than re-creating someone else's ideas to a "T." Never overdo.

9. Hire help if you need it. Hiring the right help for the right event allows a host to be a host and ensures a party's success.

10. A party without a host is like a ship without a captain. The time and care that you devote to preparing for a party will ensure that you shine as a host.

5 Pointers for Developing Your Own Entertaining Style

1. Don't let popular trends lead you by the nose. Respond to things you really love when acquiring items for entertaining.

2. It's not what you have but how you use it. If all you have is one rose and one vase, make it a focal point. Remember that simplicity makes a more distinctive statement than going overboard.

3. Pay special attention to lighting. It sets the tone for a party and is an all-important element in transforming an everyday scene into a special-occasion setting.

4. Start a collection of things that can be used for entertaining. This is a practical way to lend a personal touch to your environment.

5. Arrange furniture to create conversation areas. Good conversation is vital to a party. Determine a traffic flow and set up accordingly. Don't forget that fresh flowers and candles in other rooms will encourage your guests to move around, mix and mingle.

alpha
books

The System for a Flawless Party

Use 4×6 or 5×7 index cards. Title each card with the party theme and date. Clip the cards together with a paper clip and file according to year after the party for a handy entertaining reference guide.

CARD #1: Your Guest List and Menu Card

Make a complete guest list on one side. Allow room to jot down personal information about each guest to review before the party. Check off guests as they RSVP; note where follow-up calls are needed. List the menu on the other side. Refer to the card when planning future parties to avoid serving the same menu to the same guests.

CARD #2: Your Shopping List

Divide one side of the card into 4 columns: produce, dairy, meat/fowl/fish, miscellaneous. Read through each recipe, entering the ingredient in the proper column. On the other side, write down the name, address, and phone numbers of sources for specialty orders. Enter a pick-up date and time or the scheduled delivery date and time.

CARD #3: Table Setting, Accessories, and Special Errands Card

On the front of the card, record your table design, flowers, candles, and so on. On the back of the card, make a list of needed items after taking an inventory of the bar and butler's pantry.

CARD #4: Make Ahead/Do Ahead Card

On the front of the card, list all the recipes that you will be making and where the recipe can be found. Read through the recipes to determine make-ahead preparations and date each recipe accordingly. On the back of the card, make a checklist for polishing silver or picking up linens from the laundry, making place cards, arranging flowers, setting the table, or any other related tasks.

CARD #5: Day-of Card

On the front of the card, make a complete list of everything left to do the day of the party. On the back of the card, list last-minute food preparations, such as what time the roast comes out of the oven, what time to put dishes on to warm, and when to warm the bread. Try to include everything. The simplest things are easy to forget when you're involved with your guests.

CARD #6: Comments Card

Use this card after the party to jot down your own comments about the party—stumbling blocks, where extra organization or planning would have been beneficial, guests that didn't get along, and so on. Don't forget to include special highlights or guests at the party.

CARD #7: Miscellaneous Card

This is an optional card to use for parties that have extra details that are specific to a particular type of party. For example, what dishes are being brought to a potluck dinner, things to ask friends to bring when you are cooking together, a time schedule for serving a "dinner-at-eight," and so on.

CARD #8: Ongoing Resources Card

Keep this card at the back of your card file to use as a master list of vendors and resources for party food and supplies. Include pertinent information such as name, address, phone, and the name of a contact person.

The COMPLETE IDIOT'S GUIDE TO Entertaining

by Holly Collins and Thomas Randleman

alpha books

A Division of Macmillan General Reference
A Simon & Schuster Macmillan Company
1633 Broadway, New York, NY 10019

International Standard Book Number: 0-02-861095-4
Library of Congress Catalog Card Number: 96-084581

98 97 96   8 7 6 5 4 3 2 1

Interpretation of the printing code: the rightmost number of the first series of numbers is the year of the book's printing; the rightmost number of the second series of numbers is the number of the book's printing. For example, a printing code of 96-1 shows that the first printing occurred in 1996.

Printed in the United States of America

Publisher
Theresa Murtha

Editor
Nancy Mikhail

Production Editor
Michael Thomas

Copy Editor
Christine Prakel

Cover Designer
Mike Freeland

Illustrator
Judd Winick

Designer
Barbara Kordesh

Indexer
Ginny Bess

Production Team
Angela Calvert
Kim Cofer
Laure Robinson
Pamela Woolf

Contents at a Glance

Contents

Foreword

To paraphrase Horace, good hosts are like good generals, their genius is not revealed unless a mishap occurs. Good generals have well-thought-out orders of battle, have contingency plans for any possible turn of events, and see to details. They also enjoy their work, calmly exercising order and control over the exciting rush of events.

When you open your door to welcome guests, both you and they will feel confident and relaxed if there is an air of quiet, competent control over the festivities that are about to begin. The concepts and suggestions provided in *The Complete Idiot's Guide to Entertaining* will help you become a four-star host. From strategic planning, to tactical details; from proven recipes to handling mercenaries; from examples of successful engagements to tips on comportment under fire; this book offers all you need to know to be a host par excellence.

During thirty years as a foreign service officer, I have had the good fortune to entertain and be entertained in cities as diverse as Rome, Copenhagen, New York, Prague, Ottawa, Belgrade, Sofia, Athens, Vancouver, Madrid, Cleveland, and Detroit. Wherever I've been, the mixture of food and friendship has provided the most lasting memories. Holly Collins and Thomas Randleman have produced a valuable guide to getting the mixture right.

Donald T. Wismer
Consul General of Canada

Introduction

When you think about hosting a party, what's the first thing that pops into your mind? The party itself, right? There you are among happy guests; the setting is lovely and the food delicious. You're off to a great start. But wait a minute! Is this delightful image the beginning or the grand finale? In *The Complete Idiot's Guide to Entertaining*, we intend to start with a blank canvas; long before the doorbell rings, cocktails are poured or candles are lit.

Rest assured we'll provide you with imaginative and fun party themes, design ideas, and menus to host all types of occasions. However, it's not our starting point, because that's not what makes a party successful. It's the background organization and tending to details never seen by your guests that will propel you from fledgling party giver to gracious and winning host. Certainly the flowers, the music, the food, and the wine are all important elements of any party, but the art of hosting is what truly makes for memorable occasions.

The Complete Idiot's Guide to Entertaining gives you a clear and realistic understanding of what entertaining is all about rather than simply focusing on particular events and party designs. People who make entertaining a part of their life instead of approaching party-giving as a sporadic project are those who happily flourish as hosts. The accouterments of a party that impress your guests when they walk through your door, and the food and drink they enjoy at your party, are "finishing touches" to a way of thinking about entertaining. We hope this way of thinking will soon become a rewarding part of your lifestyle.

Here are some essential concepts we'll focus on:

➤ Some of the most important time you can devote to entertaining is when you aren't planning a party.

➤ Your personal sense of style and hospitality, not someone else's, are the best asset to all your entertaining.

➤ Good old-fashioned manners never grow old.

➤ The finishing touches and design details for a party should be subtle and personal, never a monumental project.

➤ Every host should know why, when, and how to hire help for a party.

How To Use This Book

The Complete Idiot's Guide to Entertaining walks you through a step-by-step planning tour, coordinating separate elements that together comprise a successful party. We'll weigh the importance of each aspect that goes into entertaining, and ultimately send you on your way to modify, improvise, and create your own style as a successful host. The framework for planning, organization, timing, and party plans is covered in five parts.

Part 1, "It's All in the Planning," will get you into the groove of a method for entertaining that fits gracefully into a busy lifestyle. The world can't come to a screeching halt for you to plan a party. By organizing and outfitting long before there's a party in the making, you will have a system in place to serve all your parties with ease and efficiency. Then, a party file will efficiently guide you from the initial invitation to the last good-bye.

Part 2, "The Mostest…It's You," focuses on an important criteria for becoming a confident and gracious host—doing things *your* way, not someone else's. Also, we'll talk about the real dynamic that brings a party to life. How you communicate with your guests conveys your own brand of genuine warmth and hospitality. That's how your good party becomes a great one.

Part 3, "The Magic: Menus and Party Designs," provides party plans for many types of occasions, ranging from casual get-togethers to sophisticated events. These chapters also include helpful advice, fun ideas, and specific organization tips that pertain to each particular type of party. Use these schemes and themes as a starting point to inspire your own personalized parties.

Part 4, "Special Situations," deals with those certain entertaining situations that tend to test your confidence. It's that good old "How did I ever get myself into this one?" feeling. Don't feel overwhelmed. This section offers insights, pointers, and encouragement to assuage your concerns. Finally, there's a time when the host/guest relationship strikes a different balance from most entertaining situations. We'll talk about this relationship in a chapter on weekend guests.

Part 5, "Knowing What It Takes," will speed you on your way to making practical and intelligent decisions about engaging help for parties. If organized properly, most casual events don't require help. But, certainly, it's a given that you'll need expert assistance for a big-occasion party. The common downfall is analyzing the gray areas in-between. Most of us tend to err by downplaying service needs when we feel we can slip by without, or not hiring help appropriate to the occasion. Part 5 also examines an important responsibility of a good host—special consideration for fellow entertainers. Having read this far, you know by now that acknowledging a host's efforts with an appropriately thoughtful gesture and considerate deportment is at the top of every successful entertainer's list. We will explore a broad range of possibilities for the right help for different party situations.

Extras

The Complete Idiot's Guide to Entertaining is filled with plenty of well-weathered advice, tips, and cautions to abet your entertaining endeavors. Look for these helping-hand elements in each section:

Sage Advice
Drawn from many sources and walks of life, these are words of wisdom or humor we can all relate to.

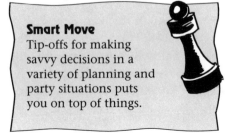

Smart Move
Tip-offs for making savvy decisions in a variety of planning and party situations puts you on top of things.

The Extra Mile
Tried-and-true things to do that are sure to make you shine as an accomplished and thoughtful host.

Good Spirits
Offers appropriate cocktail and wine suggestions to accompany the party themes and menus.

Reality Bites
Here are some realistic considerations about pitfalls to avoid. Store them in your memory bank and they'll keep you on your toes.

Cook's Notes

Supplementary advice and cautions to speed along your cooking and serving.

Designer Notes

Suggestions to aid and abet, inspire or improve your personal style and party preparations.

Acknowledgments

The writing of this book was a rather spontaneous result of another endeavor. We'd like to extend our sincere thanks and appreciation to Liz Fowler, Colette Gibbons, Richard Gildenmeister, Sidney Long, Jenny and Trevor Jones, and Dorothy Valerian for their continued support and advice over the last few years.

A very special thanks to our friends and experts who were directly involved in this book. Megan Newman got the ball rolling. Kurt Hebel, our wine authority, contributed his astute palate to many of our "Good Spirits." Paula Khanna deftly administered catering advice. Thanks to John Kelly, Alice Stefanek, and Bill Tyler for offering their famous family recipes. We appreciate Don Doskey and Charles Phillips, tasters and theme testers, for honing the art of being a good guest. Katie Collins and Holly Rogel were able recipe testers, and Scott Ballantine and Bill Russell were able eaters! Thanks to Ed Wrobel, a most patient florist, and Sue Wrobel for much friendly support. Holly Collins would also like to thank John Collins for bearing with sacrificed weekends and topsy-turvy months, Liz Collins for her recipe contribution and daughterly understanding, and Clare Collins for professional encouragement and support.

Finally, special thanks to our editor at Macmillan, Nancy Mikhail, and our feisty agent, Blanche Brann.

Special Thanks from the Publisher to the Technical Reviewer

The Complete Idiot's Guide to Entertaining was reviewed by an expert who not only checked the accuracy of what you'll learn in this book, but also provided invaluable insight and suggestions to ensure that you learn everything you need to know about entertaining.

Our special thanks are extended to:

Emily Nolan is a highly respected recipe developer and cookbook editor in New York City. A former part-time caterer in North Carolina, doing everything from food prep to full-service banquets, she soon found herself as a head chef in Maine where she cooked for the Fresh-Air program. Later on, she worked for Philadelphia's well known *Le Bus*, supplying Dean and Deluca, Le Bec Fin, The Four Seasons, and other prestigious clients with their bakery needs.

Part 1
It's All in the Planning

This section walks you through the basic elements of entertaining. Once your bar, kitchen, and party accouterments are up to speed, keeping them there so they require little or no last-minute attendance eliminates a lot of pre-party errands, tasks, and hassles. The objective is to be set up and ready to entertain at the drop of a hat.

Advice on menu planning and organizing cooking activities streamlines the process. But, most important of all, a schedule and index card system pave the way to being a calm, cool, and collected host of any event.

Chapter 1

Stocking Your Bar

In This Chapter

➤ Your basic bar tools

➤ Glassware

➤ Classic cocktails and seasonal libations

➤ The elaborate bar

➤ Cocktails and dinner wines

➤ Toasting

The first recorded use of the word *cocktail* was in 1806. American gents, inspired by the English affinity for punches, were mixing up drinks they called "bracers." One was dubbed a *cocktail*. However, there are many tales that claim the origin of this peculiar word, fated to become an American ritual. An amusing story that dates back to the Revolutionary War credits a Frenchman smitten by a charming American innkeeper.

"To Betsy and her marvelous drink!" he exclaimed. "It offers to the palate the same delightful sensations as the cock's tailfeathers offer to the eye! Vive le cocktail!" With that, Betsy proceeded to stir his drink with a cock's feather.

Sage Advice
Dorothy Parker on the fairest of them all: "I like to have a Martini/Two at the very most/After three I'm under the table/After four I'm under my host."

Whatever the truth of its beginnings, the cocktail managed to indomitably survive a racy past and evolve into an American social tradition. But until World War I, cocktails remained within the domain of men and taverns. The cocktail party hadn't made the scene, and mixed drinks weren't imbibed before a dinner party. Once cocktails came home, hostesses welcomed a sociable activity that occupied the awkward lingering between the arrival of guests and the serving of dinner. But it wasn't until Prohibition and the dawn of the speakeasy that women publicly joined a pastime once dominated by men.

It was the poor quality of bathtub gin that propelled the invention of a great variety of concoctions to embellish lousy booze. Between the 1920s and the 1930s over 100 recipes for mixed drinks were invented. Immortalizing the cocktail, Cole Porter sang about them, Ernest Hemingway wrote about them, Bette Davis performed with them, and FDR made history over them. Despite the cocktail's waxing and waning in popularity through the ages, we've been stocking our bars ever since.

Your Basic Bar Tools

If you want to be able to concoct classic cocktails and today's popular mixed drinks, make sure your bar is stocked with the following spirits, mixers, garnishes, and equipment:

Spirits:

➤ Vodka

➤ Gin

➤ Amber Rum

➤ Bourbon

➤ Scotch

➤ Canadian or Irish Whiskey

➤ Tequila

➤ Triple Sec or Cointreau

➤ Dry and sweet vermouth

➤ Dry white and red wines

Basic mixers:

➤ Mineral water, club soda or seltzer, tonic

➤ Sodas: cola, ginger ale, lemon/lime

➤ Flavored and unflavored sparkling waters

➤ Fruit juices: orange, grapefruit, cranberry, tomato

Cocktail garnishes:

➤ Oranges, lemons, and limes

➤ Cocktail olives, onions, and cherries

➤ Bitters

➤ Tabasco, Worcestershire, horseradish

➤ Sugar cubes

Basic bar equipment:

➤ Ice bucket and tongs

➤ Jigger and pony measures (a *jigger* is 1 $^1/_2$ ounces; a *pony* is 1 ounce)

➤ Can and bottle openers and corkscrews

➤ Paring knife and zester

➤ Muddler or pestle (a tool for smashing or grinding)

➤ Bar towels

➤ Cocktail shaker and strainer

➤ Coasters or cocktail napkins

➤ Long-handled bar spoon

Basic bar equipment.

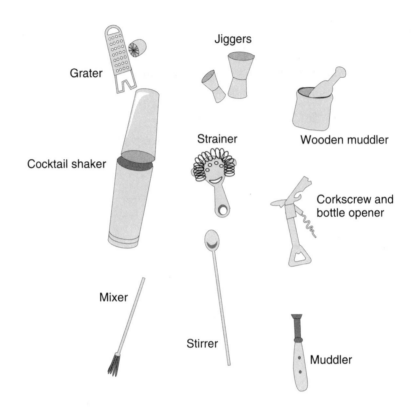

The art of mixing a good cocktail depends on the quality of the ingredients and the ratio of alcohol to mixer. Always buy quality brand-name liquors and use fresh juices, sodas, tonics, and homemade sugar syrup. When making a cocktail, follow a recipe and use the appropriate measures. Only the most experienced bartender can "eyeball" proportions. Today, many people are opting for lighter alcohol drinks during the cocktail hour. Always keep a supply of white wine on hand for parties. Also, offer a selection of interesting sparkling waters and special juices for non-drinkers.

Cook's Notes

To make sugar syrup, combine 2 parts sugar and 1 part water in a saucepan. Bring to a boil and boil for five minutes. If the sugar isn't completely dissolved, turn the heat to a simmer and cook a few more minutes.

When Your Budget's Tight

Stocking a bar from scratch calls for a hefty expenditure, so if you know your guests' preferences, stock accordingly and collect bottles over time rather than all at once. One way to gradually supply a bar is to feature a "special occasion" drink such as Mint Juleps for Derby Day, Margaritas for a south-of-the-border party, or Bloody Marys for a birthday brunch. Have a supply of white wine as an alternative choice. Throwing a large cocktail party doesn't always demand a full bar. If your budget is tight and this type of fête is your heart's desire, consider serving champagne only (with some still wine available). Invitations could read, "We're popping corks on (date) to celebrate (occasion)." Use the following guide to determine how much liquor and wine to buy for a party:

1 Fifth = 750ml

1 Pony = 1 ounce

1 Jigger = 1 $^1/_2$ ounce

1 Fifth serves 10–16 drinks

2 Fifths serves 15–24 drinks

3 Fifths serves 20–40 drinks

4 Fifths serves 40–65 drinks

1 750 ml bottle of wine serves 6 glasses

1 case of champagne serves 90–100 drinks

Good Spirits

"Come quickly, I am tasting stars!" said the blind monk Dom Perignon upon his first taste of champagne. Legend credits the Benedictine head of the wine-making Abbey of Hautvillers with the invention of our bubbly celebration drink.

Glassware

You can embellish your bar scene with a score of glassware designated for various types of cocktails. The classic tall-stemmed Martini glass with a "v" shaped bowl is also used for serving Manhattans and Margaritas. Old Fashioneds and "on-the-rocks" drinks are generally served in a wide-mouthed tumbler. Tall, iced tea glasses are appropriate for high-balls mixed with soda, Bloody Marys, tonic, and fruit juice drinks. Classic stemless Mint Julep cups can double for serving eggnog. A champagne coupe with a wide, cupped bowl can also be used for Margaritas and Daiquiris. The tall, narrow champagne flute allows sparkling wines to hold their bubbles longer.

There is also a confusing array of wine glasses to choose from. However, the best glasses for serving wines are clear glass with about a ten-ounce bowl to allow room for swirling a wine to release its bouquet. Wine glasses that very slightly close in at the rim help to concentrate the bouquet and will also help a white wine keep its chill. When purchasing any stemmed glass, if the diameter of the base is fairly equal to the widest diameter of the bowl, it indicates good design. For starters, an all-purpose tumbler and an all-purpose wine glass should suit your bar needs.

Wash good glassware by hand in warm, soapy water. Rinse completely and dry with a linen towel. Allow glasses to cool on a clean towel before wiping dry because glasses are more likely to fracture when handled while they are warm. Drinks and wines should always be served in sparkling clean glassware. Store glassware that is infrequently used upside down to prevent dust from collecting. Always check your glasses before a party to see if they require dusting or washing.

Cocktail glassware.

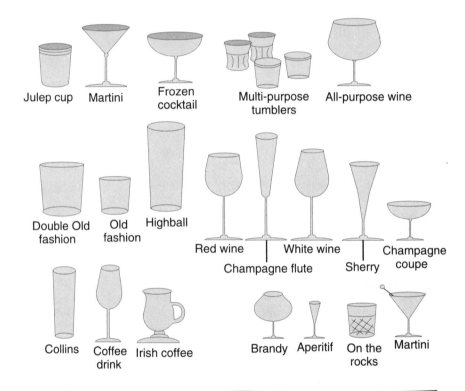

Julep cup Martini Frozen cocktail Multi-purpose tumblers All-purpose wine

Double Old fashion Old fashion Highball Red wine White wine Champagne coupe
Champagne flute Sherry

Collins Coffee drink Irish coffee Brandy Aperitif On the rocks Martini

Designer Notes

Legend has it that the first champagne coupe was modeled after Helen of Troy's breast. Years later, Marie Antoinette re-created a far more generous coupe shaped to her own breast.

The Bar Set-Up

When setting up a bar for a party, your most important consideration is traffic flow. People simply tend to collect around "the bar." If necessary, rearrange furniture so your guests don't become corralled. Place hors d'oeuvres and canapés away from the bar area to encourage movement.

Don't set up the bar near any cooking activities. Make sure that the area you choose for setting up the bar allows enough space to neatly arrange everything you need: bar tools, drink garnishes, spirits, wine, mixers, and a damp towel for wiping up spills; plus enough elbow room for mixing drinks. Have a bottle of white wine chilling in an ice bucket (keep extra wine bottles in the fridge for quick replenishments) and another ice bucket to use for making mixed drinks. For a big party, buy an inexpensive cooler to ensure that you have plenty of ice on hand.

Smart Move

Always plan on more ice than you think you'll need. A good cocktail demands lots of ice—too little ice and the cubes actually melt faster. Stow your cooler of ice in a convenient place. If you set up the bar on a card table, cover the table with a cloth and keep the cooler under it. An alternative is to station the bar near a door and keep the cooler of ice outdoors.

Designer Notes

Galvanized pails make great ice buckets and wine coolers. Dress them up to suit your theme with flowers, spray paint, napkins, crepe paper, and so forth.

Plan the same arrangement for a self-serve bar, allowing some extra room for people to move around the bar area. People usually linger and chat while mixing drinks. Self-serve bars can quickly become disheveled. Check the bar periodically and tidy up as necessary. For large parties it's a good idea to set up two self-serve bars. Distance them from each other to balance traffic flow. Use wine coolers large enough to accommodate two to three bottles of wine so they don't require constant tending. Depending on the occasion, you may choose to limit the choices available rather than offer a full bar. For example, prepare a pitcher or two of a seasonal mixed drink and offer a selection of wine and beer.

Classic Cocktails and Seasonal Libations

Since the advent of the cocktail, literally hundreds of drinks have come in and out of fashion. Nowadays, even though wines and specialty beers are the preferred spirits, the cocktail seems to be enjoying another renaissance. The following is a guide for preparing the classics, plus a few seasonal drinks.

Classic Dry Martini

Pack a cocktail shaker with ice and add 4 ounces of gin and $1/2$ ounce of dry vermouth. Stir or shake (much debate goes on over which is correct—stirrers claim shaking bruises the gin; shakers say it releases just the right amount of water from the ice cubes) and strain into a chilled martini glass. Garnish with a green olive or twist of lemon— a pickled onion turns a Martini into a Gibson.

Manhattan Cocktail

Pack a cocktail shaker with ice and add $1^1/2$ ounces Canadian whiskey, $3/4$ ounce sweet vermouth, and a few dashes of bitters. Stir well, strain into a chilled glass, and garnish with a stemmed cherry.

Old Fashioned

Place a sugar cube in a cocktail tumbler and saturate with bitters. Add an orange and a lemon wedge and crush with a muddler. Add 2 ounces of bourbon and stir well. Pack the glass with ice and fill with soda or water. Garnish with a stemmed cherry.

Margarita

The origin of the Margarita is subject for hot debate in California and the Southwest. Most agree the drink hails from the 1940s. One story credits the Margarita to a bartender at the Kentucky Club in El Paso, Texas. He rustled up the drink for a fetching young lady (so named) who desired something less punishing than her boyfriend's tequila shots. Rub the rim of a chilled glass with lemon or lime juice and lightly dip into salt. Our favorite formula combines equal parts Tequila, Triple Sec, and freshly squeezed lime juice. Use $1^1/2$ ounces each per drink.

Gin, Vodka, or Rum and Tonic

Pour 2 ounces of liquor into a tall glass filled with ice. Add fresh tonic and garnish with a lime wedge. The proper proportion of liquor to mix is 60 percent liquor, 40 percent mix.

Bloody Mary

Combine $1/4$ ounce lemon juice, and dashes of Tabasco, Worcestershire, horseradish (optional), and celery salt to taste. Add $1\,1/2$ ounces vodka and 4 ounces tomato juice. Stir well, pour over ice, and garnish with a celery stalk.

Seabreeze

Fill a tall glass with ice. Add $1\,1/2$ ounces of vodka and 4 ounces cranberry juice. Top with 1 ounce grapefruit juice. Garnish with a lime wedge.

Daiquiri

Fill a cocktail shaker with cracked ice. Add $1/2$ jigger (or $3/4$ ounce) sugar syrup, $1\,1/2$ jiggers (or $2\,1/4$ ounces) freshly squeezed lime juice, and 6 jiggers (or 9 ounces) rum. Stir well and strain into 3 or 4 chilled coupes.

Southern Style Mint Julep

Place 4–5 large, fresh mint leaves in a tall glass. Add two sugar cubes and crush with a muddler. Fill the glass with ice and pour in 2 ounces of Kentucky bourbon. Stir well and garnish with mint leaves.

Mimosa

Pour $1\,1/2$ ounces of orange juice into a champagne flute. Slowly fill the glass with champagne.

Rum Eggnog

Fill a cocktail shaker with ice cubes. Add 1 egg white, $1/4$ ounce sugar syrup, 1 barspoon powdered sugar, $3\,1/2$ ounces milk, $3/4$ ounce cream, and $1\,1/2$ ounces amber rum. Shake well and strain into a glass over ice. Garnish with a dash of freshly grated nutmeg.

Mulled Wine

In a medium saucepan, place 1 lump sugar, the juice of $1/2$ lemon, 1 dash bitters, $1/2$ teaspoon cinnamon, $1/2$ teaspoon nutmeg, and 5 ounces red wine. Bring to a boil, stirring to dissolve sugar. Serve at once in an attractive mug or heatproof glass.

Irish Coffee

Place $1\,1/2$ ounces Irish whiskey into a heat-resistant glass mug or coffee cup. Add 1 barspoon brown sugar. Stir and fill with strong, hot coffee. Float lightly whipped heavy cream on top.

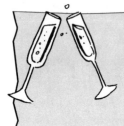

Good Spirits

Ten shakes is the appropriate number for a drink mixed in a cocktail shaker. The proper proportion of alcohol to mix is 60/40.

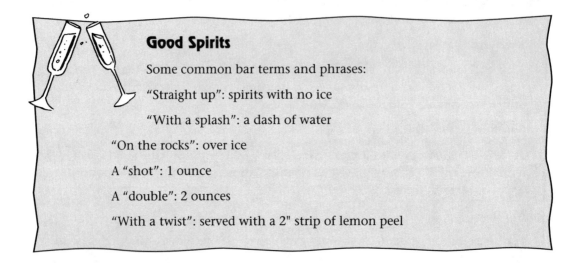

Good Spirits

Some common bar terms and phrases:

"Straight up": spirits with no ice

"With a splash": a dash of water

"On the rocks": over ice

A "shot": 1 ounce

A "double": 2 ounces

"With a twist": served with a 2" strip of lemon peel

The Elaborate Bar

If you entertain frequently or have a knack for flair, you may want to invest in a more extensive bar. People who develop a taste for a particular distilled spirit usually become aficionados of a favorite brand. For instance, scotch drinkers have a wealth of different specialized malts to choose from. Bourbon drinkers tend to find their preferred mash or blend. Bombay Sapphire gin is infused with an extra dose of herbs, giving it a pronounced flavor. Russian vodkas and flavored vodkas have also enjoyed popularity in recent years.

You may want to embellish your bar with an international mix of popular cordials or digestifs such as B&B, Sambucca, and Tia Maria to serve with coffee. Exploring the vast realm of aperitifs, sherries, Madeiras, ports, and cognacs introduces a note of sophistication to your bar. The initiate may find some of the aperitifs quite bitter or herbal-tasting. However, many of them are so delightful they're definitely worth investigating. The following is a brief introduction to aperitifs and digestifs. Let your taste buds be your guide.

Aperitifs

The word *aperitif* comes from the Latin *aperiere* meaning "to open." They open the appetite for the meal to come and offer a pleasant variation from cocktails or wine before dinner. Europeans have imbibed aperitifs for centuries. They can be a mixed drink based on wines or champagnes or a fortified wine such as vermouths, sherries, or Dubonnet. Aperitifs are lower in alcohol than hard liquor and higher in alcohol than wines. Some aperitifs may be difficult to find depending on where you live. You'll find a better selection in larger cities, and it's a good idea to explore the possibilities when you travel. Three of our favorites are the French Lillet and Pineau des Charentes, and the Italian Limoncino. Serve them ice cold.

Good Spirits
Serve sherries, Madeiras, and ports in small, narrow, 4–6-ounce stemmed glasses.

Here is a sampling of mixed cocktail aperitifs, and a rundown on fortified wines and after-dinner digestifs distilled from wine.

Kir

Place one bar spoon of cassis (a black currant liqueur) into a wine glass and fill with chilled dry white wine. Champagne instead of wine makes a *kir royale*.

Bellini

Purée a ripe, white peach (peeled) in the blender until completely smooth. Place the peach juice in a champagne flute. Add a few dashes of lemon juice and peach brandy. Whisk together with a bar whisk and fill the flute by $^1/_4$ with champagne. Vigorously whisk. Add $^1/_4$ more champagne and whisk again. Repeat until the glass is filled.

Sherry

From the sunny south of Spain, sherries are produced from the white Palomino grape, which is baked in bright sunlight before fermentation. During fermentation, sherries develop a yeast film called a *flor*, that gives them their distinctive flavor. Sherries are classified as *fino* (dry), *amontillado* (medium), and *orloso* (heavy).

Madeira

From the northwest coast of Africa, Madeira's unique flavor comes from a baking process. The wine is heated in special ovens for three months at 122°F. It must be cask-aged for eight years. Madeiras range from dry to very rich, and accordingly can be enjoyed as an aperitif or an after-dinner cordial.

Port

Several varieties of grapes are used in the production of port wines. Ports have been made in the Douro Valley in Portugal for over 200 years. They are heated and fortified with alcohol like Madeira but using different processes. Tawny ports have a longer cask aging and are less sweet than Ruby ports. Ports are excellent as an after-dinner cordial or for special-occasion late-afternoon or -evening sipping.

Cognac and Armagnac

Both are wines that go through a complex distillation process and aging in oak. Cognac is from the Charente department of France, north of Bordeaux, and armagnac from the region of Gascony. Armagnac is a much older digestif than cognac, dating back to the 14th century, and it is less smooth than cognac.

Cognacs and armagnacs are the perfect after dinner complement to a special meal. Always serve them in a squat, bowl-shaped brandy snifter. To pour, lay the snifter on its side and fill until the liqueur is a straight pool across the glass.

Calvados

From Normandy, Calvados is a brandy distilled from apples with a distinctive apple nose. Serve after dinner in a snifter as you would cognac and armagnac.

Eau de Vie

Distilled from grapes and infused with fruit, eau de vies are a crystal-clear sensory experience. Chill until frigid, raise a snifter to your nose, and experience a burst of fragrance reminiscent of a tumble through an orchard or berry patch. A sip goes down like white lightning. The most popular of these cordials are Poire Williams, Framboise, and Mirabelle—respectively, pear, raspberry, and plum scented.

Grappa

The Italian cousin of eau de vie, grappa is another clear, fragrant fire water. It is distilled from the dregs from a former fermentation of grapes, then matured in wood casks for two to four years. The type of wood used influences the flavor.

Cook's Notes

Enjoy a good port on a snowy afternoon by the fire with an excellent blue cheese and walnuts.

Designer Notes

Eau de vie and grappa bottle shapes are quite beautiful. Save them for future use as vases or simply displayed as a collection.

Cocktail and After Dinner Wines

A good rule of thumb for before dinner wines is to lean toward the light side for both whites and reds. They should be neither bone dry nor sweet. Avoid wines heavy in oak or tannin that can overwhelm rather than enhance the appetite. Alsatian white wines, Italian Pino Grigios, and American Sauvignon Blanc are good all-around choices for a cocktail wine; Beaujolais, Côte du Rhônes, Chiantis, and light Merlots are suitable reds.

For a country of soda pop drinkers, our general distaste for "sweet" wines is ludicrous. It eliminates a lot of incredibly delicious after dinner sipping and some remarkable taste experiences such as a heady tot of German Trockenbeerenauslese or the combination of a French Sauterne and foie gras. In recent years, many American vineyards began producing luscious sweet wines from Muscat, Reisling, and Sauvingnon Blanc grapes. They're generally more affordable than imported counterparts. Give them a try for a sumptuous finale after a special dinner.

The Extra Mile
Micro-breweries springing up around the country are very much in vogue. Technically speaking, a micro-brewery produces 10,000 barrels of beer or less per year. They design and bottle "craft" beers, or, in other words, beers that do not copy existing styles such as Molsen, Heineken, and so forth. These beers are unique, stay local, and are not distributed around the country. Explore the possibilities in your locale. An ice-filled tub brimming with a varied selection lends added cachet to a picnic or casual party. These beers require refrigeration. They have a shelf life of about 6 weeks.

Toasting

Toasting is one of our most ancient customs. We can assume that our primitive forebears proposed some form of toast to fellowship and their gods after a successful hunt. Early Greeks were in the habit of raising three cups in homage to Mercury, the Graces, and Zeus. Less gracious were early Danes, who used the opportunity of a raised goblet to slit the throat of those they toasted.

Modern toasting has spanned the gamut from the ridiculous to the sublime. A long-winded bore or downright silliness isn't necessarily an asset to a dinner party. Nevertheless, the essence of toasting is a noble gesture. Offering blessings, sentiments, or admiration with simplicity and sincerity does promote feelings of warmth and fraternity around a dinner table.

A personally composed toast is always more meaningful than stock, overused sentiments. Something straight off the cuff like "I'd like to propose a toast to Margit and Don. It's always such a pleasure to be at their table, and I must compliment them for the very special way they always bring together such delightful company. Would everyone like to join me in thanking them?" A good toast shows appreciation for the person being toasted, can include a brief anecdote or personal memory, and should bring a smile to everyone's face. If you know in advance that you'll be called upon to propose a toast, consider looking for a significant poem or passage around which to compose your toast.

Smart Move

A guest raised their glass one too many times? Draw them aside and say, "I remember the last time I had one too many and I'm truly concerned about you driving home. How about a switch to ice water. We'll both feel better in the morning." If the situation warrants, order a taxi and don't take no for an answer.

If you're a bundle of nerves, it's perfectly okay to write it on a small card to read from.

The appropriate time to propose a toast is right before a meal begins or before coffee is served. It's acceptable to offer a toast during a meal if it doesn't interrupt important conversation or interfere with serving. The person offering a toast should stand.

A good toast should be straightforward, meaningful, and to the point. Storytelling is fine, if brief—don't recount the details of someone's entire childhood as dinner turns cold.

The person being honored should wait for everyone to finish their sip of wine, acknowledge the toaster with a raise of their glass, then drink.

The Least You Need To Know

➤ Stock your bar gradually and buy top shelf liquors.

➤ Take the time to mix cocktails properly.

➤ Give thought to the number of guests and type of party you're having when setting up a bar.

➤ Venture the realm of aperitifs, digestifs, and after dinner wines.

➤ The next time you're a guest, offer a toast to your host.

Chapter 2

Equipping Your Kitchen

In This Chapter

➤ What to look for in pots and pans

➤ Knife know-how

➤ Essential kitchen tools and gadgets

➤ Kitchen electronics

➤ Kitchen garb and clean-up

After entertaining for 20-some years, we agree that when you're planning a fete, you become much more intent about acquiring the kitchen wares that you've been getting by without. Therefore, to avoid outfitting your kitchen with a hodgepodge of impulse buys, let's give equipment purchases some careful forethought. Whether you're starting from scratch or embellishing your existing *batterie de cuisine,* it's easy to become mind-boggled by the considerable expense and plethora of merchandise available. With an eye toward entertaining, we realize that some cookware pieces are far more serviceable than others. This chapter gives the bottom line on what we consider the basic food prep requirements that will get you through just about any party menu and perform well for years to come. Serving necessities are covered in Chapter 3.

Sage Advice

"You need to learn to cook first, and then you will learn what equipment is genuinely important to you."

—Alice Waters, *Chez Panisse Menu Cookbook*

The ABCs of Pots and Pans

Most major lines of pots and pans are available in sets that are less expensive than purchasing individual pieces. You may contemplate, "For a bit more than the price of this costly sauté pan, I can have a set of seven less-expensive pots and pans." Or perhaps you think, "These pans are so expensive; I'll save in the long run by buying the whole set." However, before you buy a set of popular cookware, consider the following questions:

➤ What are the different materials used to manufacture pots and pans? How is each piece designed and how is it intended to perform?

➤ What cooking methods do you employ most frequently?

➤ What cooking methods do you employ least frequently?

➤ Do you need the level of quality of each piece in the set? Is the overall quality of a set inadequate for important pieces?

➤ Are aesthetics an important part of your decision?

➤ How often do you entertain?

➤ Does the equipment satisfy your personal and family needs?

Frequently used pans should be the best quality you can afford. It's senseless to buy an inferior product that will find its way to the town dump a few years down the road. Generally, the heavier the gauge of metal (or the thicker the wall of the pan), the better the pan performs. Pan quality should be a determining factor in purchasing frequently used pieces. Sets of pots and pans aren't always the best investment because some are good for their intended use where others may be a poor choice for the job. For instance, a sauté pan must stand up to daily use, so it's well worth investing in a good one. A sauté pan with high, straight sides and a lid is also suitable for stewing, braising, and many other tasks. Most sets, however, offer flare-sided sauté pans that are less versatile.

Good-quality saucepans are also a wise choice. Rounded inside edges are an important saucepan feature so that a spoon can smoothly run over all surfaces. Also, in a good-quality saucepan, sauces will simmer and reduce more effectively. Saucepans that come with sets may not include the wider, low-sided shape we find so versatile for a saucepan. Gratins and casseroles perform faithfully for the entertainer time and again, but they are rarely part of cookware sets. The enameled cast iron type we prefer isn't the best choice for sauté and saucepans anyway. On the other hand, the stock pot that's often part of a set doesn't need heavy-duty construction or fancy coatings to do the job. An inexpensive stock pot works fine. How often do you roast? Here's another place to save. Supplement your important key pieces with less expensive additions. Get the picture?

Good Cookware vs. Bad Cookware

The most important thing to consider when evaluating cookware to suit your particular needs is to choose the right pot and pan material for the right job. The following is a rundown on the materials or combination of materials used to make pots and pans. (The "browning reaction" mentioned refers to the flavorful caramelization of meat juices a cook desires to achieve in the process of sautéing.)

➤ Copper

➤ Aluminum

➤ Hard-coat anodized aluminum

➤ Cast iron

➤ Enameled cast iron

➤ Stainless and enameled steel

➤ Synthetic non-stick coatings and treatments applied to metals

Copper

Copper cookware is not only beautiful, it's the most effective heat conductor of all pot materials. On the downside, copper is the most expensive cookware, plus it tarnishes easily and poses a maintenance problem. In addition, copper ions can leach into cooked foods. Although copper is a vital trace element, excessive intake of copper can be toxic. Thus, copper pans are lined with tin or stainless steel to render them non-reactive. Whipping up a batch of egg whites in a copper bowl won't harm you, but daily cooking in unlined pots can be dangerous.

Smart Move
Tin is a soft metal. Always check tin-lined copper pans for scratches that expose the copper and promptly have them repaired. Don't buy antique copper pots for cooking unless you intend to have them re-tinned or properly restored to ensure a non-reactive interior finish.

If you do use a copper bowl for whipping egg whites, whip them as soon as you put them in the bowl. Don't let them sit for any length of time in the bowl. Much-used and well-cared-for copper pieces are a beauty to behold.

Cook's Notes

To clean copper pots to a shine, rub the pot with the cut half of a lemon to moisten. Sprinkle the pot generously with salt and then use the cut lemon as a scouring pad.

Aluminum

Aluminum ranks second to copper as a heat conductor. Aluminum pans are lightweight, durable, and relatively inexpensive—all positive features. However, direct contact with aluminum can discolor light-colored foods, and the metal oxidizes over many years. The ideal use of aluminum is as a base or core material for pots and pans. Cookware manufacturers apply a variety of exterior finishes and/or interior linings. The higher the gauge of aluminum, the better the pan.

Reality Bites

In recent years you may have read negative information linking cooking in aluminum to Alzheimer's disease. To date, no scientific evidence proves this claim. Because ingesting an excess of any metal can be a health hazard, common sense dictates that a protective lining is the best choice for frequently used pots and pans.

Hard-Coat Anodized Aluminum

Hard-coat anodizing is a treatment that applies a very hard and thin protective shell to aluminum pans to prevent negative effects such as discoloration of foods and oxidation. Individual companies have patented processes, and prices vary. These pans are capable of producing a very good browning reaction, essential for capitalizing on flavor in cooked foods. Acid foods will wear the finish of anodized aluminum over time.

Cast Iron

Cast iron is also a good heat conductor but is not as effective as copper and aluminum. The chief advantage is that cast iron absorbs and retains heat well. Cooking with cast iron actually provides an iron supplement, plus cast iron has no toxic reaction with foods, it produces a good browning reaction, and it's inexpensive. A cast iron skillet is great for deep frying small batches of potatoes and other foods. The major drawback is that these pans are very heavy, and unless they are properly seasoned and maintained, rust is a perpetual problem. Some cooks claim they can detect the taste of iron in a sauce reduced or a dish braised in a cast iron pan.

Cook's Notes

To season cast iron, first coat the interior of the pan with a layer of vegetable oil. Place the pan over high heat just until it begins to smoke. Remove from the heat and, using a wad of paper towels, vigorously rub one tablespoon of salt throughout the pan. Discard the salt and repeat the process two more times.

Don't use scouring pads or abrasives to clean cast iron. After cleaning, rinse, dry, and place over low heat to dry completely. The more frequently it is used, the better the pan performs.

Enameled cast iron solves the rust problem and eliminates the possibility of the metal affecting the flavor of foods. Nevertheless, these pans are even heavier, and enamel is subject to chipping and discoloration without proper care. However, because these pans are classically attractive and hold and maintain steady heat quite capably, they are an excellent choice for cooking and serving in the same pot.

Stainless Steel

Stainless steel is a non-reactive, very durable metal but it is a poor heat conductor. To counter this problem, manufacturers coat the base of the pan with copper or fuse an aluminum plate to the bottom of the pan. These pans do not perform as well as those with layered construction throughout the pan. Any thin gauge stainless pan simply doesn't perform well. However, stainless steel is an excellent pan liner.

Enameled steel claims miraculous heat conduction properties. Realistically, you may have a hard time maintaining a slow simmer in these pots. Further, enamel is not the top choice for browning reactions.

Synthetic Non-Stick Coatings

Synthetic non-stick coatings are the rage. You can find a patented proprietary coating applied to almost all lines of pots and pans on the market. These coatings all perform pretty much the same; they are excellent for low-fat cooking because food can be cooked without sticking in no or very little fat. They are also great for omelets, crepes, and so on, but they rank last for achieving a browning reaction. Coating quality ranges from cream-of-the-crop lines to the lowest of the low. You don't need non-stick pans for every purpose. Generally speaking, buy top-of-the-line, rather than inexpensive, non-stick cookware. Cutting edge in non-stick cookware is *ceramic titanium,* a relatively new treatment applied to aluminum. The non-stick surface produces a better browning reaction than other non-stick products on the market. These pans are expensive but worth it, particularly if you are an avid low-fat cook.

Smart Move

Before you buy any piece of cookware, check out the manufacturer's guarantee. After your purchase, follow the manufacturer's instructions for care.

Your Basic Collection

Following is a recommended "starter set" of pots and pans that will adequately serve most entertaining needs. Mix and match, after reviewing the lowdown on pot and pan materials and investigating your options. Invest more in one great sauté pan, saucepan, and casserole. Save some dollars when choosing a roasting pan, stock pot, extra sauce pan, and gratins. Spend for a non-stick pan according to how much you will use it.

➤ 10"–12" sauté pan with high, straight sides (2"–3") and lid

➤ 8"–10" non-stick sauté pan with flared sides

➤ Two saucepans, 8"×3" and 6"×4", with lids

➤ Tall 10–15-quart stock pot with lid

➤ Shallow roasting pan with rack

➤ Heavy-duty oven-proof 5–6-quart casserole with lid

➤ Two heavy-duty oven-proof gratin pans, 10"–12" and 14"–16"

➤ Heavy cast-iron skillet

Look for saucepans with lids that fit comfortably on the pot, have rounded inside edges, and quality riveted (not welded) handles. Welded handles are acceptable if they are mount-cast into the pot. After you have the basic collection and want to add an extra pan, spend less. For instance, a cast iron skillet or a less-expensive saucepan is fine for extra duty. If you own, use, and like a pan that isn't exactly the cream of the crop, certainly carry on with it. Also, know that if you're starting with just one good sauté pan and one good casserole, you can prepare virtually hundreds of wonderful dishes.

Staying on the Cutting Edge

High-carbon or high-carbon no-stain knives are the only ones to consider buying. For good performance, you should sharpen knives frequently—ideally with a few swipes on the steel before each use.

Cook's Notes

How to sharpen knives:

1. Use a steel recommended by the knife manufacturer.

2. Position the blade at a 90° angle on top of the steel.

3. Draw the blade, bottom to tip, along the steel.

4. Reverse blade to the bottom of the steel to sharpen the other side.

5. Test for sharpness after about 10 swipes.

6. Professionally sharpen knives every one or two years.

High-carbon metal is relatively soft, allowing the blade to be sharpened. Beware of knives that advertise the claim "Needs no sharpening." All blades dull with use. Harder metals, such as stainless, adamantly resist the sharpening steel and require a professional sharpening to restore a good edge. Not only is a dull knife frustrating to work with, but you are far more likely to cut yourself as the knife slips off the food instead of slicing through it. "Dishwasher safe" is also hocus-pocus. The intense heat plays havoc with the molecular alignment in the blade, and it's lousy treatment for a nicely designed handle that you grasp every day. Wiping a blade clean takes but a second. The final case against throwing knives into the dishwasher is when you absentmindedly swoop your hand into the flatware basket and impale yourself on a blade.

Cook's Notes

Remember these important knife features:

➤ Good balance between the handle and the blade

➤ Full tang of the blade should be visible the length of the handle (in other words, the blade material runs the length of the whole knife and a strip is exposed in the middle of the handle)

➤ High-carbon and quality material and riveting of the handle

➤ Manufacturer's guarantee

Blades To Cut Through Any Task

Virtually hundreds of types of knives and cutting devices exist, but these blades are all you really need:

➤ 8"–10" chef's knife

➤ 4"–6" utility knife

➤ 3"–4" paring knife

➤ Serrated bread knife

➤ Carving knife

➤ Cleaver

Most crucial is the chef's knife, which will become one of your best friends in the kitchen once you learn to use it properly. A quality chef's knife may be costly, but with this knife and a good utility knife, you can chop, slice, crush, and trim just about anything.

Cook's Notes

Slicing, chopping and dicing food with uneven or rounded surfaces can be difficult. Try slicing the food in half to create a flat surface which will make further slicing easier. For example, cut an onion in half through the root; pare a thin slice from the bottom of a potato.

Wield a knife by bending knuckles to stabilize the blade.

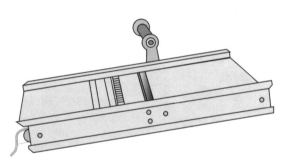

The mandolin is a great tool for fancy cutting such as paper-thin slices, julienne match sticks, and lacy waffle cuts.

Reality Bites

Wood cutting boards, especially those used for meats and poultry, harbor bacteria. After each use (and before moving on to your next preparation), clean your board thoroughly and apply a light rinse of bleach (use a 20/80 mix of bleach and water) or use an antibacterial cleaner to disinfect it. Wipe dry with paper towels.

Acceptable alternatives to wood cutting boards are thermal plastic and polyethylene. They are far superior to glass as a cutting surface. The softer, more forgiving surface doesn't dull or damage your knives.

Basic Tools for Food Preparation

The miscellaneous bowls, measures, hand tools, and gadgets used for preparing food needn't be top-drawer or top-buck items to get the job done. Quality does not influence performance. Stainless utensils are more expensive and more durable but not a necessity. The exceptions are whisks, which should be sturdy, and the avid baker may want to be more choosy about bread and cake pans, tart tins, and so on.

For basic preps, your collection should consist of these items:

➤ One or two nests of mixing bowls

➤ Wet and dry measures in various sizes

➤ Measuring spoons

➤ Balloon whisk and long whisk

➤ Vegetable peeler

➤ Wood spoons in various sizes

➤ Ladle, serving spoon, slotted spoon, toothed pasta server

➤ Stainless spatulas, short and long

➤ Colander

➤ Large and small strainers

➤ Grater

➤ Juicer

➤ Citrus zester

➤ Bulb baster

➤ Food mill

➤ Instant-read thermometer

➤ Kitchen timer

➤ Cutting board

Cook's Notes

Use glass measures with weight markings to correctly measure wet and liquid ingredients. Correctly measure dry ingredients with individual measures by scooping the cup into the ingredient and scraping off the excess with a flat edge.

For baking, these items will get you through:

➤ Flexible rubber scrapers in various sizes

➤ Off-set spatula

➤ Rolling pin

➤ Sifter

➤ Pastry scraper

➤ Pastry cutter

➤ Pastry brushes

➤ Baking sheets

➤ Cake pans, pie pans, and tart tins

➤ Metal and glass loaf pans

➤ Pie weights

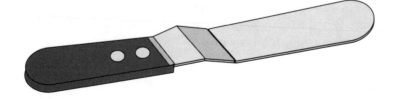

An off-set spatula is a great tool for transferring unmolded cakes or tarts to serving plates or for flipping small pieces of sautéed food.

Cook's Notes

➤ Baking pans with non-reflective surfaces offer the best heat conduction and browning of crusts.

➤ Pie weights are little metal pellets used to prevent shrinkage when pre-baking unfilled pie crusts.

➤ A straight rolling pin without sloping sides or handles gives you the best control.

These kitchen items are not necessary, but they sure make things easier:

➤ Blender

➤ Food processor

➤ Heavy-duty mixer

The blender is a boon for quickly dispatching puréed soups and sauces. When you're chopping mounds of vegetables, puréeing heavy foods, or dashing off a small loaf of bread, pizza, or pasta dough, the food processor is a blessing. Many times anything *you* can do, *it* can do better. This fact is particularly true for once laborious mortar-and-pestle or grinding jobs such as pestos, hummus, patés, and mousselines. For whipping egg whites or heavy cream, or if you love baking cakes and buttery breads, the heavy-duty mixer is a great benefit. Although many kitchen machines are on the market, these three are all you'll ever need—even for the advanced cook. Too many toys become clutter, and frankly, they are often more of a project to use than they're worth. Technology brings new appliances to market at an alarming rate, and there are many competitors for blenders, processors, and mixers. Buy the best you can afford, based on up-to-date research and personal recommendations from your friends who own these appliances.

Kitchen Wear and Clean-Up Necessities

Some successful and avid entertainers get by with hardly a flicker of the burners on their stoves, by using quality take-out items or delegating most of the cooking to a catering or carry-out operation. Others render themselves elbow-deep in the makings of a meal. If you are the latter, we offer some common-sense advice about practical cooking garb and cleaning up.

Kitchen Garb

Believe it or not, these essentials are most often sorely neglected and rarely considered an important part of a kitchen repertoire. But when they are missing or inadequate, it makes for one unhappy cook.

➤ Quality mitts

➤ Durable aprons

➤ Dish towels that withstand many washings

➤ Washable clothing

➤ Comfortable shoes

Have two sets of short, washable oven mitts (if you have just one set, your mitts are destined to be in the laundry pile when you need them) and a longer set of asbestos mitts. Make sure to stow mitts close to where you need them. White, 100 percent cotton aprons are the most practical because spots and stains respond to bleach far better than polyester blends. When you don an apron, cross the ties in back, bring around front, and tie. Run a folded towel through the tie at your waist to have a convenient clean-up for messy fingers and unexpected spills. You can never have enough dish towels—buy lots.

Have you ever pulled on a sweater and found yourself engulfed by the memory of last week's stew? Change to a casual cotton shirt before dashing to the stove for any major cooking. Last of all, always wear comfortable shoes. Party preparations often require at least double the time on your feet than you spend rustling up an everyday meal.

Clean-Up

As you get caught up in the whirl of planning a party, avoid making one of the most common entertaining faux pas: neglecting to take an inventory of clean-up supplies. Keep a good supply on hand at all times and replenish items regularly. Here is a list of clean-up essentials:

➤ Sponges

➤ Cleansers

➤ Paper towels

➤ Baking soda

➤ Small plastic scraper

➤ Dish and dishwasher detergent

Smart Move
Using zip-seal plastic bags to freeze stocks, soups, and sauces takes up far less freezer room than bulky containers.

➤ Plastic wrap, foil, zip-seal plastic bags

➤ Hand cream

Smart Move

The kitchen sponge harbors more bacteria than any other household item. Use paper towels for clean-up, or color-code sponges to specific tasks—for example, blue for the cutting board, orange for the floor, yellow for the sink, pink for the counter tops. Run your sponges through the dishwasher each day. Sponges that retard bacterial growth are now available.

The Least You Need To Know

➤ Spend your dollars on cooking equipment according to its function, performance, and your cooking style.

➤ Quality knives are a smart investment for years of happy cooking.

➤ Use and maintain your equipment properly.

➤ Don't bog yourself down with gadgets you don't need.

➤ Wear sensible garb for cooking.

➤ Keep a running inventory of clean-up supplies.

AT YOUR SERVICE...

Chapter 3

Developing Your Butler's Pantry

In This Chapter

➤ What is a butler's pantry?

➤ Why a butler's pantry is necessary

➤ How to stock a butler's pantry

➤ Where to put a butler's pantry

Few of us have a butler these days, much less an elaborate collection of china, crystal, and table ornamentations for a butler to keep in order. However, along with the disappearance of the butler and his pantry from most modern homes went a practical principle of organization that lent a comfortable ease to entertaining. If you're lucky enough to own an older home or apartment with one of these charming passages, perhaps you're not using it to its best advantage. Although most of us don't have a butler's pantry, we can, however, plan an appropriate area to improvise one, which is a step in the right direction for all future entertaining. Acting as your own butler, you will gain from the scheme of things; but even more, you have a private little space that recalls a tradition from more gracious and less hectic times.

What Exactly Is a Butler's Pantry?

In the heyday of lavish pre-income tax entertaining, every distinguished household had a butler. A good butler was much sought-after because his skill ultimately showcased his employer as a notable entertainer capable of climbing society's ranks. The butler, as *majordomo* (chief of the house), ruled from his pantry—the hub of his existence. Here the butler diligently tended the accouterments of the dining room. China, crystal, silver, wines, and linens were never left to their fate in the turmoil of a busy kitchen. These items were assigned their own room that was generally a form of passageway between the kitchen and dining room. Some butler's pantries were quite grand and some very small. In any case, this designated space existed solely to service a household's entertaining needs that related to dining rather than cooking; it was never a multi-functional space. Over time, this chamber vanished from homes along with the affluent era that kept a domestic staff.

Sage Advice

"A majordomo is often part magician, part fairy god-mother. Using all the tricks of his trade he must find a way to make his employer's every wish come true."

—Desmond Athall, *At Your Service: Memoirs of a Majordomo*

Why Should I Have a Butler's Pantry?

Reality Bites

How often do you find yourself:

Undone by setting the table?

Short one candle?

Without matches to light the candles?

Frantically rummaging for the right serving piece?

With silver polish under your fingernails when guests arrive?

With nothing to offer a drop-in guest?

As entertainers who fit parties into busy schedules, more often than not your energies are focused on the guest list, the menu planning, the shopping, and the preparation of food. Suppose that you're having a small dinner party and plans have fallen into place nicely. Everything is running along smoothly and under control. Then, the afternoon before your party, you find napkins rumpled in the back of a drawer that need ironing. Melted wax and burned wicks are glued into the votives. The platter on which you were going to arrange paté de campagne is missing—you lent it to Fred two months ago. Only minutes before, you were cruising along; now you're hustling around and making do. Interestingly, human nature tends to make these situations repeat performances. After we squeeze by the caught-short circumstance, it goes forgotten until the next time.

Who needs this last-minute fracas? The logic of a butler's pantry is simple. By relegating table-setting accessories, serving pieces, and other related items to a specific spot, they're at your fingertips when you need them. Just the idea that you have allocated space to a butler's pantry initiates a good habit. Once a butler's pantry *exists*, so does an ever-present reminder to keep it replenished and up to speed. You can easily take inventory at a glance. This step can become routine, preferably immediately following every party, or two weeks before a party. By taking stock routinely, you're aware of anything that needs cleaning or polishing. Things you need to replace go immediately on the weekly errand list instead of requiring a special trip. Certainly you don't *need* to have a butler's pantry. But it's one more step to organization that makes entertaining a breeze rather than an ordeal. And it offers a busy host a reassuring peace of mind when it comes time to have a party.

Smart Move
Place a small amount of water in votives or candlesticks, or spray them with cooking spray for easy clean-up right after the party.

Smart Move
Put used linens directly into the washing machine to soak after a party. Or put them in a bag by the back door to take to the laundry the next day.

Remove candle wax from linens or carpeting by placing a brown paper bag or paper towel over the spot and ironing with a warm iron. As the paper absorbs the wax, apply fresh paper and continue ironing until all the wax is removed. Use hydrogen peroxide and a stain stick to remove stubborn red wine stains.

The Makings of a Pantry

Because entertaining isn't a full-time occupation for any of us anymore, we tend to stash most of our party paraphernalia in out-of-the-way places. Nevertheless, for those of us who enjoy entertaining, the logic of pooling these items in an accessible spot makes sense. Depending on where you decide to locate your butler's pantry and how much room is available, apply the principle according to your circumstances.

For instance, let common sense dictate that china remain in the archives if necessary to make room for other essentials. After all, plates don't require special maintenance or replacement. On the other hand, it's convenient to have hors d'oeuvre plates handy, to know that linens are clean and ready to go, and to be able to detect silver that needs polishing or be aware that your candle supply is low.

Designer Notes

A pleasant addition to your pantry is inexpensive collectibles that can add great flair to a table setting. For example, look for antique crystal celery vases, cruets, or toothpick holders in various shapes and sizes to fill with cut flowers.

Glass celery vases.

Cook's Notes

For a nostalgic cocktail hors d'oeuvre, fill your antique celery vases with celery sticks and serve with a blue cheese dip enhanced with a spoonful of cognac and a sprinkling of chopped, toasted walnuts.

In the spirit of things, a butler's pantry should allow a little extra room for ongoing creative collecting. The following is a broad list of things to centralize in your butler's pantry:

Tablecloths, placemats, napkins

Napkin rings

Serving pieces

China and crystal

Silver and silver flatware

Trivets

Trays and bowls for cocktail nibbles

Ice bucket, wine coaster

Salt shakers, pepper mills

Vases

Candlesticks and votives

Place cards and place card holders

Silver polish

Stain removers

Matches or igniter

Non-essential collectibles acquired for party decoration

Reality Bites

Synthetic material tends to hang onto stains with a vengeance. Natural fibers such as linen and cotton clean much easier.

Smart Move

Tend to spills with the following steps:

1. Blot up liquid with an absorbent towel.

2. Flush with clear water or club soda; blot, don't scrub.

3. Apply stain remover.

4. Soak the fabric.

5. Apply more stain remover before laundering.

6. Repeat soaking and laundering if necessary before drying. The heat of a dryer sets stains.

Your Own Special Touch

Generally, we build our serving and table setting repertoire as we go along. Developing your own tastes and style is very apropos today. You don't need the outfittings of a Duke or Duchess to be a successful party-giver. With a little imagination and a sense of fun, many atypical items unrelated to serving and table setting can stylishly accommodate your needs where traditional pieces once ruled. Never feel that your things aren't up to snuff to entertain even the most distinguished of guests. If a guest invited to your home sets his or her table with Waterford crystal and Limoges china and you don't, it doesn't matter. Entertaining is about making things special in your own way. Your gesture of hospitality is every bit as gracious as that of the most well-heeled host. Sophisticated entertainers with true confidence and élan are genuinely appreciative of the efforts of a host who has far less elaborate trappings and experience.

Smart Move
One woman we know collects antique silver place settings one at a time. Each setting is different but all have a flower. Another couple collects different white plates. The common bond is that each plate has a gold rim.

Blue-and-white porcelain pieces that can be used for serving as well as displayed as collectibles.

Smart Move

Consider collecting these versatile serving pieces if you're starting out:

➤ A large, oven-proof meat platter with a lip is a versatile item. This piece serves the holiday bird, then the rest of the year you can surround smaller roasts, chops, sautéed chicken breasts, poached salmon, etc., with colorful vegetables to fill in the extra room on the platter.

➤ You can use small pottery pitchers as sauce boats.

➤ Save plant and flower arrangement baskets for breads.

➤ A large, wide, shallow bowl is multipurpose for tossed salads, composed main course salads, pastas, risottos.

➤ Closeouts on miscellaneous plates from sets are good buys for hors d'oeuvre platters.

➤ Buy inexpensive trays and lacquer them in a primary color.

➤ To add interest to your table, mix and match miscellaneous serving pieces such as vegetable dishes, sugar and creamer, and condiment bowls. When you mix and match, keep to the same genre—all antique pieces or all glazed pottery, etc.

➤ Serving spoons, forks, and ladles should also suit your theme. Avoid plastic except for barbecues and picnics.

The Extra Mile

If space permits, keep a supply of specialty food items in your butler's pantry for drop-in guests:

Cured olives	Specialty nuts and chips
Cornichons	Interesting salsas
Breadsticks and crackers	Smoked oysters
Chutney	Exotic teas, coffees, and biscotti
Mini corn-on-the-cob	

You can create a quick cocktail nibble by surrounding a bowl of chutney with mini corn-on-the-cob.

Will I Have to Hire a Contractor?

Don't panic. We're not suggesting a remodeling project. The essence of the whole idea is a matter of organization. Better yet, reinventing the butler's pantry is a whimsical and romantic notion that should be fun as well as practical. You have many sensible solutions for creating a butler's pantry if you think of it as defining a space rather than a room. Of course, the ideal solution would be to designate an area near the dining room, but that option may not be in the picture. However, just about everybody has a closet that begs for a better use. A butler's pantry may be just the incentive to weed out the closet and outfit it with inexpensive shelving to store your entertaining things. If you don't have a closet available, you can consider many other feasible alternatives.

For instance, an inexpensive armoire, chest with deep drawers, or a buffet can act as a butler's pantry. Also, an inexpensive cabinet or space-saver storage unit can be tucked into a laundry room or out-of-the-way spot. An attractive baker's rack or open-shelving unit, with your pantry items neatly arranged, can actually become a pleasant accent in a kitchen or dining room. Wicker storage baskets make handsome containers for storing items in an open-shelving unit.

Designer Notes

An open-shelving unit can become a design element on its own. Consider these possibilities:

➤ Arrange linens in attractive wicker baskets.

➤ A collection of decorative tin or cardboard containers can hold candles, stain removers, matches, silver polish.

➤ Vases and stacks of trays, bowls, or other serving pieces can be attractively interspersed among wicker baskets and decorative boxes.

➤ Colorful plates and glassware will be admired rather than hidden away.

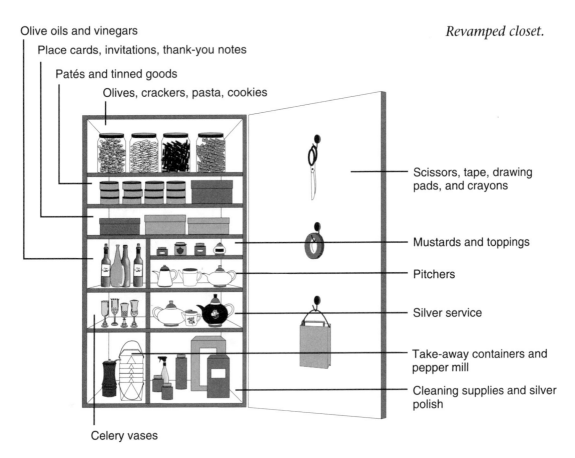

Olive oils and vinegars

Place cards, invitations, thank-you notes

Patés and tinned goods

Olives, crackers, pasta, cookies

Revamped closet.

Scissors, tape, drawing pads, and crayons

Mustards and toppings

Pitchers

Silver service

Take-away containers and pepper mill

Cleaning supplies and silver polish

Celery vases

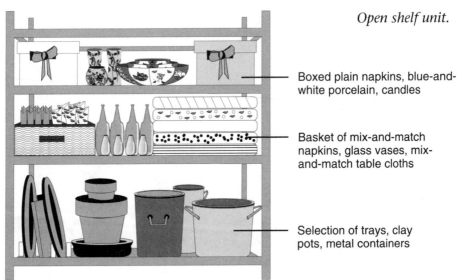

Open shelf unit.

Boxed plain napkins, blue-and-white porcelain, candles

Basket of mix-and-match napkins, glass vases, mix-and-match table cloths

Selection of trays, clay pots, metal containers

41

The Least You Need To Know

➤ Think of a butler's pantry as a concept.

➤ Organizing things for setting the table and serving a meal is a great convenience for the entertainer.

➤ Always have your butler's pantry prepared for drop-in guests.

➤ Delight in your own stuff and your own style.

Chapter 4

So, You're Having an Affair

In This Chapter

➤ Planning your menu

➤ A note on dinner wines

➤ How to read and follow a recipe

➤ Your shopping list

➤ Your schedule for a flawless party

In the last couple of chapters, you gained a handle on the behind-the-scenes organization that goes into entertaining. And now it's time to get down to business. Let's turn our attention to the specifics that constitute the backbone of a successful party: designing an appropriate menu, acquiring the raw materials, cooking efficiently, and planning a schedule to follow from pre-party preparations till the last dish is cleared.

We've learned from experience that most first-time entertainers tend to err with an enthusiasm that can override reality. When you overdo, you overlook. When you are too caught up in one aspect of your party, other areas go neglected. So if the careful consideration we attribute to these party details seems to be overkill, trust us—it's not. Nothing can render you bedraggled or catch you off guard more than failing to evaluate your plans with a cool eye.

The objective is to strike a balance between what you want to do and the time you have to do it. The details that go into a party need not be elaborate. But when everything merges as a subtle whole—theme, menu, flowers, table setting, music, and a relaxed host—that's what delights the subconscious. The atmosphere makes your guests feel special. To overwhelm is intimidating and uncomfortable. Aim for low-key, organize in detail, and you'll have complete control of how your party unfolds. Before you know it, the process will become second nature, and you'll be able to quickly detect and deter potential hazards well before your party is in progress.

Planning Your Menu

Let Escoffier's motto, "Keep it simple," be yours whenever you plan a menu for a party. Never bite off more than you can chew because realistically, each dish you plan to make will take longer than you anticipate. Take into account the inevitable interruptions that are part of our day-to-day lives. Begin by asking yourself these questions to bring your party into perspective:

➤ What is the nature of the occasion?

➤ How many people are invited?

➤ What is the season?

➤ Is your kitchen space and equipment appropriate to efficiently prepare the menu?

➤ How much time do you have to devote to cooking?

Sage Advice
Over 100 years ago, a famous French chef named Auguste Escoffier revolutionized kitchens and streamlined an overbearing cuisine. His motto was *"Faites simple"* (Keep it simple).

What's the Occasion?

Are you gathering close friends or getting people together for the first time? A sit-down dinner is more intimate than cocktail parties or buffets. When guests are seated before a full place setting, everyone has the opportunity to get comfortable and delight in the meal. You can serve several courses and be more elaborate with dishes and sauces. The dinner sets the stage for camaraderie, conversation, and lingering at the table. Serve only the number of people you can comfortably manage at a sit-down dinner. Don't squeeze people around a table and expect them to relax and have a good time. Consider hiring kitchen and serving help for more than 8 to 10 guests if you're planning several courses that require attention. An alternative is to plan a first course that doesn't demand last-minute work and let your guests serve themselves the main course from a sideboard. For smaller, more casual get-togethers, such as inviting friends to enjoy a film or sports event along with a meal, consider how your main course will fare on a lap tray. The food should be fun and spirited if it's not the focus of the occasion.

Are you having a cocktail party, open house, or event that calls for lots of mixing and mingling? When guests are moving about and serving themselves, plan food accordingly. For every hors d'oeuvre or cocktail tidbit you plan into a cocktail party menu, imagine yourself eating it. Can you gracefully swallow the item in one bite, or is that stuffed cherry tomato likely to dribble down your chin? Will the cheese in the pastry stretch a foot from your mouth as you attempt to eat it? Does the dip have enough texture to be scooped up with crudités, or will you be wearing it? What time of day will you hold your party? If a cocktail party or open house overlaps the dinner hour, serve one or two more substantial items.

Smart Move
At large buffet parties, allow guests to circulate around the buffet table. For smaller buffets, place the table against a wall.

How Many People Will Attend?

When you're providing a full meal to a crowd, picture serving yourself from a buffet. What flatware is required and do you need a knife to cut the food? Must you balance the plate on your lap or will you sit at a table? Where will you put your drink? Is a runny sauce likely to spill on your clothing or make a soggy mess of a paper plate? Paper and plastic plates are a poor choice for any food that requires a knife. If the occasion calls for a big picnic or pot luck, think about adequate refrigeration and/or warming space and the mechanics of serving and protecting food outdoors. The following list suggests how much food to plan per person:

At dinner:

6 ounces uncooked boneless weight of protein

$^1/_2$–1 cup complex carbohydrate

$^1/_2$–$^2/_3$ cup vegetable

1 cup salad

(Children eat half as much and teen boys eat double.)

For a vegetarian meal, plan 8–10 ounces plus a salad, bread, and side dish.

At a buffet:

People eat more when serving themselves. Plan 2–3 extra servings overall.

For cocktails:

4 cocktail hors d'oeuvres per person preceding a dinner

4 hors d'oeuvres per guest the first 2 hours at a cocktail party and 2 per hour after

Keep the Change of Seasons

Always allow the season to dictate your menu. When planning a party, keep an eye out in the market for the best, the freshest, and the ripest produce available, and feature it in your menu. When you hold a sun-warmed tomato from the vine in the palm of your hand and understand the difference from its hydroponic counterpart, that's all you need to know. An attractive platter of sliced ripe tomatoes with a light dusting of fresh herbs, freshly ground pepper, and sea salt is the essence of simplicity and an apropos late-summer first course. Also, when you're entertaining out-of-town guests, incorporating a regional specialty or product into your menu is always a welcome treat.

As a rule of thumb, serve light and delicate dishes in the springtime, cool and refreshing dishes in the summer, and rich, warming, soulful food when the cold winds blow. In other words, if you're crazy about onion soup, don't plan it for a dinner party in May. Cold poached salmon is quite welcome in July, but not January. Although grilling is hot, you may regret flipping marinated chops in the throes of a blizzard.

An Eye Toward Balance

Another important aspect of a good menu is contrasting flavors, textures, and colors. Don't follow a cream soup with a cream sauce. A rich and hearty entree calls for a light first course and simple dessert. If you're serving an absolutely decadent dessert, skip the hollandaise or opulent sauces on preceding courses. Food should be visually appealing, but don't go overboard. Contrast the colors on a plate and use garnishes with discretion. A dinner plate isn't a canvas; it offers nourishment for the body and soul. Let your food be real.

Finding Kitchen Space

When you are planning a menu, it's important to consider your kitchen capabilities. Read through each recipe, taking note of preparation details. Do you have the appropriate pots and burner space? Is your oven large enough to warm specific dishes? Will you need to use a broiler in the same oven? How many pots must you use on the stove top?

Determine what dishes you will use for serving. If you are plating food in the kitchen, reserve an uncluttered area adequate for the task. Do you have room in your oven to keep the plates warm until serving time?

Tick, Tock

Consider how much time you have to devote to cooking. How many recipes will you prepare ahead, when will you make them, and how will you store them? When you're on your own, don't plan dishes that require a lot of last-minute preparation. No matter how much you love to cook, all the enjoyment goes down the drain when you're rushed. Things go wrong when you're in a hurry—the butter burns, the cake falls. Don't forget to take into account oven temperatures called for in recipes. Don't plan two dishes that must cook at the same time at different temperatures if you have one oven. Consider using one or more prepared dishes from a reliable carry-out restaurant to fill in a menu when pressed for time. Of course, when you entertain a group of good friends who like to hang out in the kitchen and lend a helping hand, cooking can become a fun project. In any case, good hosts spend most of their time with guests.

Designer Notes

If you entertain buffet-style frequently, a set of large buffet plates and a collection of extra-large napkins are good investments. Consult houseware catalogs to find both at a fairly reasonable price.

Menu Building Blocks

Here are some considerations to take into account that will take your menu planning over the top.

A good menu:

➤ Suits the occasion

➤ Is practical to serve to the number of guests

➤ Is always seasonal

➤ Doesn't push you beyond your limits of time or ability

A great menu:

- ➤ Balances flavors, textures, and colors
- ➤ Balances light and rich dishes
- ➤ Doesn't repeat ingredients or techniques
- ➤ Features the best your market has to offer

A marvelous menu:

- ➤ Is planned with regard to timing and serving
- ➤ Balances make-ahead or prepared food with time-consuming dishes
- ➤ Keeps last-minute preps to a minimum
- ➤ Takes refrigerator, burner, and oven space into consideration

On Dinner Wines

Making intelligent choices about wines is no longer a simple matter of knowing varieties and recognizing reliable vineyards. The choices available today are boundless and vary regionally. Today's favorite may vanish from the market tomorrow. It's virtually impossible to stay on top of the range of styles from vineyard to vineyard, vintage to vintage, and country to country. To complicate matters, most of the rules governing wine and food pairing are history.

The best way to enjoy good wines and ensure value for your dollar is to establish a relationship with a local wine merchant. Never feel uncomfortable about asking questions, and always trust your palate. Either you like a wine or you don't. No one needs to be an expert to appreciate wines. When a wine merchant gets to know you, he or she becomes familiar with your taste preferences and price range, making wine-shopping a simple exercise rather than a dilemma. Before a party, discuss your menu with the merchant, allowing enough time to order wine.

The Extra Mile

How to properly serve wine:

➤ Pour wine from your guest's right.

➤ Do not pick up the glass to pour.

➤ Fill wine glasses $1/2$ to $2/3$ full.

➤ A slight twist of the bottle as you finish pouring prevents dribbles on the tablecloth.

➤ When removing wine from an ice bucket, wrap a napkin around the bottle to catch drips and condensation.

➤ Consult your wine merchant about the proper temperature for storage and serving of individual wines.

Mix and match wine and water goblets for interesting arrangements.

Smart Move

How to open champagne:

➤ Untwist the wire. Remove wire and foil.

➤ Drape a linen towel or napkin over the cork.

➤ Position the bottle at a 45° angle away from your body.

➤ Gently twist, or position both thumbs under the lip of the cork's base and gently rock the cork out.

➤ Drink champagne as soon as it is poured.

Copper bin for chilling champagne flutes.

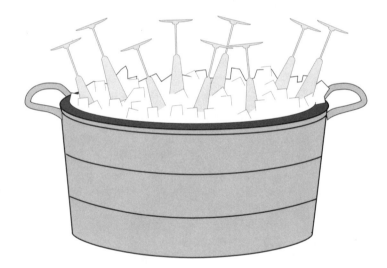

How To Read and Follow a Recipe

The cardinal rule before beginning to prepare a recipe is to *read the recipe from beginning to end*. This does not mean skimming. It means reading every word. Recipes are concepts that combine techniques with ingredients. All good recipes list ingredients and instructions in sequential order, appearing in the most logical order of preparation. Essentially, recipes are blueprints to improvise according to your creative inclinations. But for a novice cook or even a practiced cook, it's always a good idea to follow a recipe the first time around. Get a feel for the recipe before applying your own touch. Let common sense be your guide when it comes to using substitutions. Certainly you can use logical equivalents such as young tender green beans rather than asparagus. However, the chemistry involved in baking requires more diligent attention to ingredients and measures. When a recipe calls for a specific pan design or size, it will affect the outcome of the dish. The length of a recipe does not indicate difficulty. It's simply an organization of different steps.

To tackle your recipes with utmost efficiency, follow these steps modeled after what professional chefs call a *mise en place* (putting everything in place). It's the most proficient way to cook.

➤ Read the recipe from beginning to end.

➤ Place all the ingredients on a tray or arrange them neatly near your work space.

➤ Collect all equipment required to complete the recipe.

➤ Have a trash can, bag, or bowl on hand for scraps.

➤ Follow the sequential order of the recipe to prep all the ingredients before beginning to cook. Arrange the prepped ingredients in individual bowls (Styrofoam food trays make great prep containers).

➤ Clean up as you go to keep your work area uncluttered.

➤ Follow the sequence of the recipe as you cook.

Sage Advice

"When the logic of each step is understood in its relation to a total formula, everything falls into place....There are no secrets, no sleights of hand, no special talents unique to a culinary elite."

—Richard Olney, *Simple French Food*

Cook's Notes

To quadruple a recipe for 6 to serve 24, you get better results preparing a double batch twice.

Your Shopping List

We live in an age when list-making is inevitable. You probably have one too many in your pocket already, and now we're going to suggest yet another. This list will expedite the ubiquitous grocery store trek and focus exclusively on your party needs. Keep this list separate from your weekly grocery list. Prepare the list on a 4"×6" index card with a code heading for your party and the date of the occasion (for example, Spring Dinner, May 1997). Divide one side of the card into four columns:

➤ Produce

➤ Dairy

➤ Meat, Fowl, Fish

➤ Miscellaneous

Consult your menu and collect all the recipes you plan to use. Read carefully through the recipes, itemizing ingredients in the appropriate columns. Check your supply of staples called for in the recipes before preparing your grocery list. If you happen to be ordering any out-of-the-ordinary ingredients or special cuts of meat, fowl, fish, and so on, on the back of the card enter the name and phone number of the butcher, fish monger, farm, specialty store, or wine shop where you will place orders. Always check the phone book first to save time when looking for specialty ingredients, and place orders early for uncommon items or a volume purchase. After calling in your order, indicate on the card whether it is a delivery or pick-up. Include the date of delivery or pick-up.

Smart Move

Check out magazines and catalogs for interesting specialty items to enhance your parties and add them to your party file for easy reference.

Your Schedule for a Flawless Party

Your shopping list is the beginning of a party file. Let's fill in the file with a countdown schedule devised a week or two before your event that designates party preparations to an appropriate day and time slot. Organizing this way prevents all the details from converging upon one another in a hopeless muddle. Your cards are clear, uncluttered reminders that guarantee you will survive cool, calm, and collected. Record-keeping of the party's details will come in handy as a future reference every time you entertain. Keep the file in your butler's pantry. This file is a rewarding little dossier to consult or add to as you discover new "finds" in the realm of suppliers, kitchen help, caterers, party supplies, and so on.

To begin your party file, prepare six more 4"×6" index cards according to these instructions:

➤ *Guest list and menu card.* On one side write down your menu. On the other, jot down your guest list. Place a check next to anyone who needs a follow-up call the week before the party.

➤ *Shopping list card (see preceding section).* Review and decide when to purchase items according to your make-ahead schedule. Double-check all orders.

➤ *Table setting and decorations card.* On the front, record your table design, flowers, and decorations. On the back, make an errand list. List new items and anything needed for the bar and butler's pantry.

➤ *Make-ahead/do-ahead card.* On the front, list the recipes you can make in advance, where to find them, and the day you will prepare them. On the back, list what day to set the table, arrange flowers, prepare place cards, polish silver, pick up linens from the laundry, etc.

➤ *Day-of card.* Make a detailed list of everything to do before guests arrive. On the back, list last-minute kitchen tasks, such as what time the roast comes out of the oven and when to warm the bread.

➤ *Resources card.* Use this card as an ongoing master list of vendors and resources for party food and supplies.

➤ *Comments card.* After your party, jot down a few notes. Were there any stumbling blocks? Did guests mingle or stay with the people they already knew? What was particularly special about your party?

Put a party code and date on each card except *Resources*. The week before the party and the day before the party, review all your cards. The day of the party, follow the *Day-of* card, and you're ready! After your party, clip together the cards that pertain to that event. You can use colored paper clips to code the files by month or year.

The Extra Mile
Make sure the hassle of parking a car doesn't ruin a guest's evening before he or she arrives at your door. Kids who work as restaurant valets welcome the extra cash. Local police departments may provide assistance or advice.

The Least You Need To Know

➤ Let simplicity, practicality, and a respect for natural ingredients be your menu-planning guides.

➤ Strike up a relationship with a good wine merchant.

➤ Adhere to an organized system when you cook.

➤ Let your party file be your entertaining guru.

Part 2
The Mostest...It's You

Now that you have the upper hand on the behind-the-scenes organization of party planning, it's time to think about the heart and soul of entertaining: how you relate to your guests. It's the vital dynamic that brings your party to life.

This section covers extending invitations, creating an ambiance and setting an attractive table, and being a gracious host. The focus is on developing your own special way of saying "Welcome."

A memorable party begins with a host who conveys their own sense of style and hospitality to their guests.

Chapter 5

Extending Invitations

In This Chapter

- ➤ Components of a good invitation
- ➤ Types of invitations, from traditional to creative
- ➤ Etiquette for extending and responding to invitations
- ➤ Composing a great guest list

Rigid rules governing invitations no longer exist. Unless you're entertaining dignitaries or heads of state, even formal invitations can diverge from traditional dictates. Passé are most formalities that once gave us little room for error. However, maybe such a broad spectrum of acceptability is less than ideal. It's easy to neglect to include important details that ensure your guests are well-informed, from dress code to what to bring and exact time and place of the gathering. Being a considerate and gracious host begins with an invitation that provides your guests with all the information about your party.

A good invitation conveys a sense of the party. When the style of the invitation complements the event, your guests have a better idea of what to expect. We also encourage taking the extra step to make your invitations personal. Unless your event calls for

Sage Advice
"The ornament of a house is the friends who frequent it."

—Ralph Waldo Emerson

engraved invitations, pick up a pen and put on your thinking cap. Electronic communications and computer graphics do not transmit the warmth and generosity that are the soul of entertaining. This chapter fills you in on the important details that compose an informative and gracious invitation. We also discuss a few pointers for putting together an interesting guest list.

The Elements of a Good Invitation

The most important element of a good invitation is the amount and quality of information it contains. No one can know what you don't tell them—here is what you should make known:

➤ The name(s) of host(s), legibly written.

➤ Description of the event: "Join us for a festive outdoor picnic to welcome our new neighbors, the Fowlers" or "We're having a dinner to celebrate Kate's birthday."

➤ The date, the hour and duration of the party, and the location.

Reality Bites
Don't ask a notorious late arriver to bring the hors d'oeuvres to your party.

➤ "RSVP" or "Regrets only" in the lower left corner. With the pace of our busy lives, "Regrets only" is becoming increasingly popular. However, for a sit-down dinner party, you may be more comfortable receiving a reply.

➤ Other essential data in the lower right corner: "Casual," "Come in a '30s mood," "No gifts, please," "Valet parking," and so forth.

➤ For a first-time guest, enclose a small separate card with directions or a map. For a large party, indicate where guests should park.

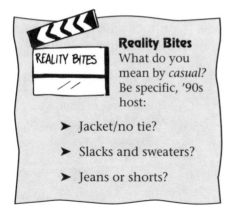

Reality Bites
What do you mean by *casual?* Be specific, '90s host:

➤ Jacket/no tie?

➤ Slacks and sweaters?

➤ Jeans or shorts?

Both formal and informal invitations should bear the same information. For a formal party, follow the sequence of the above bullet points on the invitation. On formal invitations, don't use abbreviations (for example, "On Saturday, the sixteenth of March at eight o'clock"). Follow suit addressing the envelope: "Shaker Boulevard, Shaker Heights, Ohio." A host is most likely to err with an informal invite: "We're having a party on the 21st. Hope to see you there." Who? What month? Where? Although it's fine to use a conversational tone, be sure you don't omit any details. If you decide on engraved invitations for an event, do business with a reputable and experienced establishment. These companies have the expertise to suggest a selection appropriate for the occasion, and they also are less likely to make errors in typeset or deliver late.

Basic informal and formal invitation format.

Informal invitation

Formal invitation

Invitation Styles

Fill-in invitations are a dime a dozen and widely used. Though certainly acceptable, these invitations are rather impersonal. Have you ever received two of the same invitation to different parties? You have plenty of over-the-counter alternatives to the ubiquitous fill-in-the-blanks cards. A hand-written invitation is a thoughtful gesture.

Sending an out-of-the-ordinary announcement for your party inspires a sense of anticipation. For instance, if you're having a dinner for eight people and your menu is country French, browse the blank card section of your local card shop for a reproduction of a Monet or van Gogh painting. For your neighborhood picnic, choose a small-town- America scene. For a Sunday brunch for colleagues, use an amusing collection of black-and-white photos related to a common bond. At any rate, don't let your invitation appear to be an afterthought. Take the time to add a personal touch.

The Extra Mile
Buy special-issue stamps for your special invitations.

For a personal invitation that never goes out of style, invest in premium-quality white or ecru cards with matching envelopes. As long as the handwriting is impeccable, these cards are perfectly suitable for a formal occasion. You also can customize plain cards for your party or use other materials to create an invitation that's completely unique. Here are a few ideas to get you started:

For a party with a foreign or regional theme:

➤ Buy a foreign newspaper or journal and pen-markers in the color of the country's flag (e.g., red and blue for France, red and green for Italy). Separate the sheets and compose the invitation with the markers directly on the newsprint. Roll each invitation and place it in a small mailing tube.

➤ When you travel, stock up on interesting postcards to use as invitations. Buy envelopes to fit the cards for mailing.

➤ Look for packets of canceled foreign postage stamps of the world at dime stores and craft shops. Center the stamp at the top of a plain white card or perch at a jaunty angle. Fill in the card with your party information.

For an era party theme or anniversary:

➤ Buy old 45-speed records from a thrift or junk shop. Make a cut-out from a plain white card to cover the inner circumference of the record and compose the invitation in a circular design. For a special anniversary, spraypaint the record silver or gold. Send the invitation in a cardboard mailer.

To personalize any invitation:

➤ Color copy art reproductions that relate to your theme. Reduce and affix the art to your plain white cards. To dress up the invitation, border the art repro in silver, gold, or a color. Paper-punch a corner of the invitation and attach curled ribbons in the same color. For example, at the library, find a painting of the founding fathers to copy for a Fourth of July party. Reduce the copy, affix to plain cards, and border in red and white. Attach curled red, white, and blue ribbons or a length of small silver stars on wire (used as Christmas decorations).

➤ Record your invitation on a cassette, playing appropriate music at the beginning and the end. For a reunion, include a remembrance about the person you're inviting.

➤ Collect small stencils for creating designs on plain cards.

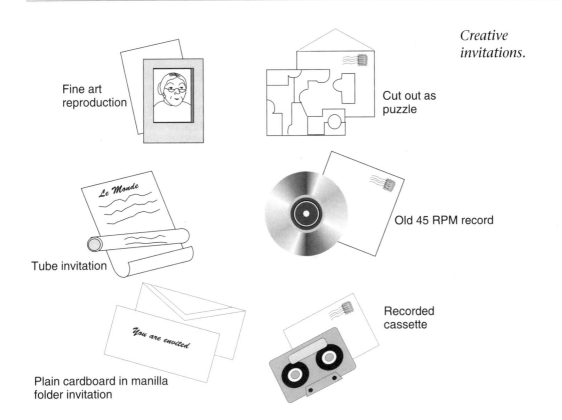

Creative invitations.

Fine art reproduction

Cut out as puzzle

Tube invitation

Old 45 RPM record

Recorded cassette

Plain cardboard in manilla folder invitation

Etiquette for Extending Invitations

Proper timing for sending invitations can make or break your party, particularly around the busy holiday season. For a formal event, reception, or an important dinner, send invitations six to eight weeks in advance. Send invitations for other occasions three to four weeks ahead. Extend telephone invites two to three weeks before the party. Remember that all the party information over the phone is just as important as sending it through the mail. It's easy to get side-tracked by conversation and forget to deliver the details. Use a checklist to avoid receiving eight phone calls the day of your party inquiring about dress, time, parking, or whether you have oven space to warm a covered dish. When someone is hard to reach, try your best to talk to them personally. Belting off party details to an answering machine or voice mail sounds more like marching orders than a request to share someone's company.

If you haven't heard from a guest after 10 days, calling him or her is not out of place. You can spare the guest embarrassment by saying, "I was afraid the invitation may have been lost in the mail" or "I know you travel frequently…"

Smart Move

A telephone invitation:

"We're having a potluck supper on October 29 and hope you can come…Could you possibly bring your wonderful apple tart?…Can the custard sauce be warmed in the microwave or should I plan burner space for you?…We're serving a fireside buffet so come in sweaters and jeans… See you at 7:30 for cocktails."

When you invite weekend guests to your home, be equally as specific. Guests who stay a day or two welcome some direction from their host. Having an idea of your arrangements allows guests to respond appropriately. If they are driving, indicate what time you would like them to arrive. If the visit requires airport pick-up and delivery, say what times are convenient for you to make the trip before they book their flights. Give guests an idea of the itinerary: "We'll have some homemade soup and plenty of time for catching-up when you arrive Friday evening"…"Let's go to the Egyptian exhibit at the Art Museum on Saturday then have lunch at a great new place downtown"…"We love sleeping in on Sunday mornings"…"Unfortunately I have a meeting from 3:00 p.m. to 5:00 p.m. Saturday afternoon." Providing this information allows guests to plan what clothing to bring and whether to throw into the suitcase their walking shoes, a book, or a report they're working on.

The Extra Mile

When you invite out-of-town guests to a big event, and they're not staying at your home, enclose these things:

➤ List of hotels with phone numbers or hotel brochures

➤ Airport transport services

➤ Maps to weekend events

➤ List of babysitters, when appropriate

If the event is for adults only, indicate on the invitation that this is your wish.

Should you feel awkward asking a friend to join your party when you've had a last-minute cancellation? The best way to extend a last-minute invitation is to be sincere and natural. Bumbling explanations and apologies doesn't make anyone feel welcome. Be positive: "I've got my fingers crossed that you're not busy tonight. Pete just canceled for dinner and I think you'd really enjoy meeting the Gillum's." The most gracious way to accept a last-minute invite is an enthusiastic, "I'd love to join you!" Decline by saying, "I'm busy but thanks for thinking of me."

Another "unexpected" inevitably crops up now and then. A guest calls the day of the party with a dilemma—a college pal arrived in town unannounced. This is hardly a problem for large gatherings or cocktail parties, but suppose you're having a sit-down dinner? You're in a catch-22. You certainly aren't eager to be down a guest or two. On the other hand, a roast to serve eight people is in your oven. Be honest with yourself and with your guest. Either you can handle it or you can't. Try a diplomatic approach: "I don't want to miss out on having you with us tonight and I'd love to meet your friend. I'm concerned I might run a little short on food. Here's what I'm having (menu). Could you possibly bring another vegetable dish to fill things out?"

The Extra Mile
Unexpected guests are bound to feel uncomfortable. Treat them to a little extra warmth and generosity.

How about toddlers or pets tagging along? Again, don't say "Yes" if you mean "No." We know people who truly delight in all creatures great and small. If the situation isn't for you, don't agree, then inflict your discomfort on the rest of your company.

Etiquette for Responding to Invitations

When you receive an invitation, respond within one week. An engraved invitation for a big event usually has a reply card enclosed. If not, issue a hand-written response on a simple white or off-white card of good-quality paper stock. Compose a formal reply in the same style of wording that the invitation was written in. If you are replying to a more casual invitation (bearing RSVP), drop a hand-written note or reply by phone to your host or your host's secretary. Reserve fax and e-mail for business transactions.

If you are invited to an event and you're faced with an "unexpected" situation (like the unannounced visitor described in the preceding section), you're in the catch-22 this time. It's inconsiderate to cancel at the last minute. When you offer an explanation, it may sound like an attempt to manipulate an invitation for the extra guest. If you don't know your host well (or it happens to be your boss) pick up a carry-out meal and a video for your friend and leave the party as early as possible without being rude. When your host is a friend, state the situation in a nutshell—a 30-minute

Reality Bites
For a black-tie event, consider the nature of the occasion before donning a polka-dot cummerbund.

explanation is uncomfortable for both of you. Offer to bring an extra dish and, of course, take a thoughtful gift for your host.

Composing a Great Guest List

The greatest reward for a host is a party that lives up to his or her dreams. Anyone who plans a party imagines it actually taking place, and this thought usually includes a mental picture of guests happily interacting with one another. Before composing a guest list, reminisce about some of the memorable parties where you were a guest. Most likely the rapport among the company stands out in your mind.

Because flowers are an important part of your party scheme, let's approach a guest list the same way you approach a flower arrangement. Flowers of different heights and complementary colors, with a dramatic splash here, a soft touch of green fern there, create a charming composition. Use the same congenial mix for your guest list: complement the serious nature with a sense of humor; a heavy hitter with the light-hearted; the old guard with the up-and-coming; and the intellectual with the spontaneous. Balance is the key for an interesting and animated party. Consider what happens when the balance is out of kilter. Your friend the sculptor may be bored silly in the sole company of seven computer engineers. When you invite a new friend or couple to dinner, asking them to join your six old buddies from way-back-when won't tip the scale in the new friends' direction. Add another friend or two from "outside" to bring things into balance.

If your party is all couples and one single, invite your solo guest to bring a friend. No one enjoys feeling like a fifth wheel. Of course, good old common sense always pays off. We hope it wouldn't cross your mind to seat a fervent Greenpeace supporter next to a military officer at dinner. Aiming for balance and an interesting mix of different people keeps the mood light. No one has the opportunity to take themselves too seriously. After all, this is a party.

The Least You Need To Know

> ➤ A good invitation includes all the details about your party.

> ➤ Use a checklist when making phone invitations.

> ➤ A personalized invitation goes the extra mile.

> ➤ When the unexpected crops up, be gracious, tactful, and *honest*.

> ➤ The best parties begin with an interesting mix of guests.

Chapter 6

Schemes, Themes, and Dreams

In This Chapter

➤ Creating the life of a party with schemes and themes

➤ Gilding your lily

➤ Designing a table setting

A memorable party has an extra dimension that sets it apart from the ordinary. That *something* beyond food and drink makes the company and the whole occasion sparkle—the party seems to have a life of its own. Before you call in a marching band or clear out your garage to make room for an arts-and-crafts studio to set the stage, consider this: you probably can't put your finger on exactly what that *something* is. To understand this concept better, think about your favorite restaurants. Most likely what you find so pleasing is a particular *je ne sait quoi* ("I don't know what") that delights when everything clicks. For instance, you may favor a bare-bones joint with a worn pinball machine, faded neighborhood photos, crusty bartenders, and the best fish fry in town. Or maybe you cherish an intimate enclave that lures you with fragrant bursts of garlic and herbs, soft jazzy tunes, and sensual colors. Or your favorite may be the grand room with a sculpture floating in the center surrounded by a sea of diners engaged in animated conversation.

From simple to sublime, each scenario has its own cachet. Doing what comes naturally makes the magic. Whenever you entertain, consider it an opportunity to share a special mood of your own devising. Begin by developing a personalized scheme at home, and your surroundings will take on an intimate, welcoming appeal. You have one all-important rule: Be true to your individual sense of style. Your own magic wand is what puts a twinkle in your guests' eyes. When it's time for a party, your basic scheme can stand on its own or you can dream up a festive theme to add to the occasion. Be yourself and have fun.

Sage Advice

"The idea came to him in June, and it immediately captured his imagination. Nothing, he reckoned, could be a better symbol of the new, grown-up Truman. In one evening, he could not only repay his peacock friends for all their years of entertaining him, but also satisfy a wish he had nursed most of his life."

—from *Capote: A Biography* by Gerald Clark

Using Schemes and Themes to Bring Life to a Party

In November 1966, Truman Capote's "Black and White Ball" was the talk of the town in New York. Guests were required to wear nothing but black and white, including black masks for the men and white masks for the ladies. He invited a dazzling roster: five hundred celebrities, the rich and famous. The black-and-white mask theme was a stroke of genius, serving as a clever equalizer among the notables. Capote's motivation may not have been hospitality, but he was certainly in his element. You may not have such a grand scale in mind for your next fête, but the substance of schemes (the big picture) and the spirit of themes (the specifics) can make your party every bit as special. Let's begin with the concept of a comfortable scheme for your habitat.

The Essence of a Scheme

Keep in mind these general tips when you are developing your scheme:

➤ Zero-in on your own style.

➤ Create a furniture arrangement conducive to conversation.

➤ Good lighting makes a significant difference.

➤ Don't overlook your guest lavatory.

A good design scheme brings a method to the madness of enhancing your surroundings. The scheme should be an expression of your personality, not what's in vogue. Personality is what makes a house a home and a fun place to entertain. If your tastes are decidedly classic, contemporary, provincial, or arts-and-crafts, add special touches to your home accordingly. Aim for consistency. If you love antique china, don't feel guilty about returning a gift of chunky hand-blown glassware. You don't have to use an elaborate candelabra that's a family relic when your passion is hand-thrown pottery. When you're most at home with clean, contemporary lines, focus on simplicity. The essence of the idea is to create an agreeable harmony in your surroundings with things that are right for you. Here are a few pitfalls to avoid:

➤ *Lowest common denominators*: Polyester masquerading as linen, fake veneer finishes on serving pieces (i.e., wood grain), plastic pretending to be marble, and so on.

➤ *Loving hands at work:* Do friends or relatives bestow you with items they feel you *must* have but are totally foreign to your lifestyle? Gifts aren't given maliciously. Be diplomatic, then quietly put them away.

➤ *Pretending to be:* There's a vast world of things that aren't what they appear to be and simply lack integrity. Plastic is a good example; it passes for stemware, wood, flatware, and china. And artificial flowers don't cut it.

Accents of flowers, candles, and music are the icing on the cake for entertaining. Don't relegate them to the dinner table. Flowers and a few votives on a front hall table say "Welcome." Every room your guests pass through should have a special touch. For instance, if your overall decor leans toward classic design, place a collection of inexpensive Chinese blue-and-white cachepots filled with seasonal flowers around the house. If the mood is provincial, fill rustic baskets with colorful fruit or pastoral flowers to tuck here and there. A collection of artistic candles throughout the house complements an arts-and-crafts milieu. In a contemporary abode, showcase a modernistic display of single-color amaryllis on a sleek sideboard.

Chinese blue-and-white pieces.

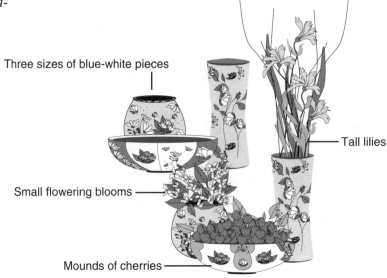

Three sizes of blue-white pieces

Tall lilies

Small flowering blooms

Mounds of cherries

Tie music into a menu or a theme. Mariachi music may not be right for a formal sit-down dinner, but it certainly can add pizzazz to your fiesta. Mood-evoking music enlivens an occasion, but remember that a party isn't a concert. Your guests shouldn't have to shout over pulsating rhythms or vibrate in their seats through dinner.

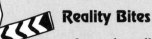

Reality Bites

Scented candles are only one of two things: divine or devastating. Stick to natural, citrus, or botanical fragrances. Burn them before guests arrive then blow out for a subtle, evocative whiff. Never burn scented candles at the dinner table. Buy good candles; inexpensive scented candles tend to be terribly cloying.

The Right Move

Give some thought to rearranging furniture before a party. A strategic arrangement can make all the difference in the world when it comes to getting conversations going in smaller groups or effortlessly serving food and drinks for larger parties. For fewer than 12 guests, move furniture into groupings that allow two to three people to participate in conversation. Some colorful pillows and throws that tie into your scheme add a cheery warmth. When you entertain more than 12 guests, prepare for them to move around.

Think about your traffic patterns and remove any obvious road blocks. When you're serving a buffet, everyone should have a place to sit and eat their meal. You may need to use other rooms for seating. Make sure to deck them out with flowers, candles, and any other party touches to indicate these rooms are equally a part of the festivities.

Nothing contributes to a relaxed ambiance more than proper lighting. Lights that either blare or are set too low make people feel uncomfortable. Unless you have 12-foot ceilings, overhead lighting is harsh and unflattering. One of the best investments you can make is 3-way lamps and/or dimmers, which enable you to adjust lighting to suit the occasion and strike a mood. You can purchase dimmers that attach to lamps at most hardware stores instead of re-doing your switches. To softly illuminate a wall or corner with no lamp, arrange a grouping of candles in varying heights on a table.

Smart Move

An ottoman on wheels is a good investment for a party-giver. It provides extra seating without cluttering a room and can easily be moved where needed.

Designer Notes

You can get a lot of mileage out of clear glass votives at very little cost. Scatter plenty of these votives around a room at different levels—from a high mantle to a low table. The whole room will sparkle.

The extra thoughtfulness you administer to a guest lavatory is a considerate gesture. Pile fluffy hand towels in a basket, or arrange them on a counter or small table. Have a wicker basket on the floor for used towels. Place an attractive dish of imported soaps and hand cream near the sink. The guest lavatory is a perfect spot for scented candles or votives. If you really want to go over the top, connect a small tape player with a chamber music cassette to your light switch.

The Essence of a Theme

You've created the perfect backdrop for entertaining with your personal scheme. This alone makes for a good party. The next step is adding a theme. Essentially, themes bring a little more substance to a party. The simplest of themes ties in a mood, season, or menu. A special celebration honoring a birthday, anniversary, graduation, or the like can prompt you to create a more elaborate theme. Keep in mind that a fine line exists between delightful and overkill. A theme should never monopolize the whole party.

Entertaining is about play, not work, for both host and guest. If you spend three months making doodads for decorations, your guests are more likely to think you went over the deep end than to be impressed.

When seasons change, the time is ripe for a note of celebration. To get the gist of simple seasonal theme, in springtime deck the whole house with flowering hyacinth bulbs massed in wide pot trays—the fragrance delivers the spirit of spring. Intersperse small containers of lily of the valley around the dinner table. Serve spring lamb stew *(navarin printanier* in France) to highlight tiny new potatoes, peas, baby carrots, and plenty of chives, including the purple blossoms—they're edible.

In the early fall let apple-picking season guide your theme. Use a basket of brilliant-red polished apples as a centerpiece and white napkins tied with red bows on the table. Feature a pork roast surrounded by caramelized apples in your menu or homey baked apples for dessert. Place "apple" candles around the house and perhaps a few red throw pillows.

You can link a simple theme to a menu designed around a country or region. Add appropriate cultural accents to your decor, on your table, and with music. In the summer, an Italian theme could center around an al fresco meal featuring a variety of salads made with vegetables, pastas, greens, and seafood. For hors d'oeuvres, wash a large branch and secure it in a weighted container. Drape prosciutto over the branches for guests to twirl onto breadsticks. Decorate with rustic hurricanes or lanterns and play bocci on the lawn. Focusing on a mood or feeling is what's significant.

The Extra Mile

If you're an electronics wizard, hook up your VCR to your audio system. With a two-hour video cassette you can tape six hours of music tailored to a specific mood or theme. You never need to get up to change discs, and the tape serves as a clock for your party.

When celebrating a special event that recognizes a milestone, tailor the party theme to the interests of the person or persons being honored. Here are some ideas for inspiration:

Focus on a hobby, vocation, or passion:

➤ If Grandpa is a fisherman, for his birthday dinner buy paper fold-out fish from a craft outlet. Attach the fish to long twigs and secure in small galvanized buckets to decorate your table. Use ribbons to tie brightly colored flies on each napkin (Grandpa gets to take the flies home). Feature several favorite fish dishes on your menu.

➤ If you are honoring a musician or music-lover, collect old sheet music from an antique shop and use as place mats. Let the era of the honoree's favorite musician inspire your table design and menu. If your friend is a fan of Mozart, have a dessert buffet featuring lavish tortes and cakes. Decorate the buffet table with cake plate stands placed on the sheet music.

Repeat a single design element and color:

➤ At an outdoor party to celebrate a birthday or shower, trail yellow crepe paper ribbons from the table into the garden and the trees. Attach a gift to the end of each ribbon to initiate a festive search. Use the ribbon theme in your menu—a ribbon of yellow pepper sauce on poached salmon, a bundle of green beans tied with chives, lemon mousse in cups tied with a ribbon for dessert, and so on.

Focus on a mood or an era:

➤ Several years ago, we began designing menus and party themes around classic and foreign films. This idea makes for a fabulous party because movies touch everyone in a special way. Making those remembrances a first-hand experience is a delight. Use a favorite film as inspiration for a party. An example might be an English picnic with an atmosphere drawn from *Room with a View*, or a party for teens modeled after *American Graffiti*.

➤ For an anniversary, hire a solo artist or ensemble from a local music school or institute to play music from the era of the couple's marriage. Decor and menu could follow suit. Or hire a pianist to wrap up an evening with a sentimental sing-along.

Focus on camaraderie:

➤ Prepare a scrapbook of your special guest's interests and achievements. Ask friends or relatives to contribute photos or write-ups and invite all the guests to sign the scrapbook before the party concludes. Gear your menu and decorations to the guest's favorite things or favorite color.

➤ For family or school reunions, fill a large basket with disposable cameras. Mark cameras with the type of shots to take: food, special moments, funny moments, and so on. Supply stamped envelopes for picture exchanges. Ask for contributions of family recipes for your menu.

Gilding Your Lily

We're all prone to impulse buys that can sooner or later comprise a mumbo-jumbo of unrelated *stuff* that gets in the way. Let your scheme direct these purchases toward things that reflect your personality and taste. Then, whatever you acquire has significance. A *collection* makes a statement; it also lends a charming personal signature to your entertaining when you use it for decoration or serving. A collection should have a common chord as a governing factor. If country is your style and your scheme includes earthenware plates, hand-crafted baskets, blown glass, and hand-woven tablecloths, consider collecting pewter candlesticks. Look for different single candlesticks at antique shops. They're less expensive than buying pairs and make a far more interesting display or table setting.

If your scheme leans toward classic, a collection of antique clear crystal toothpick holders makes charming vases or condiment containers. You can mix and match sterling flatware and serving pieces if you stay within a specific design genre. For instance, the uniting factor for servers could be a pearl handle. Don't let monograms deter a good buy (you have many initials in your family). Pawn shops are an overlooked source for silver and good-quality tea services. Keep a notebook of things you'd like to collect as a reminder when you're in out-of-the-way places, particularly when you're abroad. A hunt makes for an exciting jaunt when you're exploring a new city. Whatever you find has added value as a memento.

Smart Move
Explore import chains and local arts-and-crafts shows for reasonable buys.

Here are some ideas and guidelines for collecting:

➤ *Pitchers and jugs:* Limit yourself to a single category: crystal, silver, pottery, or china. Collect different shapes and sizes. Use your pitchers at the bar for water, sangria, or lemonade. Arrange flowers in them. Use small pitchers for serving sauces. Display your pitchers in a flat wicker basket when not in use.

➤ *Pottery and earthenware:* Mix different pieces at random but tie them together—all honey-colored or all with a band of the same primary color. Mix antique and new pottery all of the same color and type.

➤ *Blue-and-white china and porcelain:* Canton and Blue Willow are the real thing and can be pricey. Quality knockoffs are very acceptable. Look for well-saturated color and sharp detail. Use the library as a reference to identify classic shapes, and collect a variety of different pieces in different sizes. Besides being useful for serving or as a centerpiece, these items have a timeless quality and look great just on a shelf.

➤ *Demitasse cups and saucers:* Stick to china and porcelain and mix shapes, sizes, and colors. Complement the collection with a variety of demitasse spoons.

Mix and match demitasse cups and saucers.

➤ *Baskets:* Antique or contemporary baskets should be of the same design category—Shaker, Asian, etc.—and the same color range. A collection of different shapes doubles for flowers, fruit, breads, crackers and snacks, napkins, flatware.

➤ *Soup tureens:* Stay with a scheme such as fruit motif, scenic, creamware, and so on. Tureens make a beautiful display on a shelf and are elegant for serving not only soup but breads and vegetables. Flowers and fruit look elegant in a tureen.

➤ *Antique celery vases:* Grandma's Sunday dinner wouldn't have been without them, to hold trimmed, crispy sticks of carrot, celery, or green onions. I bet Grandma never knew how useful and decorative they really are. Styles range from simple clear glass with a fluted edge to elaborate cut glass designs. Use these pieces as vases or to hold small votives, as a container for breadsticks, for parfaits, filled with small scoops of sorbets or berries, or for the ultimate Bloody Mary.

Designing Your Table

When collecting linens and other accessories for your table, stick to the classics, which will serve you well for years to come. Avoid wasting money on items with limited use that too strongly suggest seasonal or holiday themes.

Linens

It's a good idea to have two or three different sets of table linens and napkins and a set or two of place mats to alternate according to the occasion or season. You'll never get bored with the classics. A white or off-white cloth, a windowpane or small check, and a rich solid color are all good choices that agreeably mix and match. Buy fabric compatible with your scheme or style and stick with natural fibers. The integrity is obvious, and they are easier to clean. If you simply *don't* iron, wash your linens and have them pressed at the laundry. Shop household emporiums, catalogs, and specialty shops for basic cloths. Antique fairs usually have one or two booths selling linens. Mixing different antique linens of the same color makes a sentimental and charming table. If the linens are not too fussy, they fit into any design scheme. Antique fairs are also a good source for large 24"×24" linen napkins. These napkins have an old-world reality about them that makes any meal an occasion. For a truly personalized table setting, buy a wonderful fabric and have a cloth made up. On a round or rectangular table, drape square cloths in a triangle, handkerchief style. Mix and match cloths for different effects. Combine solid color and patterned napkins on the table for different effects.

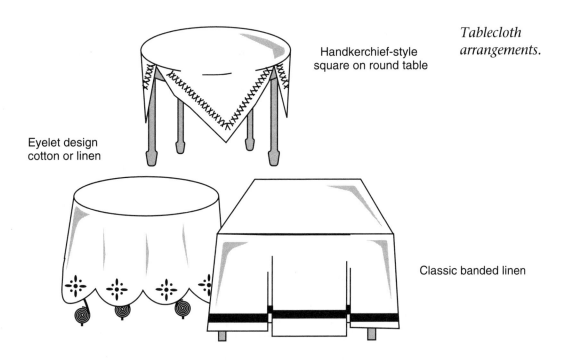

Tablecloth arrangements.

Handkerchief-style square on round table

Eyelet design cotton or linen

Classic banded linen

Designer Notes

Pile neatly folded stacks of linens in flat wicker baskets and store on your pantry shelves. Toss a few lavender or herbal sachets in the basket, but steer clear of strong floral sachets.

Centerpieces and Accessories

Short jars, vases, and containers on a table convey a warm and cozy ambiance. Adding height with tall vases and long stems brings drama to the table. Using your collectible pieces to create a table design is more interesting and personal than a single flower arrangement. Be wary of the heights and placement on the table. When guests have to bob their heads like woodpeckers to converse around your table design, it's very disconcerting. A huge mass of flowers in the center of the table just about eliminates any repartee between guests seated on either side. Don't make the table too busy, or it may distract from the food and conversation.

Allow yourself enough time to thoughtfully arrange flowers, although the results should appear natural and effortless, never contrived. Experiment with different arrangements of containers on the table. A French flower canister (tall, narrow, galvanized pail with two handles) is practical for keeping flowers and greens fresh until you arrange them. Stems stay upright and separated for easy selection. These ideas may inspire your table setting:

➤ *Blue-and-white Chinese porcelain or pottery.* Juxtapose short bowls and taller vases down the center of the table. Use single-color blooms, such as white in the taller jars or vases, for an elegant setting that blends with any other color accessories in your dinner service. Use branches of greens sparingly to add depth. Or pick up a color in your dinnerware, such as orange and yellow flowers. Use a white cloth and napkins tied with orange and yellow bows.

➤ *Small, clear glass or crystal containers.* Use varying shapes and sizes. Haphazardly run the containers down the table and trail English ivy among them. Reflected candle-light on the glass makes a table sparkle.

➤ *Tall, clear glass classic vases and cylinders.* Fill vases with lemons, tangerines, or blood oranges and some interesting shiny leaves. Or feature a tall blooming amaryllis in the cylinder. First remove the flower from its pot and rinse the dirt from the roots. Place the flower in the glass cylinder and cover the roots and bulb with water. Place a graceful branch alongside the amaryllis and attach it to the stem with a small tie of twine.

Amaryllis display.

➤ *Feature a single color.* Use all red flowers but different types of flowers. It's a dramatic look that highlights linens and china. If you're lucky enough to have garden flowers to cut or know a generous friend who does, certainly use them.

➤ *A garden bower.* Create a bower on your table with neutral terra-cotta pots filled with colorful garden flowers. Surround the mouth of the pots with dampened moss. Or use herb plants of different heights for a topiary effect. To highlight crafted clay pots (with garlands or raised designs), fill with potting soil and top with damp moss. Place single blooms in glass florist's vials and "plant" down into the moss. Decorate a buffet table with a few potted blooms, and use a large pot as an ice bucket for wine. Terra-cotta is porous. Put a plastic liner in the pots to protect table surfaces from moisture.

➤ *Flowering plants.* Here's an economical alternative to cut flowers for arrangements. Use the blooms and leaves from a bushy cineraria plant or miniature rose bush to fill small vases. Not only is a plant less costly than cut flowers, but with care it continues to grow.

A flowering plant used as a garden bower and to fill a vase.

1. Whole potted blooming plant.

2. Clip single blooms and place in glass container.

3. Place remaining plant into a decorative cachepot.

➤ *Candles.* Use all white candles or candles of the same color as your flowers. Mix several candlesticks of the same material—crystal, silver, wood, etc. The more candles the merrier. Small, clear glass votives scattered on a table complement any design scheme.

The Least You Need To Know

➤ A scheme provides a backdrop for spirited parties.

➤ A theme should be simple and thoughtful, never overwhelming.

➤ A collection of favorite things enhances your entertaining scenario.

➤ Let your table setting bear your own signature.

Chapter 7

Being Gracious

In This Chapter

➤ Guests' arrival and introductions

➤ Party in progress

➤ Uncomfortable situations

➤ Weekend guests

Those who delight in entertaining rarely worry about being gracious. It's in their blood. Why second guess the social graces that come so naturally to party-givers? So, when you've set a smashing table and the soup is sublime, it's easy to take for granted the fleeting moments that launch a party or the dynamic that guides its course. Least of all does an enthusiastic host waste time dreaming up possible calamities that could taint the party.

Nevertheless, an occasional glitch can befall the most well-planned event. These obvious party bugs we learn to avoid; if a guest takes a flyer on the ice, you'll remember to salt the walk next time, or when you greet Julie as Jessica, you'll review your guest lists forever-more. Once a party's underway, if a kitchen-bound host emerges to a room full of restless guests, you'll plan a simpler menu for future parties. No problem. But sometimes, like a bolt from the blue, a sticky situation pops up to bedevil the most confident host. Maybe a cutting remark stops conversation dead right in the middle of dinner, or a guest cuddles your 4-year-old who throws up in the guest's lap. The most important thing to keep in mind is that, handled properly, no oversight or mishap is going to deal a deadly blow to your entertaining career. You don't need the poise of a Jacqueline Onassis to get by, either. Rely on a bit of tact and a sense of humor, and fluky episodes can actually become a party perk. Finally, a little extra thoughtfulness goes a long way when you have weekend guests. We'll offer some tips for making overnight stays special.

Sage Advice

There's a classic tale about a hostess who entertained with great aplomb. Her guests were seated at the table for Thanksgiving dinner. The butler entered bearing a grand turkey, which to her horror, unceremoniously slithered from silver platter to the floor. "Good heavens, James!" said the lady, "Dispense with this and go get the other one." James retreated to the kitchen, dusted off the bird, rearranged the platter, and marched back to the dining room. Dinner was a great success.

Arrival and Greetings

If tending to last-minute details has set a tempest in a teapot brewing when the doorbell rings, no fairy godmother is coming to the rescue. A harried greeting and mad dash to assemble hors d'oeuvres is bound to put your company on edge. Even if you feel completely organized and under control, make a pre-party double-check *de rigeur* when you entertain. First run through the *Day-of* card in your party file. Then, plan a survey of preparations and a review for administering final touches. Between the survey and final touches, make a relaxing hour to yourself a top priority. An unruffled host sets the stage for a successful party. Allow about 30 minutes for the survey before you unwind. Reserve 20 minutes before guests arrive to set out hors d'oeuvre trays, organize final food preparations, light candles, and so on. Make sure to include these areas in your review:

Before you relax:

➤ Is there adequate space for coats?

➤ Do you need extra room for umbrellas or boots?

➤ Does foul weather call for any other arrangements?

➤ Check the guest lavatory.

➤ Check the bar set-up.

➤ Assemble hors d'oeuvres.

➤ Lay out your clothes.

➤ Select the music.

After you relax:

➤ Set out hors d'oeuvres and fill ice buckets.

➤ Organize last-minute food preparations and garnishes.

➤ Light the candles (except on the dinner table).

➤ Adjust lighting indoors and turn on outdoor lights.

➤ Turn on the music.

The host has the responsibility to welcome every guest. Of course, be enthusiastic, but don't bombard them in the doorway. Let them cross the threshold. Greet your guests with eye contact, a warm hand-shake or light kiss, and a thoughtful, sincere remark. "It's so good to see you, Terry. I'm anxious to hear about your latest adventure. You have a knack for getting people involved in a good story." When a couple entertains, one of you can usher guests off to the bar to serve drinks, returning to the door as other guests arrive. If you're single and hosting a party for more than eight people, it's wise to ask a good friend to come early and help out. Make sure you have a place to put host gifts, or have your spouse or friend dispense with them. Standing at the door with an armload of trinkets looks ridiculous. Don't feel compelled to use gifts of food or wine if they don't fit into your menu. If the dinner table has no room for flowers, display them elsewhere. It's not a bad idea to have a vase handy to quickly arrange cut flowers.

Smart Move
Your attire should be in complete accord with how you re-quested your guests to dress.

Smart Move
Faring the weather. Use a tall French flower canister or large clay pot with a plastic liner for an impromptu umbrella stand. Buy a length of plastic runner to have on hand for wet boots.

Introductions

When making introductions, think of something to say about each person that generates conversation. Share something personal, mention a hobby or an interest: "Colette has a son the same age as your James" rather than "Colette is an attorney." Or "Brad and Todd began designing artistic lamps and before you know it, their hobby's a hit in New York."

If you know a guest who is new to your significant other or cohost, share some information about that person before the party so you're both capable of initiating conversations. "The Murphys are planning a trip to Africa. The Joneses will probably enjoy telling them about their experience."

The Extra Mile

Introduction P's and Q's:

Present men to women. "Judy, this is Don Doskey."

Present younger people to older. "Bob, meet our daughter Rosie."

Present other guests to a distinguished individual. "Your Majesty, may I introduce John Kelly?" "Albert Einstein, please meet Blanche Brann."

Party Underway

Now your party is rolling. Thoughtful introductions reward the occasion with a lively hum of conversation. If you do encounter an uncomfortable lull, be prepared to pose a question or broach a topic to reinstate the flow. Think about your guests. Is anyone an expert or has someone recently had an interesting experience or accomplishment? "David, I understand you're teaching yoga at the university." "Clare, tell us about your retreat in the Berkshires." With your guests in mind, avoid raising controversial subjects that might press a wrong button.

Always be diplomatic when rescuing a wallflower. However well intended, a pointed question or remark that puts a guest in the limelight can mortify a shy person. It is far better to engage them with a gregarious guest, perhaps asking them both to give you a hand in the kitchen to break the ice.

The Extra Mile
Traditionally a guest of honor sits to the right of the host. You may want to seat the guest between two people who are particularly special to him or her.

Allow about one hour for cocktails before dinner. Accordingly, work out a time schedule for serving your meal. You and whoever tends bar should be in concert regarding timing, or you may be bringing plates to the table just as another drink is poured. Estimate how long serving will take so you can time your departure to the kitchen. Don't abruptly break off a conversation. Engage another guest in your discussion before making an exit. At a small dinner party, rejoin your guests and wait for a pause in conversation to announce dinner.

Seat people next to others whose company they will enjoy. Two people who routinely see one another may have more fun getting to know someone new. When guests are meeting for the first time, they will appreciate you taking charge of seating. If everyone is fairly well acquainted, let them seat themselves. Bigger parties call for place cards to avoid awkward moments when it's time to sit down to dinner. It's common at large gatherings for guests to simply ignore an announcement of dinner. For some reason, even the most forward individuals balk at "going first." Don't shout or ring bells. Rather, direct a group of guests to the buffet and insist they start. Follow with another group, and so on.

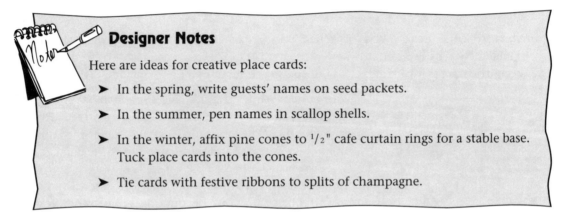

Designer Notes

Here are ideas for creative place cards:

➤ In the spring, write guests' names on seed packets.

➤ In the summer, pen names in scallop shells.

➤ In the winter, affix pine cones to $1/2$" cafe curtain rings for a stable base. Tuck place cards into the cones.

➤ Tie cards with festive ribbons to splits of champagne.

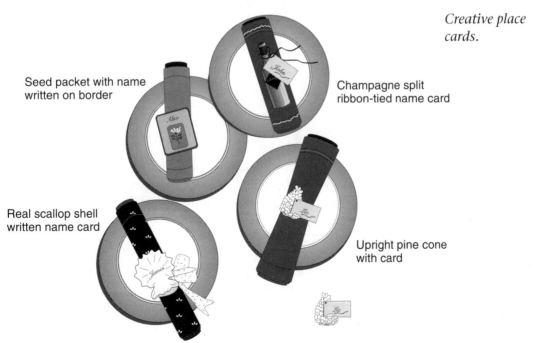

Creative place cards.

Seed packet with name written on border

Champagne split ribbon-tied name card

Real scallop shell written name card

Upright pine cone with card

Sticky Situations

Being calm is the most gracious response a host can offer to a sticky situation. Your next best ally is a healthy sense of humor. Fostering these two qualities will gracefully carry you through any predicament, keeping integrity intact for both you and your guest. Staying calm tempers a guest's reaction to a break, spill, or heated debate. A sense of humor exercised with kindness (not a flippant remark) eases embarrassment and quickly restores the tempo of the party.

Breaks and Spills

When someone breaks a glass or valued object, make light of it and discard the shards immediately. The less said, the better. A guest isn't expected to replace a broken item, but accept the offer if it becomes clear the guest is going to make an issue out of the incident.

Reality Bites
Having a small wisp broom and dust pan handy is far preferable to, and causes less commotion than, dragging out a large broom or vacuum.

Your butler's pantry should have a supply of stain removers to deal quickly with spills on a guest's clothing. Don't drag your guest off, making a huge fuss. Offer the appropriate stain remover and towel, and direct the guest to a sink or private bathroom. Cover spills on the table with the same color napkin as your tablecloth, and carry right on with dinner. In any case, don't let conversation focus on the mishap or empathetic stories from other guests relating similar incidents. Use hydrogen peroxide and a stain stick to remove stubborn red wine stains. To lift candle wax from linens and clothes, cover the wax with a brown paper bag and press with a warm iron.

Offers to Help

Sometimes well-meaning helpers actually become a hindrance to getting dinner on the table. This decision is a personal one for the host. You may be quite comfortable directing someone through your kitchen, or you may be more efficient and at ease on your own. If you accept help, immediately give your helper a specific task to avoid becoming dis-

The Extra Mile
Supply small plates for hors d'oeuvres. Spills are far less likely to occur.

tracted by conversation. If you prefer not to have help say, "Thanks, but everything is set to go." Also consider the mixed message in an offer to help. Many people volunteer assistance to be polite when it's the *last* thing they want to do. Another guest may be looking for a temporary escape hatch. If this is the case, assign a simple task that keeps the guest out of your hair, yet assuages his or her need.

Vagaries of Human Nature

The least desirable situation to have on your hands is when two guests become engaged in a heated discussion or exchange insults. Hopefully, you can head off this scenario with a "look" or a light-hearted remark: "You two look much better with your feathers un-ruffled." If the situation is beyond that, you may need a more blatant means of conveying the message that argumentative repartee is not welcome in your home. Here's where your kitchen timer or a small dinner bell comes in handy. Move between the offenders and hold up the timer or bell. Sound the timer or bell and say, "Okay, time's up! Wish I had some mistletoe, but the bell's going to have to do." Then, touch both guests simulta-neously, with a friendly squeeze to their hand or shoulder. Get a neutral conversation going to prevent them from setting up enemy camps at opposite ends of the room. The two are obviously feeling foolish, so the objective is to get them out of the predicament gracefully.

Of course, right up on top of the list of undesirable situations is the intoxicated guest. You must find a safe ride for the person. If no one offers, don't impose the responsibility. If a taxi isn't available, you have an overnight guest.

What if a member of your company is, quite simply, obnoxious? Occasionally we can thank fate (or luck) for taking charge. The best story we've heard comes from a friend who had a particularly vociferous guest on her hands. He carried on all evening, bounding from one topic to the next, barely pausing for breath. None too soon he prepared to leave, yapping and gesticulating as he started down a flight of stairs. Suddenly, while emphasizing a point a bit too strongly, the obstreperous fellow lost balance and tumbled backward landing in a heap at the door. The hostess graciously prevailed. There are times when patience pays.

Sage Advice

"At the Newport Casino Mrs. Belmont grandly accused Mrs. Fish of having said she looked like a frog. Mrs. Fish appeared very alarmed. 'No, no,' she declared, 'not a frog—a toad, pet, a toad.'"

—Ceil Dyer, *The Newport Cookbook*

Weekend Guests

When you're having guests for the weekend, a few thoughtful gestures can ensure a relaxing time for both host and guest. Overnight guests shouldn't need to ask a score of questions about weekend plans. And they wouldn't feel comfortable interrupting you on the phone to ask for a roll of toilet paper. Without enough direction, visitors are likely to feel they're imposing rather than welcome. When your company arrives, let them know where to park the car so they don't need to move it with every coming and going of family members.

Don't swoosh your guests off to the guest room. Plan some time to unwind over tea, lemonade, or cocktails. This time provides a good opportunity to make or discuss any plans for their stay. When you take guests to their room, help with their luggage and point out closet space or drawers for their things and the bathroom they can use. Of course, going over these fine points may not be necessary with an old college roommate of four years, but most people appreciate being shown the ropes. Bumbling around like a thief in the night for an extra blanket at 3:00 a.m. can be rather unnerving. Here's a list of particulars for equipping a top-notch guest room:

➤ Luggage valet or place to put a suitcase

➤ Adequate hangers and a free drawer

➤ A good reading light and comfortable chair

➤ Water carafe and tumbler

➤ Stack of fresh towels

➤ Extra blanket

➤ Small basket of toiletries

➤ Box of tissues

➤ Bowl of fresh fruit or candies

➤ Fresh flowers

The Least You Need To Know

➤ Being gracious means being relaxed and organized.

➤ Good introductions communicate something interesting about the people you're introducing.

➤ Keep conversation flowing by drawing out an engaging story from a guest.

➤ Be calm and employ a sense of humor to conquer sticky situations.

➤ Let weekend guests know what to expect.

Part 3
The Magic: Menus and Party Designs

Part of the fun of entertaining is the many different options for parties. From casual, homey get-togethers to the ultimate bash, just about anything goes. These chapters offer menus, party designs, guidelines, and recipes to suit your fancy of the moment. Special details particular to each type of party are included in the chapters.

Each party focuses on a simple theme to add a note of finesse to the occasion. The idea is to get your own wheels turning. Before you know it, you'll be confidently on your way to devising your own themes, schemes, and dreams.

Chapter 8

Sunday Suppers

In This Chapter

➤ Rediscovering Sunday supper

➤ A cozy, family-style table

➤ Hosting a lap-tray supper

➤ The recipes

It's Sunday. Most likely you're making a run to the supermarket or catching up on laundry rather than heading over to Grandma's for dinner. For many of us, getting together with family for Sunday supper may mean a trip around the globe, not a leisurely drive. An American institution for generations, Sunday supper has been sadly lost to a seven-day-a-week shuffle and the transient life. Hey, even Grandmas are too busy jet-setting to fix dinner. It would be nice, though…a day devoted to *nothing* but a homey meal and an easy rapport. That's why the idea of relaxed entertaining on a Sunday is an especially welcome respite from our weekly hustle-bustle. It's not just Grandma's table we're missing. It's a comfortable, cozy mood. After the week's hectic pace, a Sunday supper is just the ticket for restoring our equilibrium. Maybe we can't turn back the clock, but we can have fun re-creating the idea to suit our lifestyle. Whether you recall Grandma's table or gather friends together to take in a game or a good flick, Sundays are a great day to entertain.

Sage Advice

"Food is still our ritual relaxation (a 'break' in the working day), our chance to choose companions and talk to them, the excuse to re-create our humanity as well as our strength, and to renew our relationships."

—Margaret Visser

Rediscovering Sunday Supper

After we took such pains with party planning in Chapters 1–7, it may seem bizarre to begin the menu chapter with the advice to relax on the details. However, at the heart of Sunday supper is the luxury of time and a friendly, leisurely mood. You have plenty of chances to strut the organizational stuff in the other chapters. In this chapter, forgetting about super structure is part of the deal.

Let Sunday supper have a hands-on spontaneity that's unhurried; even food that cooks slowly fits into the scheme. The event begins with a friendly phone call that implies there will be no big production, just homey food and good companionship. This kind of entertaining is for your family or old friends, or for bonding with new ones. Start sometime in the afternoon and gently drift into evening. You can gather around an intimate table or assemble a small group to share a special sports event or an engaging film, along with a cozy lap-tray supper. Either way, you'll find that the relaxed camaraderie of a Sunday supper will be as refreshing for you as it is for your guests.

The Extra Mile
A Sunday gathering that brings together different ages broadens everyone's horizons.

A Cozy, Family-Style Table

The menu:

Herb-Roasted Pork Loin

Caramelized Apple Spoonbread

Green Beans, Corn, and Field Mushrooms

Raspberry Chocolate Cake

Grandma's Relish Tray

The recipes for this menu can be found at the end of this chapter.

The mood of this Sunday supper is rooted in homemade, fresh, *real* things. There's nothing like the aroma of a good, old-fashioned roast wafting through the house, or the simple charm of a relish tray for communal nibbling. Treat yourself to a special day of rejuvenation devoted just to Sunday supper. Marinate your pork roast on Saturday afternoon. Then, on Sunday morning, take a trip to a farmer's market to make the process of preparation pleasurable in itself. Be spontaneous. Allow whatever strikes your fancy to embellish your menu. If you see a bin of plump, juicy lemons, make homemade lemonade. Has the first batch of cider come to market? Mull it with spices and lace it with rum. Is a block of local cheese on display? Buy some for hors d'oeuvres. If the green beans are past their prime, substitute whatever vegetable is freshest instead of heading for the freezer case.

These recipes are simple and straightforward so that preparing your Sunday supper can be fun and relaxing. If you're snapping beans when company arrives, all the better. Let them pitch in. Last but not least, serve dinner early enough so you have time for lingering around the table. This is what Sunday supper is all about.

Good Spirits
Serve local wines or beer at your Sunday supper. Or serve a homemade punch, aperitif, or mulled wine for a personalized, homey touch.

The Extra Mile
On a beautiful day, invite friends early enough to enjoy a walk in a nearby park before dinner.

Your Table Design

Here are a few ideas for setting your table in keeping with a nostalgic mood.

➤ *Linens:* A tablecloth and cloth napkins are in keeping with tradition and the sense of nostalgia. If you happen to have a family heirloom, now is the time to use it.

➤ *Mood:* Serve this meal family style, passing dishes from person to person.

➤ *Flowers:* Fill a simple glass vase with a bunch of fragrant, old-fashioned garden flowers. Or use a pot of miniature roses in a small glass bowl.

➤ *Grandma's relish dish:* You can use any low, glass dish to compose a variety of relishes. Use one dish for four people; two dishes for six to eight people.

➤ *Candles:* Center a glass candlestick in the middle of the table with a single white taper.

➤ *Music:* Depending on your mood, choose anything from Chopin waltzes to Broadway show tunes.

Decorate your table with old-fashioned garden flowers such as cosmos, lily of the valley, or peonies.

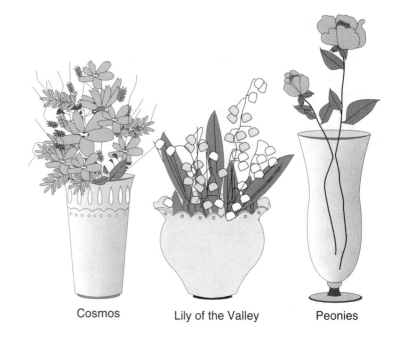

Cosmos   Lily of the Valley   Peonies

A Lap-Tray Supper

The menu:

Cheddar-Pistachio Spread with Apple Slices

Spinach and Leek Salad with Grapes and Walnuts

Vegetarian Cassoulet

Crusty Rolls

Solange's Pear Cake with Vanilla Ice Cream

The recipes for this menu can be found at the end of this chapter.

Smart Move
Use bistro-style tumblers for wine. They're less likely to tip over than wine glasses.

When you're getting friends together to take in a movie or sports event, this menu is easy to manage on a lap tray. One way to orchestrate this Sunday supper is to plan an intermission at an appropriate break point to serve the meal. First, set up a bar with napkins and a tray of the cheese spread surrounded with crisp apple slices. Make sure the spot is convenient for everyone to leisurely serve themselves before intermission. Assemble a buffet with a stack of lap trays, plates, and flatware rolled in extra-big napkins. You can make all the recipes ahead. Have the cassoulet and rolls warming in the oven and the salad ready to toss at the last minute. After everyone serves themselves and gets settled you can pass beverages. Saving dessert and coffee for after the show or game opens the door for lively discussion of the outcome.

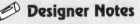

Designer Notes

Inexpensive flat wicker baskets lined with napkins or tin trays spray-painted in different colors of lacquer are good choices for lap trays.

Practical lap trays have a gallery edge.

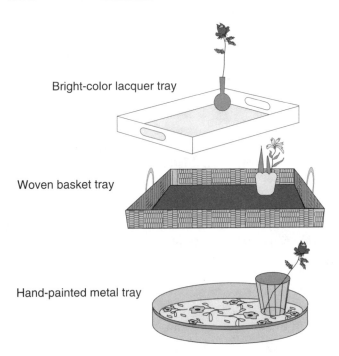

Bright-color lacquer tray

Woven basket tray

Hand-painted metal tray

The Least You Need To Know

➤ For low-key get-togethers, Sundays are a great day to entertain.

➤ An uncomplicated Sunday supper recalls simple sensibilities.

➤ Forget detailed planning and enjoy a little spontaneity.

➤ Enter the comfort zone with a homey meal and relaxed camaraderie.

Family-Style Table Recipes

Herb-Roasted Pork Loin

Requires overnight marination

3 quarts water

$^1/_3$ cup salt

$^1/_3$ cup sugar

1 tablespoon black peppercorns

1 tablespoon coriander seed

1 tablespoon allspice berries

1 tablespoon fennel seed

2 teaspoons dried thyme

2 teaspoons dried rosemary

1 small onion, peeled and quartered

3 large garlic cloves, peeled

2 tablespoons fresh rosemary leaves

2 tablespoons fresh thyme leaves

5 sage leaves

$^1/_2$ cup flat leaf parsley leaves

1 tablespoon cracked black peppercorns

$^1/_4$ cup olive oil

4 pounds center cut pork loin on the bone
(have the butcher crack the "chine" bone
to facilitate carving)

1. In a large pot, combine the water, salt, sugar, black peppercorns, coriander seed, allspice berries, fennel seed, dried thyme, and dried rosemary and bring to a boil. Stir until the sugar and salt dissolve. Remove the pot from the heat and allow the mixture to cool.

2. Place the pork, bone side facing up, in a deep pan (such as a high-sided roasting pan) and cover with the brine. Cover and refrigerate overnight.

3. Preheat the oven to 350°.

4. Combine the remaining ingredients, except the olive oil, in the work bowl of a food processor fitted with the knife blade. Pulse until the ingredients are finely minced. With the machine on, pour in the olive oil in a thin, steady stream until the mixture forms a spreadable paste. Alternatively, mince the ingredients very finely with a chef's knife and stir in the olive oil.

5. Remove the pork from the liquid and pat it dry with paper towels. Rub the herb paste on both sides of the roast. Allow the roast to come to room temperature.

6. Place the meat in a roasting pan, rib side down. Roast the pork on the center oven rack, uncovered, to an internal temperature of 140–145°; about 1–1 $^1/_2$ hours. (Use an instant-read thermometer placed in the thickest part of the meat, not touching the bone, to test the temperature.)

7. Remove the roast from the oven and raise the oven temperature to 450°. Cover the roast loosely with foil and allow it to rest for 15 minutes before carving.

8. To carve the roast, place the roast meat side down on a carving board with the rib bones pointing up. Beginning at the tip of the rib bones, angle a carving knife toward the bones and carve down, following the curvature of the bones, to separate the meat from the rib bones in one piece. Carve the rack of bones into individual ribs. Place the ribs in the roasting pan and return them to the hot oven to brown while you slice the roast. Thinly slice the pork and arrange the slices on a warm platter surrounded by the bones. Serves 6.

Cook's Notes

Trichinosis is killed at 137°. Pork cooked to 140–145° will be white throughout and still juicy. Pork cooked to 160° will be dry.

Caramelized Apple Spoonbread

1 $\frac{1}{2}$ cups peeled, cored, and chopped medium-sized Granny Smith apples

7   tablespoons unsalted butter

2   tablespoons sugar

1 $\frac{3}{4}$ cups whole milk

$\frac{1}{2}$ cup cornmeal

$\frac{1}{2}$ teaspoon salt

1   tablespoon sugar

2   tablespoons melted unsalted butter

3   eggs, separated

1. In a small skillet, melt 2 tablespoons of the butter. When it foams, add the chopped apples. Sprinkle the apples with the sugar and cook them, stirring over low heat for about 10 minutes until the apples are glazed and flecked with golden brown.

2. Preheat the oven to 350°. Melt 3 more tablespoons of butter and double butter (see *Cook's Notes*) a one quart soufflé mold.

3. In a medium sauce pan, heat the milk over medium heat until it is steaming; do not allow it to boil. Sprinkle in the cornmeal in a thin stream, whisking. Add the salt and sugar; cook, stirring with a wooden spoon until mixture is completely smooth.

continues

95

continued

Melt the remaining 2 tablespoons of butter.

Remove the pan from the heat and beat in the melted butter and the egg yolks. Stir in the apples.

4. In an electric mixer, or using a balloon whisk and a large bowl, beat the egg whites until they hold firm peaks. Whisk $1/4$ of the egg whites into the cornmeal mixture to lighten the mixture. Then, using a large rubber spatula, quickly but gently fold in the remaining whites using as few strokes as possible.

5. Pour the spoonbread into the prepared mold and bake in the preheated oven for 40–45 minutes, or until puffed and lightly browned.

Cook's Notes

To double butter, brush the interior surface of the pan with melted butter. Put the pan in the freezer for a few minutes. The butter will harden and streaks will indicate any bare spots. Brush with butter again, covering the bare spots.

Green Beans, Corn, and Field Mushrooms

1 $1/2$ pounds young, fresh green beans, stem ends snapped off

2   ears of corn, husks and silk removed

8   ounces of any exotic fresh mushroom (shiitake, oyster, enoki, etc.)

3   tablespoons unsalted butter

3   tablespoons snipped chives

salt and freshly ground black pepper to taste

1. Bring a large pot of water to a boil and plunge in the beans. Return the water to a boil and watch the beans carefully, tasting and testing for doneness every few minutes. As soon as they are tender (3–5 minutes depending on the freshness and youth of the beans), drain them and run under cold water until the beans are completely cool. Transfer the beans to paper towels to drain.

2. Place the ears of corn in a pot and cover them with water. Bring the water to a boil and boil for two minutes. Turn off the heat and cover the pot. Let the corn sit for ten minutes. Remove the corn from the pot and allow it to cool. Using a small, sharp knife, cut the kernels from the cob.

3. With a damp paper towel, wipe away any soil clinging to the mushrooms. Trim off the tough stems of the shiitake mushrooms, the tough base of oyster and enoki mushroom stems, and thinly slice the mushrooms. Leave tiny enoki mushrooms whole.

4. Melt one tablespoon of butter in a medium sauté pan over medium-high heat. When the foam subsides, sauté the mushrooms until they are flecked with brown (about 5 minutes).

5. Combine the beans, corn, and remaining two tablespoons of butter with the mushrooms. Toss the vegetables together until they are warmed through and glossed with butter. Add the chives and salt and pepper to taste. Toss again and transfer the vegetables to a warm serving dish. Serves 6.

Grandma's Relish Tray

Compose a relish tray with a combination of raw vegetables and preserved relishes and chutneys. At a good produce market you're likely to find less common vegetables and boutique relishes. Be adventuresome, combining the atypical and the classic. Here are a few ideas:

Veggies:

thin wedges of fennel	matchsticks of raw turnip
match sticks of celery root	carrot, celery, and radishes
tender baby asparagus	sugar snap peas
red and yellow pepper strips	

Preserves:

rhubarb chutney	pickled watermelon rind
onion jam	green tomato relish
pickled Brussels sprouts	

*Old-fashioned
relish dishes.*

Designer Notes

Flea markets and second-hand shops are great sources for old-fashioned relish dishes. They can do double duty for arranging a variety of hors d'oeuvres, crackers, olives, cornichons for pate, and so on, or for a display of pretty blossoms.

Raspberry Chocolate Cake

7 ounces unsalted butter, softened (14 tablespoons)

8 ounces fresh or frozen raspberries

6 ounces whole blanched almonds

8 ounces good quality semi-sweet chocolate, broken into small bits

$^2/_3$ cup granulated sugar, plus a little extra to sweeten the raspberry sauce to taste

3 eggs

the grated rind of one orange

$^1/_3$ cup firmly packed fresh bread crumbs

1 tablespoon Grand Marnier or Kirsch

1. Preheat the oven to 375°.

2. Melt 2 tablespoons of butter and butter the bottom and sides of an 8-inch round cake pan with a light coat. Line the bottom of the cake pan with parchment or waxed paper and place in the freezer for a few minutes. Remove the pan from the freezer, butter again, and reserve.

3. Puree the raspberries in a blender or food processor fitted with the knife blade. Reserve $1/3$ cup puree for the cake. Transfer the rest of the puree to a container or storage bowl and sweeten to taste with granulated sugar. Reserve.

4. In a food processor fitted with the knife blade, chop the almonds very finely using on/off bursts.

5. In a small heatproof bowl, melt 4 ounces of the chocolate over a small saucepan of gently simmering water (use a bowl large enough that it rests on top of the pot and the bottom does not touch the water).

6. In an electric mixer, cream 4 ounces or one stick of the butter with the sugar until it is light and fluffy. Begin adding the eggs, one at a time, beating after each addition to incorporate one egg before adding the next. Remove the work bowl from the machine and fold the ground almonds, crumbs, 1/3 cup raspberry puree and the 4 ounces of melted chocolate into the batter.

7. Pour the batter into the prepared pan and bake on the center oven rack for 25–30 minutes. When a toothpick inserted in the center comes clean, the cake is done.

8. Cool the cake for 30 minutes before unmolding. Run a small, sharp knife around the perimeter of the cake, place a plate on top of the cake pan and invert the cake onto the plate. Discard the paper. Place a cake rack on the cake and flip right side up. Chill the cake for 10 minutes before glazing.

9. To glaze the cake, melt the remaining 4 ounces of chocolate with the remaining butter over simmering water as described above. Remove from the heat. Add the liqueur and beat with a wooden spoon until the chocolate is cool, thick, and glossy.

10. Place the cake on its rack over a piece of waxed paper. Pour the glaze over the cake and tip the cake gently back and forth to coat the top and sides with glaze. With an off-set spatula, scrape up the glaze that has dripped on the waxed paper and use it to fill in any bare spots.

11. Serve slices of the cake on top of a spoonful or two of the raspberry sauce. Serves 8.

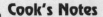

Cook's Notes

This is a fragile cake. Use two large spatulas to carefully transfer the cake to a serving plate. The cake freezes well but should be frozen unglazed. Double wrap in plastic film and seal tightly. Defrost before glazing. If refrigerated, the glaze will regain its sheen when it reaches room temperature.

Lap-Tray Supper Recipes

Cheddar-Pistachio Spread with Apple Slices

1 ½ cups of grated sharp cheddar cheese

2 ounces of unsalted butter, softened

2 tablespoons brandy

1 tablespoon Dijon-style mustard

2 teaspoons Worcestershire sauce

⅓ cup shelled pistachios, finely chopped

3 Granny Smith apples

3 Red Delicious apples

1. In the work bowl of a food processor fitted with the knife blade, combine the cheddar cheese, butter, brandy, mustard, and Worcestershire sauce. Process until light and fluffy.

2. Remove the mixture to a mixing bowl and fold in the pistachios with a rubber spatula. Pack into an attractive crock or serving dish and refrigerate. Bring to room temperature before serving.

3. Core the apples and cut them into ½" slices. Cut the apples right before serving so they don't darken.

4. To serve, place the crock of cheese on a tray and surround with the apple slices, alternating red and green slices.

Cook's Notes

If you want to slice the apples ahead, keep the slices in a covered storage container of ice water with the juice of one half lemon to prevent them from darkening. Drain and pat the apples dry before serving.

Spinach and Leek Salad with Grapes and Walnuts

1 pound fresh young spinach leaves, washed and dried

1 small head of loose-leaf lettuce, washed and dried

2 leeks, cleaned (see Appendix for information on cleaning leeks)

1 cup seedless grapes cut in half

1 cup walnut halves, broken into bits and lightly toasted in a 300° oven

3 tablespoons lemon juice or berry vinegar

  salt and freshly ground black pepper

1 small garlic clove, peeled and crushed

1 generous teaspoon grainy mustard

5–6 tablespoons walnut oil

1. Remove and discard the tough green leek leaves. Trim off the root and cut the leek into two pieces about two inches long each. Place the halves cut side down on a work surface and slice into fine julienne slivers.

2. In a large salad bowl, whisk together the juice or the vinegar, the salt, pepper, garlic, and mustard. Dribble in the oil in a thin stream, whisking. Taste and correct the seasoning.

3. Place all of the salad ingredients on top of the dressing in the salad bowl. Toss the salad right before serving. Serves 8.

Vegetarian Cassoulet

Cook's Notes

Cassoulet hails from Southwest France, where much debate ensues about exactly what ingredients constitute an authentic version. A cassoulet consists of beans, meat, sausage, and *confit* (duck or goose preserved in their own fat). In this vegetarian version, portobello mushrooms stand in for the confit. Extra spices and squash replace the richness of animal fats. The cassoulet can be completely prepared in advance.

continues

continued

$^3/_4$	pound navy pea beans	1	bottle olive oil
1	medium onion stuck with one clove	1	cup tomato puree
1	bay leaf	1	teaspoon dried thyme
1	teaspoon dried thyme	1	teaspoon dried rosemary
2	teaspoons salt	2	teaspoons spice mix
	a generous grinding of black pepper	1	small butternut or acorn squash, halved, seeds removed, peeled and diced
4	large portobello mushrooms		
1	head of garlic (cloves separated but left unpeeled) plus five extra cloves, peeled and minced	$^1/_2$	pound tubular pasta
		1	cup bread crumbs
4	teaspoons spice mix (see the following *Cook's Notes* box)		

Cook's Notes

For the spice mix, combine 1 teaspoon cinnamon, 1 teaspoon allspice, and 1 teaspoon ground coriander seed with $^1/_2$ teaspoon cardamom and 1 crumbled bay leaf. Store in a tightly sealed jar.

1. Rinse and pick over the beans, discarding any stones. Soak the beans in water to cover overnight. Place the beans in a large pot, cover with 3 inches of water and bring the pot to a boil. Drain the beans, return them to the pot, cover with water again, and bring to a simmer. Add the onion, bay leaf, thyme, salt, and pepper. Simmer the beans gently for 30–40 minutes, or just until they yield to the bite. Remove the pot from the heat and reserve the beans in their cooking liquid. The beans may be made a day ahead. Cool, cover, and refrigerate.

2. Wipe any soil from the portobello mushrooms with a damp paper towel. Remove the stems (reserve them for making stock). Place the mushrooms in a wide pot in one or two layers. Scatter the unpeeled, whole garlic cloves and 2 teaspoons of spice mix over the mushrooms and add enough olive oil to just barely cover. Bring the oil to a very gentle simmer over medium-low heat. Simmer slowly for about 30 minutes or until a toothpick glides easily into the mushrooms. Remove and reserve the mushrooms and garlic for finishing the cassoulet. Store the oil in a covered jar in the refrigerator and use for other meat or vegetable sautes.

3. In a deep pot, heat 2 tablespoons of the reserved spiced oil over medium heat and gently sauté the minced garlic just until it begins to turn golden. Add the tomato puree, the herbs, and 2 teaspoons of the spice mix. Raise the heat to high and "fry" the tomato puree until it reduces to a paste. Add the diced squash to the tomato mixture and add just enough water to cover. Adjust the heat and simmer for 10–15 minutes or until the squash is tender.

4. Cut the reserved mushrooms into one-inch chunks and add them to the tomato mixture. Squeeze the garlic from their skins into the tomato mixture. The vegetable mixture may be made a day ahead. Cool, cover, and refrigerate.

5. To assemble the cassoulet, bring a large pot of water to a boil and cook the pasta until tender to the bite. Meanwhile, in a large heatproof casserole dish, combine the cooked beans and tomato mixture. When the pasta is done, drain, reserving one or two cups of the pasta cooking water. Stir the cooked pasta into the cassoulet. Add enough pasta liquid to obtain a creamy textured mixture. Taste and adjust the seasoning, adding more salt, pepper, and spice mix as desired. The cassoulet should be highly seasoned. The entire cassoulet can be assembled a day ahead, if desired. Cool, cover, and refrigerate. Bring the cassoulet to room temperature before baking.

6. Preheat the oven to 350°.

7. To finish the cassoulet, sprinkle the bread crumbs over the top. Bake the cassoulet, uncovered, for 40 minutes to 1 hour or until it is warm and bubbly and a crust has formed. Serves 8–10.

Solange's Pear Cake

3 pears (not overly ripe), peeled, cored, and cut in 1" chunks

7 ounces unsalted butter (14 tablespoons)

vegetable spray for preparing the cake pan

$1^1/_4$ cups flour

3 eggs

$^3/_4$ cup granulated sugar

1 teaspoon vanilla extract

$^1/_4$ teaspoon almond extract

$^1/_4$ cup sliced almonds

4 tablespoons confectioners sugar

3 tablespoon water

3 tablespoon brandy

1. Melt two tablespoons of the butter in a large sauté pan over medium heat. Toss the pear chunks in the butter until they are flecked with brown and tender when pierced with a toothpick. Reserve.

continues

continued

2. Preheat the oven to 375°.

3. Spray a 9" cake pan with vegetable spray to coat. Line the bottom of the pan with parchment or waxed paper. Spray the pan again and reserve.

4. In an electric mixer, cream the remaining 6 ounces or 12 tablespoons of butter and the sugar until they are light and fluffy. Add the eggs, one at a time, beating until each egg is incorporated before adding the next. Add the vanilla, almonds, and almond extract and mix on medium speed just until they are combined. Remove the work bowl from the machine and fold in the flour with a large rubber spatula.

5. Spread the batter evenly in the prepared cake pan. Distribute the reserved pears over the top and gently press them into the batter. Bake the cake on the bottom oven rack for 25–30 minutes or until a toothpick inserted in the center comes clean.

6. When the cake is done, place a plate on top and flip it over to unmold the cake. Place a heatproof plate on the cake and turn right side up.

7. In a small sauce pan, combine 3 tablespoons of confectioners sugar with the water and the brandy and simmer the mixture over medium heat until the sugar dissolves. Drizzle the sugar syrup over the cake.

8. Heat the broiler on high. Sift the remaining one tablespoon of confectioners sugar over the top of the cake. Position the cake 3" from the heat element and glaze the top of the cake for 30 seconds to one minute or until it is lightly flecked with golden brown. Serves 8.

Cook's Notes

Serve the cake slightly warm, topped with a dollop of whipped cream or vanilla ice cream.

All-American Gatherings

The Pilgrims were completely unprepared for the challenges of the New World or nourishing themselves with the mysterious new foodstuffs they found there. Corn, beans, squash, potatoes, and tomatoes were all new to them and many of the fish, shellfish, and game were uncomfortably foreign. Lousy fishermen, hunters, and farmers, the newcomers were a sorry lot. Thanks to the Native Americans, they learned and survived.

We've come a long way from the stodgy palates of our Puritan beginnings, but it certainly didn't happen overnight. Maybe the melting pot started brewing almost right off the bat, but we Americans took a good long time to become a culinary melting pot. Despite the fright of near starvation, the colonists promptly reverted to their Anglo-Saxon tastes with a vengeance. Immigrant dishes were reinvented to adapt to less colorful tastes. Then, mere decades ago, when authentic exotic cuisines began creeping into vogue, we suddenly embraced them with religious fervor. All the while our native flavors stayed out of the limelight.

Sage Advice

"Sometimes God gives them fish or flesh,
Yet they're content without.
And what comes in, they part to friends
And strangers round about."

—Roger Williams, *A Key Into the Language of America*

In recent years a renaissance and talented chefs have brought native ingredients to the fore, preparing them with sophisticated and imaginative techniques. American food has become a celebrity. Nonetheless, when it comes to an all-American gathering—holiday celebrations, reunions, neighborhood and community get-togethers, or any sociable feast with family or friends—one thing holds true. Humble family favorites passed from generation to generation speak strongly of our intermingled roots and native flavors. They still come to our tables, embellished over the years by each hand they pass through, and the melting pot thickens. The familial dishes we bring to potluck are wrought by a blending that may not be celebrity status, but it's definitely American.

Sage Advice

"It is not the cooking that appears on television or in gourmet magazines or posh restaurant guides, because its purpose is neither showbiz or celebrityhood nor fashion. It is not designed to streamline bodies or delay cardiac arrest. This is cooking for the pleasure of cooking and eating."

—from *I Hear America Cooking*, by Betty Fussell

The P's and Q's of Potluck

Originally, "potluck" was a meal offered to a neighbor or caller who dropped by at dinner time and had the good fortune to be offered the "luck-of-the-pot." It was a wise host who decided that vice-versa—guest bringing food to the host—was more to their advantage. Even though you're spared much of the cooking that goes into preparing for other parties, a potluck get-together still benefits from planning and organization. We'll point out the particulars to address for potluck entertaining, as well as some special considerations that will make it a happy occasion for everyone from tiny tots to seniors.

How To Orchestrate a Potluck

A potluck host's responsibility is primarily coordinating. First, if you are providing a central dish, keep it simple so that it's compatible with a broad range of flavors. Next, knowing what people are bringing is key to managing your party. Be specific when assigning dishes in order to coordinate a fairly balanced menu. Simply asking for a side dish or dessert could deliver three renditions of baked beans or batches of brownies. "Bring a salad" may mean potato to someone when you had something green in mind to round out the offerings.

On your guest list, note each dish next to the guest's name. Be sure to ask ahead of time if the dish will require refrigerator, freezer, oven, or burner space. Jot this information down on your list next to the dish so you can appropriately plan ahead. If you can't provide the space, request "ready to serve" dishes. Don't forget to consider the serving utensils you will need. People often neglect to bring them, so consult your list and have the appropriate serving pieces available. Keep in mind that dips, barbecued foods, and finger food call for a double supply of napkins.

Smart Move
When you entertain a crowd, pitchers of beverages and beer on tap spare storing and recycling bottles and cans.

Serving and Traffic Flow

How many dishes will comprise the potluck menu? Clear adequate space on your kitchen counters to make room for organizing dishes until serving time. Also, designate a spot for clean plates, platters, and casseroles that guests will retrieve to take home. The most practical way to serve an informal potluck get-together with a broad variety of dishes is to set up a buffet where people can serve themselves from both sides of the table. (Check out Chapter 18 for rental information if you need a long buffet table or extra tables or chairs.)

Before setting up, rearrange or remove any furniture that inhibits traffic flow around the buffet. Plan an orderly scheme for collecting and organizing used dishes and enlist a friend to help out so that clean-up goes smoothly. When table seating isn't provided, a typical pitfall at large casual gatherings is the inevitable multiplication of used plates, cups, and glasses around the house or haphazardly dumped in the kitchen. You almost always find guests poking around to find a spot to deposit used dishware, or it's simply left where the food was consumed. If you're using paper plates, it's not a bad idea to decorate a

Smart Move
Co-host a potluck with a favorite relative, friend, or neighbor. One of you can be in charge of setting up, requesting entree and side dishes and their organization and serving. One of you will take over appetizers and desserts and their serving and manage clean-up. You'll both have time free of party-tending to enjoy friends or relatives.

large trash can and put it in a place where it's both convenient and obviously intended for everyone to pitch in their own throw-aways.

Finally, woe to the outdoor party that has no place to go if it rains. Always have a back-up plan for outdoor events. Be it a recreation room, garage, or basement, a pre-party clean-up and party transfer plan is well worth the effort.

Family Affairs

Reserve a quiet room for naps and a place for diaper changing when you're expecting small children or infants and have some extra pillows, blankets, or throws on hand. If there's more than a few little ones, ask an amiable party member in advance to be a "storyteller" to initiate a nap time. Also, kids love to tackle a box of dress-up clothes or puppets. Propose that they plan and perform a skit together to entertain the grown-ups. Seniors may also appreciate a quiet place to rest. Does anyone have special needs? Investigating their specific needs allows you to thoughtfully accommodate them.

The Extra Mile

Here's a great ice-breaker for family or class reunions. Choose a theme based on famous names, songs, ancestors, classmates, professors, and so on. Write the names on adhesive name tags which you will apply to each guest's back. Fellow guests must give each other three clues to their identity.

A Menu of Family Favorites

The menu:

Holly's Version of Mrs. Kelly's Ham Loaf

Peg Tyler's Pepper Relish, Tex-Mex Style

Neoclassic Cucumbers

Gertie's Baked Beans

Tom's Updated Southern Greens

Potato Salad à la Alice Stefanek

Strawberry-Rhubarb Tarte

The recipes for this menu can be found at the end of this chapter.

The highlights of potluck suppers are the sentimental aromas and flavors that strike a happy chord in our memories and the sampling of new dishes contributed by friends of their traditional family fare. This delightful hodgepodge that comprises a potluck meal proves that "grazing" is not a modern invention. If you're planning to fire up a grill for your party, here's an idea from a favorite uncle who was grilling thick pork chops to a succulent turn in the '50s, when the outdoor barbecue grill first became a common feature in American backyards: Following the Herbed Pork Loin recipe in Chapter 8, substitute thick loin pork chops for the roast and marinate them overnight. Pat dry and coat both sides with the herb mixture in the same recipe, then grill over a medium fire, turning every five minutes until an instant read meat thermometer reads 140–145° when inserted in the thickest part of the chop.

The Clambake Reconsidered

Undoubtedly, the most original and withstanding of all American gatherings is the clambake, which hails from our Native Americans. Masters of pit cooking, they dug their ovens, lined them with rocks, and built a fire. When the embers provided sufficient heat, now retained by the rocks, food was placed on top and covered to steam. Legend has it that a friendship between Roger Williams and Chief Conanicus of the Narragansett Indians saved the English from extermination in the early 1600s. It's more than likely that Roger was one of the first white men introduced to a clambake by the good Chief during their collaborations, securing the destiny of the clambake, and Americans, for generations to come. Our Conanicuit Island chowder was invented on the Chief's name-sake island that nestles in the middle of Narragansett Bay. Conanicuit Island, better known as the town of Jamestown, Rhode Island, remains a popular host to many a shellfish feast.

Granted, not all of us have access to the beach, rocks, and seaweed required for an authentic clambake. But you don't necessarily have to resort to a counterfeit commercial set-up either. That's why we're reconsidering the clambake to give you two options for indulging in an original Native American feast. You can combine the fruits of the ocean in one bowl for the simplicity of one-dish entertaining, or choose to tackle your shellfish hands-on and delve elbow-deep in shells. Thanks to today's speedy air freight and the popularity of fresh fish in recent years, even inland shellfish lovers can easily compose a simple clambake feast. Whichever option suits you, keep your party in the potluck spirit. The chowder is a "focal point" dish; have your friends fill in by bringing hors d'oeuvres, salad, and dessert. If you're staging a hands-on shellfish feast, let everyone join in the preparations.

Table Design

Reflect a seashore spirit in your table design. Keep it simple and basic and use bold colors and hand-crafted items to convey a sense of fun.

➤ *Linens*: A checked "picnic" style tablecloth and napkins suit the spirit and theme.

➤ *Flowers*: Line the table with clay pots filled with grass or chives.

Good Spirits

Fill a large oval galvanized tub (like an old-fashioned wash tub, commonly found at hardware stores) with ice, bottled beers, and crisp white wines to accompany a shellfish dinner.

➤ *Candles*: Use fat, chunky candles placed in clay pot trays lined with sand.

➤ *Tableware*: Big, colorful Fiesta ware bowls make festive chowder bowls. Use glass tumblers for beverages.

➤ *Place cards*: Clam shells or store-bought scallop shells become place cards with a seashore spirit.

➤ *Music*: How about reggae for starters, then Scott Joplin tunes or a selection of American jazz artists at dinner?

A seashore-inspired table.

The Least You Need To Know

➤ Potluck affairs are easy on the cook but still require thoughtful organization.

➤ At family and all-age gatherings, do something special for young and old.

➤ Redesign a clambake to suit your own style.

The Recipes

Holly's Version of Mrs. Kelly's Ham Loaf

$^1/_2$ pound ground pork

$^1/_2$ pound ground ham

$^1/_2$ pound ground beef

1   cup heavy cream

2   tablespoons tomato purée or catsup

3   tablespoons chopped onion

1   small clove of garlic, minced

1   teaspoon dry mustard

2   tablespoons Worcestershire sauce

$^3/_4$ cup soft bread crumbs

1   teaspoon salt

$^1/_8$ teaspoon freshly ground black pepper

$^1/_2$ cup brown sugar

2   tablespoons sherry vinegar

2   tablespoons water

1. In a large bowl, combine the ground meats with the heavy cream, tomato purée, onion, garlic, dry mustard, Worcestershire sauce, and bread crumbs. Season with the salt and pepper and beat with a wooden spoon until thoroughly blended.

Cook's Notes

For a more sophisticated "paté-like" version, process the ingredients in a food processor to a smooth purée. Maple syrup may be substituted for the brown sugar in the glaze.

2. Preheat the oven to 350°.

3. Transfer the meat mixture to a one-quart loaf pan. Give the loaf pan a few bangs on the counter to knock out any air bubbles.

4. In a small sauce pan, combine the brown sugar, sherry vinegar, and water and bring to a boil. Boil just until the sugar dissolves.

5. Place the ham loaf on the center oven rack and bake for 30 minutes. Begin basting with the glaze every ten minutes and cook for one more hour. When the ham loaf is done, remove it from the oven and pour any remaining glaze over the top. Serve warm or cold. Serves 8.

Cook's Notes

Accompany the ham loaf with a sweet/hot mustard sauce and Peg Tyler's Pepper Relish (see following recipe).

Peg Tyler's Pepper Relish, Tex-Mex Style

1 large red bell pepper

1 large green bell pepper

2 large poblano peppers

1 jalapeño pepper

1 large onion

$^1/_2$ cup sherry vinegar

$^1/_2$ cup granulated sugar

1 teaspoon salt

1 bay leaf

$^1/_4$ cup minced fresh oregano leaf

1. Protect your hands with rubber gloves when preparing the poblano and jalapeño peppers. Wash the peppers and remove the stems, seeds, and membranes. Very finely mince the peppers and the onion by hand. Combine the minced vegetables in a large pot.

2. Bring a tea kettle of water to a boil. Pour enough boiling water over the vegetables to completely cover them and let them stand for five minutes.

3. Drain off the water and return the vegetables to the pot. Add the vinegar, sugar, salt, bay leaf, and oregano; bring the liquid to a boil, stirring constantly for five minutes.

4. Remove from the heat; pour the contents into a clean glass jar and cool. Cover and refrigerate until ready to use. Makes about three cups.

Neoclassic Cucumbers

2 European cucumbers

3 tablespoons raspberry vinegar

$^1/_2$ teaspoon salt

1 bunch of scallions, cleaned and cut crosswise into slivers

1$^1/_2$ cups creme fraiche

   salt and freshly ground pepper to taste

2–3 sprigs of fresh sweet basil or opal basil

   several edible flowers

Cook's Notes

To make creme fraiche, in a small pot, combine 1 cup heavy cream and $^1/_2$ cup sour cream. On a low burner, heat the mixture to body temperature. Pour the creme fraiche into a sterilized glass jar, partly cover, and allow the mixture to mellow for 12 hours at room temperature. Alternatively, buy commercial creme fraiche.

1. With a dinner fork, score the cucumbers by scraping the fork down the length of the cucumber. Score deeply, all around the perimeter of the cucumber. Slice the cucumber into paper-thin coins.

2. In a large mixing bowl, combine the cucumbers with the vinegar and the salt, tossing to evenly coat them. Set the cucumbers aside for one-half hour.

3. Drain the cucumbers in a colander, pressing on them to extract as much liquid as possible.

4. Wipe the mixing bowl dry and whip the creme fraiche in the bowl until it is frothy. Add the cucumbers and scallions to the bowl and fold them together until the cucumbers are evenly coated with creme fraiche. Season the cucumbers to taste with salt and pepper. Cover and refrigerate the cucumbers for an hour or two.

5. To serve, pour the cucumbers into an attractive bowl or a platter with a lip. Snip thin slivers of basil leaves over the cucumbers and decorate with edible flowers. Serves 8–10.

Gertie's Baked Beans

2 pounds of dried lima beans

1 bay leaf

1 small onion stuck with one clove

1 teaspoon dried thyme

2 teaspoons salt

   a generous grinding of black pepper

1 pound of country style bacon, cut into 1" pieces

1 cup of brown sugar

2 teaspoons dry mustard

2 tablespoons Dijon style mustard

4 cups of tomato purée

1 cup cider vinegar

1 medium onion, minced

1 teaspoon dried savory

Cook's Notes

For a low-fat version, use smoked turkey instead of bacon. For a vegetarian version, replace the bacon with 1 cup sun-dried tomatoes cut into slivers.

1. Soak the beans overnight in water to cover.

2. Drain the beans and put them in a large pot. Cover the beans with water by 2 inches. Bring the water to a boil, boil for 5 minutes, and drain the beans. Return the beans to the pot and add water to cover by 3 inches. Add the bay leaf, onion, thyme, salt, and pepper. Bring the water to a boil, reduce the heat, adjusting the beans to a slow simmer, and cook the beans for 40 minutes to one hour or until they are tender to the bite. Begin testing the beans for doneness after 30 minutes to prevent overcooking them. When the beans are done, remove them with a slotted spoon to a large casserole. Reserve the bean liquid.

3. Preheat the oven to 300°.

4. Add the remaining ingredients to the beans, stirring to combine well. Cover the beans with a lid or foil and bake on the center oven shelf for 2 hours. Check the beans periodically, adding more bean liquid if necessary to keep the beans moist and soupy. Uncover the beans and continue cooking for one more hour, allowing the beans to absorb the cooking liquid. Serves 10–12.

Tom's Updated Southern Greens

Cook's Notes

Down south, different crops of hand-picked field greens are shared among neighbors. Experiment with using a variety of different greens and develop your favorite combination.

1 large bunch of greens: dandelion, collard, mustard, kale, Swiss chard, or a combination

3 $^1/_2$" slices of Canadian bacon cut into large dice or an equal amount of leftover ham, or a small smoked ham hock left whole

  salt and freshly ground black pepper to taste

1 ripe tomato, peeled, seeded, and chopped

1 small onion, minced

1 hard-boiled egg, chopped

  a cruet of balsamic vinegar

1. Fill a sink with cool water and vigorously swish the greens around to dislodge dirt clinging to the leaves. Drain and repeat if the greens are particularly sandy. Remove the tough stems from the greens and discard. Roughly chop the leaves.

2. Fill a large pot or deep skillet with 2 inches of water and bring to a boil. Toss in the greens and the ham (if you are using a ham hock, add it whole to the pot, remove it when the greens are cooked, trim off the meat in small pieces, and return to the greens).

3. Partially cover the pot, turn the heat to medium, and cook the greens for about 15 minutes. Taste for texture. They should still be slightly crunchy but not raw-tasting (traditionally, greens were cooked for a lengthy time period). Cook for a few more minutes if necessary.

4. Season the greens with salt and pepper to taste and transfer them to a warm serving dish (either drain the greens or serve in their "pot likker"). At the table, pass small bowls of the chopped tomato, chopped onion, chopped egg, and a cruet of balsamic vinegar for diners to garnish their greens as desired. Serves 6.

Potato Salad à la Alice Stefanek

3 pounds of small red potatoes, unpeeled

1 egg

1 egg yolk

the juice of one-half lemon

1 generous teaspoon Dijon-style mustard

1 $1/4$ cup safflower oil

$3/4$–1 cup sour cream

$1/2$ tablespoons Dijon mustard

salt and freshly ground black pepper to taste

3 stalks celery, thinly sliced

$1/2$ cup minced celery leaf

2 large shallots, peeled and minced

1 teaspoon celery seed

1–2 teaspoons Hungarian paprika

$1/2$ cup minced fresh dill

1. Place the whole potatoes in a large pot and cover with water. Bring the potatoes to a boil, reduce the heat, and simmer just until they can be pierced through with a skewer or a sharp knife. Drain and cool the potatoes completely.

2. To prepare a homemade mayonnaise, combine the egg, the egg yolk, lemon juice, mustard, and salt and pepper in a blender. Pulse the mixture until thoroughly combined. Turn the blender on high and very slowly trickle the oil into the mixture. Stop and scrape down the sides of the blender jar as necessary. Adjust the seasoning to taste. To make the dressing for the potato salad, combine $3/4$–1 cup of the mayonnaise with the sour cream, Dijon mustard, and salt and pepper to taste.

3. Cut the potatoes into bite-sized cubes and place in a large mixing bowl. Toss the potatoes with the dressing. Fold in the celery, celery leaf, shallot, celery seed, paprika, and dill until thoroughly combined. Taste and adjust seasoning as desired. Serves 10–12.

Cook's Notes

Alice recommends putting whatever vegetables suit your fancy into the potato salad. The key is using enough mayonnaise and sour cream to make it silky-smooth.

Strawberry-Rhubarb Tarte

Cook's Notes

To make a flour mix for tender pastry, combine 3 cups all-purpose flour with 1 cup cake flour.

1 $^3/_4$ cup pastry flour mix

4 ounces cold, unsalted butter cut into $^1/_2$" bits

2–3 tablespoons ice water

1 egg yolk

1 teaspoon sugar

1 teaspoon salt

3 large stalks of rhubarb cut into $^1/_2$" slices

3 cups of hulled and sliced strawberries

the zest of one-half lemon

3 tablespoons fresh lemon juice

3 tablespoons corn starch

1 teaspoon cinnamon

$^1/_2$ teaspoon nutmeg

1   cup granulated sugar

$^1/_2$ cup strawberry preserves

1-2   tablespoons confectioners sugar to garnish

1. To prepare the pastry, put the flour, 6 ounces of butter, and the sugar and salt on a work surface or in a large bowl. Toss the butter bits with the flour. Using your fingertips, work the butter and flour together, pinching it into a crumbly mixture that resembles coarse meal. Beat 2 tablespoons of ice water with the egg yolk. Drizzle over the flour/butter mixture and toss to evenly dampen. If the mixture feels dry, add enough liquid to evenly dampen. Gather the pastry into a rough ball on a work surface. Using the heel of your hand, press a small portion of the dough down and away from the edge of the dough ball opposite you, smearing the butter and flour together against the work surface. Smear bit by bit. Using a pastry scraper, gather the dough together and repeat the process. Gather the dough into a ball and press into a slightly flattened disc. Wrap in film and chill for 20 minutes before rolling out the dough.

2. In a large bowl, combine the sliced fruit, lemon zest, and juice. In a small bowl, combine the corn starch, spices, and sugar. Toss the corn starch mixture with the fruit until evenly coated.

3. Preheat the oven to 450° and position the oven rack in the lower third of the oven.

4. Lightly flour a work surface and roll the pastry into a $^1/_8$" thick round. Transfer the pastry to a 9" tarte pan and trim the overhang to 2". Spoon the fruit mixture into the pastry shell. Fold the pastry overhang onto the tarte, making a pleat in the pastry every two inches or so. Bake the tarte for 10 minutes, reduce the temperature to 350°, and bake for 35–40 minutes more or until the crust is golden. Cool the tarte on a rack for 30 minutes.

5. In a small pot, melt the strawberry preserves over low heat. Strain into a small bowl. Using a pastry brush, evenly glaze the fruit filling with the melted and strained preserves. Dust confectioners sugar over the crust before serving. Serve the tarte topped with softened real vanilla ice cream. Serves 8.

A Clambake

Chowder

Pilot Crackers

Steamed Clams or Mussels

Lobster

Corn on the Cob, Sliced Tomatoes, Cole Slaw

Melted butter and lemon wedges

The spirit of a clambake is inherently a potluck, hands-on enterprise. Obviously, digging a pit and nursing a "bake" along was never a solo endeavor. In keeping with the mood of your improvised clambake, gather your friends together to go scouting for all the ingredients. After a jaunt to the fish market and farm stand, let everyone pitch in with the preparations. At a traditional pit clambake, foil wrapped packages of fish, red skins, or sweet potatoes are added to the bake and brown bread is a common accompaniment. Embellish the basic "bake" we feature according to your whim or fancy.

You'll need three large pots to cook the lobsters, clams or mussels, and the corn. A shellfish feast is a messy affair, so if you're eating indoors, don't use paper plates, which become hopelessly soggy. It's also a good idea to use side plates for the cole slaw and tomatoes so they don't swim in lobster juices. If you don't have lobster crackers, you can use a hammer to crack the claws and tails before serving the lobsters. Also, fingers are just as effective as shellfish forks for seeking out every last morsel. Have several large bowls or paper bags lined with plastic bags for disposing of shells. Use small ramekins or paper or plastic cups for melted butter. Pass a separate bowl of melted butter with a small pastry brush to easily butter the corn. Don't forget plenty of napkins and a container of moist towelettes.

Here's how to proceed: Begin with a steaming bowl of chowder that you have made ahead (a basic chowder can be prepared using the Conanicuit Island recipe with fish only; about 3 pounds) and pass a basket of pilot crackers. More simply, just enjoy mugs of clam or mussel broth with your steamed clams or mussels. If you're serving chowder, put the pots of water for the lobster and the corn on the stove to come to a boil before you bring the chowder to the table. After the chowder, put the lobster and the corn in their ready pots and begin steaming the mussels or clams. The bivalves should be ready around the same time that the lobster pot returns to a boil, and the corn will be ready to turn off to finish cooking. Pile the clams or mussels into a big bowl and bring them to the table. Set a timer for the lobsters. When the lobsters are done, transfer them to a large colander or place them directly in a sink. With a small, sharp knife, poke a tiny hole behind the eyes, then turn the lobster over and let it drain for a few minutes.

Serve the lobsters as soon as they are cool enough to handle.

Basic Shellfish Facts and Preparation

Lobsters were once so plentiful that the colonists apologized for serving them to company. Homarus americanus, which we know as our "Maine" lobster, lives in cooler waters and is an entirely different crustacean than the warm water Panulirus argus, or "spiny" lobster. The texture of a spiny lobster is coarser and the flavor less delicate than the Maine lobster. When we purchase "lobster tails" from a market or menu, it is spiny lobster. The only inedible portion of a Maine lobster is the "head sac" (a waste storage container) that lies between the eyes. Beyond the tail and claw meat, there's plenty of tender nuggets of meat nestled in the lobster body cavity and you can draw the legs and tail flippers between your teeth to wriggle out more meat. The green tomalley and orange coral (roe) are edible and considered delicacies.

To cook lobsters:

Fill a pot large enough to accommodate the lobsters with water to a rolling boil. Toss in a tablespoon of salt and plunge in the lobsters head first. Cover the pot and return to a boil. As soon as the water returns to a boil, uncover the pot and begin timing the lobsters: 10–12 minutes for 1–1 $1/4$ pounds, 15–18 minutes for 1 $1/2$–2 pounds, and 20–25 minutes for 2 $1/2$–5 pounds.

Mussels are a mere 2 percent fat and a generous 12 percent protein. Loaded with minerals, Vitamin A and Omega 3's, mussels are a top pick for a quick, healthy meal. Mussels should be tightly closed or willing to do so. Mussels have a tendency to "gape." Firmly rap any open mussels on a counter. If they don't close discard them. It always pays to buy a few extra. Scrub the mussels and remove the "beards" (a protein filament that looks like a shredded scouring pad) with a small knife. "Rope" mussels are the product of carefully supervised aquaculture and are generally quite clean and beardless. Soak wild mussels in water to cover, sprinkled with 1–2 tablespoons of cornmeal for 30 minutes to one hour before cooking.

To steam mussels:

3 pounds mussels

1 shallot, minced

2 tablespoons parsley, minced

freshly ground black pepper

1   cup dry white wine

Place the clean mussels in a large pot. Add the shallot, parsley, a generous grinding of black pepper, and the wine to the pot. Cover tightly and turn the heat to high. Steam the mussels until they have all opened, checking the pot every few minutes. Transfer mussels to a bowl, discard any that have not opened, and reserve the cooking liquid. Remove mussels from shells and reserve.

Cook's Notes

For an easy meal, combine the mussels with 1 large can of diced tomatoes, 3–4 chopped cloves of garlic, 1–2 sliced jalapeño peppers, and 3 tablespoons minced coriander. Cover and steam as above. Serve with crusty bread and a crisp green salad. For mussels *à la francaise*, steam with the wine and shallots and add a healthy splash of cream and torn basil leaves after they have steamed.

Hardshell clams, or *quahaugs*, are sold in three sizes. Little Necks are the tiniest and are most often served raw, on the half shell. Cherrystones are the next largest and also served on the half shell or can be used for a variety of baked clam preparations. Both Little Necks and cherrystones can be steamed although they aren't as tender as softshell clams. Quahaugs that are 3" in diameter or larger are used for making chowder and stuffed clams, never for steaming. Like mussels, hardshell clams should be tightly closed. Quahaug shells were the Northeast Native American's wampum.

Softshell clams, also known as Ipswich clams, or "steamers," are the steamed clams we associate with a clambake and fried clams. They have a more elongated oval shape than hardshells. Softshell clams do not tightly close.

To steam clams:

Scrub and soak the clams in water to cover for 30 minutes to one hour to allow them to disgorge trapped sand. Steam littlenecks or softshell clams in about an inch of dry white wine or beer following the same procedure as for mussels. Enjoy au naturel or with melted butter and lemon. The broth is great for sipping.

Corn on the cob:

Place shucked ears of corn in a large pot and add water to cover. Add one half lemon and one tablespoon sugar to the pot. Bring the water to a boil and boil for two minutes. Cover the pot, turn the heat off, and let the corn sit for ten minutes.

Conanicuit Island Chowder

Cook's Notes

Two lobsters can stretch to feed eight. Enjoy all the flavors of a clambake at a fraction of the cost.

Cook's Notes

Follow the instructions for cooking shellfish in the clambake section earlier to precook the shellfish for the chowder.

2   live lobsters, cooked, shelled, meat and shells reserved (shell over a plate to catch juices)

4   tablespoons unsalted butter

1   tablespoon vegetable oil

1   small carrot, minced

2   medium onions, minced

1   4-ounce piece of salt pork, cut into small dice

3   tablespoons flour

2   dozen mussels, steamed, shelled, and broth reserved

2   dozen Little Neck clams, steamed in wine, shelled and broth reserved

2   pounds of scallops, halibut, cod or a combination, cut into bite-sized pieces

3   cups tiny red skin potatoes, cut into dice and simmered in lightly salted water until tender

4   cups whole milk

1   cup of heavy cream

$^1/_2$ cup snipped chives for garnish

1. Cut the lobster meat into bite-sized pieces. Break or chop the shells and carapace into chunks. In a large saucepan, heat one tablespoon of the butter over medium heat. Sauté the carrot and $^1/_2$ cup minced onion until they soften. Add the broken lobster shells and sauté for three minutes. Cover the contents of the pot with water by one inch, adding any juices that accumulated from the lobster. Bring to a boil, reduce the heat to a simmer, and simmer for 30 minutes, stirring the contents of the pot occasionally. Strain the lobster stock into a bowl and reserve. Discard the shells.

2. In a large soup pot, slowly render the salt pork over low heat until it is crisp. Remove to paper towels to drain and pour off all but one tablespoon of fat from the pot. Add the butter, and when it bubbles add the remaining minced onion and gently sauté over medium heat until wilted. Add the flour and cook, stirring for three minutes without browning. Whisk in the reserved lobster stock and the reserved mussel and clam broth. Simmer for five minutes, stirring, then add the fish and/or scallops. Continue to simmer for 2–3 more minutes.

3. While the fish cooks, scald the milk by heating just until bubbles appear around the perimeter of the pan. Add to the chowder pot along with the potatoes, the lobster meat, mussels, and clams. Taste and adjust the seasoning. The chowder can be made a day ahead. Completely cool, then cover and refrigerate. Bring to room temperature before very gently reheating. Do not allow the chowder to boil. Stir in the salt pork and the heavy cream.

Cook's Notes

For an extra special touch, whip the cream to the soft peak stage and gently stir it into the chowder. Or, whip only $^1/_4$ cup of the cream and float a small portion on top of each serving.

Cooking Together

In This Chapter

➤ Cooking together, naturally

➤ Understanding the game plan

➤ A hands-on menu for many guests

➤ A menu for two

➤ The recipes

Just about everyone has cooked side-by-side in the kitchen with a relative or friend at one time or another. Whether preparing for a holiday feast, a celebration, or just a friendly meal, these times are fondly remembered for their warmth and good humor. Have you ever considered actually arranging an evening with friends to recreate just that kind of scenario? At parties, people gravitate toward the kitchen. It's a friendly place to be. Sharing the preparation of a meal becomes entertainment in itself, adding a lively dimension to an invitation for dinner. We have found that even friends who don't "cook" are delightfully engaged by the process.

The Natural Act of Cooking Together

Once the first two sticks met to make fire, humankind didn't take long to get into the act of cooking. Cooking wasn't a solo endeavor for our primitive ancestors, either. Acquiring and preparing food was a communal effort—the gift of a meal was a celebration in itself.

Maybe that's why kitchens have a special lure, particularly when people are cooking together in them. The smelling, touching, and tasting that progress with the preparation of a meal strike an instinctual chord and a common bond. Whatever the case, the companionship between fellow makers and tasters, along with a process that reaps swift rewards, creates a happy camaraderie.

Maybe you have tried cooking with friends and found it was a lot of commotion. Not this time. We have a blueprint for cooking together that efficiently organizes everything from soup to nuts. The simple methodology enables you and your friends, or perhaps just you and a significant other, to cook contentedly without fumbling around for ingredients and utensils. And you won't get in one another's way or render your kitchen a disaster area. We'll call this methodology *the game plan,* and it has worked as well in an apartment galley as it has in a big country kitchen. Give this strategy a try.

The Game Plan

The premise of the game plan is based on three golden rules. In the following section, "A Menu for Many Hands," we demonstrate the process. Using the game plan, this menu for six is designed for three sets of partners; recipes are divided among the teams (make recipe copies to hand out). First, designate a cooking space for each pair of cooks. Next, set up everything the cooks need to complete their recipes at their specified area. Finally, partners need a cooking sequence to follow in order to coordinate everyone's cooking activities. After you get the gist of the strategy, you can apply the rules to any menu and group of friends.

Sage Advice

"For me, cooking has always been a high form of play..."

—from *Beach Music* by Pat Conroy

In Chapter 4, read the section, "How to Read and Follow a Recipe," and heed the theory of a *mise en place* (putting everything in place). It's the organizational guts of the system. Prepare your shopping list as suggested in Chapter 4 and tick off ingredients as you set up. For the icing on the cake, station a self-serve bar away from cooking activities so that fellow cooks can help themselves to drinks and nibbles as they cook. Prepare a simple hors d'oeuvre from any of the menu chapters and include it on the bar. Tune in some favorite music, and you're ready to roll.

The Extra Mile

Draw straws or names from a hat, first for partners, and then again for a set of recipes.

Golden Rules

Here are three golden rules to guide you through the game plan system.

➤ *Assign specific prep areas.* If counter space is limited, a card table and the end of a dining table with a protective cover can serve as work areas. Everyone brings their own apron and knife. Borrow two additional cutting boards if you have only one.

➤ *Set up ingredients and utensils for making the recipes at prep areas.* If you arrange things on a tray, you also can use the tray for transporting items to the stove for cooking. Supply scrap bags and damp wipes. Needless to say, everyone tends to their own clean-ups.

➤ *Devise a plan of action to coordinate everyone's cooking activities.* Read the recipes to determine burner and oven space requirements. Six people can't use four burners at the same time. The following menu uses three pots and two sauté pans, and the oven broils, bakes, and warms. To avoid traffic jams, we attach sticky notes to partners' recipes that recommend a sequence for their cooking activities.

Smart Move
Attach different-colored stickers, tags, or ribbons to wine glasses so they don't get mixed up as fellow cooks move around.

A Menu for Many Hands

The menu:

Tomato-Pepper Bisque with Shrimp and Fennel

Sautéed Duck Breasts on Warm Red Cabbage Salad

Creamy Mashed Potatoes with Garlic and Sage

A Selection of Cheeses and Champagne Grapes

Apple-Pistachio Tarte

The recipes for this menu can be found at the end of this chapter.

Fall is that time of year when we begin to yearn for warm, cozy spots like kitchens. This menu complements the season, highlighting a cornucopia of harvest produce and emphasizing fall flavors of fennel and apple under different guises. If you want, substitute chicken breasts or pork tenderloin for the duck. When the air begins to change and the first hearths kindle, the mood is ripe for lingering over a leisurely meal. With many hands at work you can

Good Spirits
Serve a Fumè Blanc with the bisque and a red Côte du Rhone or Châteauneuf-du-Pape with the duck breasts.

serve a multi-course menu that you probably wouldn't consider making and serving on your own. Let partners serve and clear their own creations course-by-course, in keeping with the nature of the undertaking. Calvados would be the perfect digestive to serve with after dinner coffee.

Setups for the Many-Hands Menu

To determine where to station prep areas, read through the recipes and note the various steps involved. For our menu, setup #1 needs an outlet for the blender or processor, setup #2 can work anywhere, and setup #3 needs a place to roll pastry.

Setup #1: Tomato-Pepper Bisque

	Ingredients	Utensils
1	red and 1 yellow pepper	Soup pot
1	large onion & 3 cloves garlic	Paper bag for peppers
1	fennel bulb	Wooden spoon
	Pernod or fennel seeds	Whisk
4	tablespoons unsalted butter	Strainer
1	bay leaf, thyme, peppercorns	2-cup measure
$^3/_4$	pound small green shrimp	Mixing bowl
6	large, ripe tomatoes	Processor or blender
2	tablespoons flour	
$1\,^1/_2$	cups heavy cream	

Sticky note #1: Roast peppers first to free oven for the tarte. Don't wash the pot after straining the soup base. Rinse and reuse the pot to finish the soup.

A sample setup.

Setup #2: Duck and Warm Cabbage Salad

Ingredients		Utensils
6	duck breast halves	1 large sauté pan
1	bottle Pinot Noir	1 saucepan
6	large cloves of garlic	Wooden spoon
2	cups all-purpose stock	Spatula
1	small head red cabbage	1-cup measure
1	fennel bulb	Measuring spoons
$^1/_4$	cup duck fat (or 2 tablespoons each butter and oil)	Oven-proof bowl and plate
2–3	tablespoons red wine vinegar	
2–3	tablespoons wildflower honey	
1	large leek	
2	Granny Smith apples	
1	small bunch fresh thyme	

Sticky note #2: Make sauce first and set aside in its pan. Reheat just before serving. Make the cabbage next and transfer to a heat-proof bowl to reheat later (reuse same sauté pan for duck). Prep garnishes. Sauté duck 10 minutes before serving time. Place duck on a heat-proof plate to hold in a low oven when soup is served. Cover cabbage and reheat at the same time as the duck. Slice duck just before serving.

Setup #3: Mashed Potatoes/Apple-Pistachio Tarte

Ingredients		Utensils
3	Golden Delicious apples	Paring knife
$^1/_4$	cup Demerara sugar	Measuring spoons
$^1/_4$	cup shelled pistachios	1- and $^1/_4$ -cup measures
	Calvados	Small pot
2	tablespoons unsalted butter	Rolling pin
1 $^3/_4$	cups pastry flour mix (see Tarte recipe)	Pastry scraper
	Sugar and salt	10" tarte pan
1	cup ice water	Wooden spoon

continues

continued

Ingredients		Utensils
6	ounces cold unsalted butter	Potato ricer or masher
$1/2$	cup apricot preserves	Kitchen shears
	potatoes (2 lbs.)	Pot for potatoes
4	shallots & 3 garlic cloves	
	Sage leaves	
	Half-and-half	

Sticky note #3: Put the potatoes on to cook while making the pastry. Prepare tarte filling as the pastry chills. Roll pastry and assemble tarte to go in the oven 1 hour before dinner time. Complete potato recipe and set aside to reheat before serving.

The Extra Mile

You can measure out the ingredients when you set up or let fellow cooks measure their own. Put salt, pepper, butter, and oils for cooking in a spot for communal use. Save Styrofoam meat trays to use as containers for everyone to organize their chopped, sliced, diced ingredients. Small paper cups also are good containers for measured ingredients.

Just the Two of You

The menu:

> Scallop Gratin with Caviar
>
> Walnut-Crusted Rack of Lamb
>
> Sweet Potato Frites
>
> Watercress with Rose-Scented Vinaigrette
>
> Chocolate-Dipped Strawberries

The recipes for this menu can be found at the end of this chapter.

Here's a menu just for the two of you; it features easy recipes, provocative food, a few things for voluptuous finger nibbling. Prepare the recipes together instead of dividing them up. As per the game plan, arrange ingredients for each recipe on separate trays, and approach the recipes as follows. First, make the vinaigrette for the watercress and get the ingredients for the chocolate glaze ready to go. Julienne the sweet potatoes. Next, prepare the lamb and set aside, ready to pop in the oven. Make the scallops last, and when they come out of the oven, reset the temperature to roast the lamb. Slip the lamb in the oven and pop the cork on a bottle of champagne to enjoy with your first course while the lamb roasts. When the lamb is done, cover with foil to rest while you prepare the frites. Put two plates in the oven to warm. One of you can toss the watercress while the other one carves.

Sage Advice

"With that meal it seemed they had discovered a new system of communication..."

—from *Like Water for Chocolate* by Laura Esquivel

Cook's Notes

On caviar: Beluga is the mildest, smoothest, and most expensive, with the largest eggs. Osetra eggs are a little smaller and firmer with a fuller flavor. Sevruga, the least expensive, has the smallest and most intensely flavored eggs. Good caviar has separate, glistening eggs and a fresh seagoing scent.

A Romantic Table Design

Here are a few ideas for creating a special atmosphere for an intimate evening.

➤ *Mood:* This is a special time to focus on togetherness. Silly sentimentality isn't at all what we had in mind. Clear the kitchen and dining area of any humdrum distractions of daily life, such as bills or upcoming events. Promise not to talk about problems. Turn off the phone and soften the lights except, of course, over your stove. If you don't have dimmers, put candles all around the room. Also burn a good-quality scented candle with a subtle, natural fragrance.

The Extra Mile

For your special evening, each of you must bring three thoughts to share: some-thing special about the other person; a dream (not the asleep kind); a trip you'd like to take together some day.

➤ *Table setting:* Make the table special with your best cloth, mats, and tableware. But keep it simple with one tall candlestick and a few votives for extra illumination. The whole ambiance should be peaceful and relaxing rather than commanding. If you're sharing the evening with a significant other of long standing, a small framed photo or two of a special memory is a nice touch on the table.

➤ *Flowers:* Definitely roses, but look for the old-fashioned variety in soft yellow or peach tones. Make a loose arrangement in a low crystal or silver bowl or a pretty basket.

➤ *Music:* Tune in to your favorite songs while cooking, then switch to Chopin nocturnes for dinner music or a selection of classic love songs by good vocalists.

A romantic table for two.

The Least You Need To Know

➤ Try cooking together at a party for plenty of hands-on interaction.

➤ Using a game plan gets fellow cooks rolling in the right direction.

➤ Many hands together can serve a delightful multi-course meal; just the two of you can share an especially intimate evening.

The Recipes

Tomato-Pepper Bisque with Shrimp and Fennel

1 red bell pepper

1 yellow bell pepper

1 fennel bulb (or substitute 1 tablespoon fennel seed)

1 large onion, chopped

1 large clove of garlic, chopped

$^3/_4$ pound small green shrimp, peeled and shells reserved

4 tablespoons unsalted butter

1 tablespoon oil

1 bay leaf

1 teaspoon dried thyme

5 black peppercorns

2 tablespoons Pernod

6 large ripe tomatoes, coarsely chopped (about 2 $^1/_2$ lbs.)

1 cup white wine

2 cups water

2 tablespoons flour

1 $^1/_2$ cups heavy cream

   salt and freshly ground black pepper to taste

1 lemon

1. Roast the peppers over an open gas flame or close to a broiler element, turning, until they are evenly charred. Seal the peppers in a paper bag and allow them to cool. Remove the charred skin from the peppers by wiping them with a damp paper towel or rinsing them under running water. Remove the stems, seeds, and membranes and coarsely chop the peppers. Reserve.

2. Strip the delicate fennel fronds from the main stalk. Mince them and reserve. Remove and discard the stalk, then cut the fennel bulb in half through the root. Place cut side down and thinly slice the fennel.

3. Cut the shrimp in half lengthwise and remove and discard the black vein.

133

4. In a large soup pot, melt 2 tablespoons of butter with the oil over medium heat. When the butter foams, add the onion, garlic, fennel, shrimp shells, bay leaf, thyme, and peppercorns to the pot. Stir to coat the vegetables with butter and oil. Press a piece of tin foil down on the vegetables and turn the heat to low. Cover the pot with a lid placed ajar and "sweat" the mixture for ten minutes, stirring occasionally. Do not allow the vegetables to brown. Remove the foil and add the Pernod. Raise the heat to high and stir for 3 minutes. Add the tomatoes, wine, and water and bring to a boil. Reduce the heat to low, cover the pot with a lid placed ajar, and simmer for 30 minutes.

5. Strain the soup base into a bowl, pressing hard on the solids to extract as much liquid as possible. Discard the solids. Purée the roasted peppers in a blender or food processor with 1 cup of the soup base.

6. In the same soup pot, melt the remaining two tablespoons of butter over medium-high heat and when it foams add the flour. Stir for three minutes without browning. Whisk in the soup base and the pepper purée. Bring the soup to a boil, then reduce the heat and simmer, stirring, for three minutes more. Add the heavy cream, the shrimp, and the minced fennel fronds to the pot. Slowly heat, stirring, until the soup is steaming but do not allow it to boil. The shrimp will turn opaque and cook in 1–2 minutes. Taste and adjust the seasoning, adding salt, pepper, and drops of lemon juice to taste. Serves 6–8.

Cook's Notes

Pernod is a French aperitif with a startling licorice nose. It was developed to replace the notorious *absinthe*, a hallucinogenic brew favored by many French country folk and American expatriates in France in the 1930s. Pernod is perfectly safe and a heavenly enhancement to shellfish soups and stews.

Cook's Notes

Order boneless duck breasts from a specialty butcher. You may substitute 6 skinless, boneless chicken breasts or 3 pounds pork tenderloin for the duck breasts. Also, the meat may be grilled rather than sautéed. Cook chicken breasts for 5–6 minutes per side; pork tenderloin to 140–145° internal temperature.

Sautéed Duck Breasts on Warm Red Cabbage Salad

6 boneless duck breast halves

   salt and freshly ground black pepper

3–5 tablespoons wildflower honey, at room temperature

1 tablespoon Dijon mustard

3 $^1/_2$ cups Pinot Noir

6 large cloves of garlic, skins on

2 cups of all-purpose stock (see Appendix)

1 red onion, peeled and sliced

1 medium head of red cabbage, cored and thinly sliced

1 fennel bulb, trimmed and sliced

$^1/_4$ cup duck fat, trimmed from the duck breasts (or use 1 tablespoon butter and
    1 tablespoon oil)

2–3 tablespoons good quality red wine vinegar or balsamic vinegar

1 large leek, cut into julienne (see Appendix for instructions for cleaning leeks)

2 Granny Smith apples, cored and cut into small dice (reserve in water to cover with
    the juice of $^1/_2$ lemon)

$^1/_2$ cup Calvados

$^1/_2$ cup fresh thyme leaves

Cook's Notes

Duck skin and fat is a luxurious indulgence, and not as sinful as you may think; duck fat (as well as poultry) has 13 percent less cholesterol than butter. Duck breasts should be served medium-rare, like a fine steak. Cook skinless breasts one minute less on the first side.

1. Score the skin on the duck breasts in a criss-cross pattern or remove and discard the duck skin. Lightly season the duck breasts with salt and pepper. Combine 1 tablespoon of wildflower honey, the Dijon mustard, and $^1/_2$ cup of Pinot Noir in a glass, ceramic, or enameled dish large enough to accommodate the duck breasts in a single layer and marinate the duck breasts for 30 minutes.

2. In a small pot, combine 3 cups Pinot Noir and the garlic cloves. Bring to a simmer over medium heat, partly cover the pot, reduce the heat to low, and gently simmer for 30–40 minutes or until the garlic is very tender. Remove the garlic, raise the heat, and reduce the wine to $1/2$ cup. When the garlic is cool enough to handle, remove the skins and force the garlic cloves through a fine sieve with the back of a wooden spoon, or mash to a purée with a fork. Reserve.

3. Add the stock to the wine reduction, raise the heat to high, and reduce the sauce until it lightly coats a spoon. Whisk the garlic purée into the sauce and season to taste with salt, freshly ground black pepper, and a teaspoon or two of wildflower honey to balance the acidity of the wine. Reserve the sauce.

4. In a large, heavy sauté pan, heat the duck fat or the butter and oil over medium-high heat. Add the red onion and sauté until it begins to wilt. Add the cabbage and the fennel and toss until the cabbage begins to wilt. Continue tossing the cabbage until it is tender/crisp. Add the wine vinegar and 2 tablespoons of wildflower honey and season with salt and pepper. Taste and adjust the seasoning, adding drops of vinegar or more honey to obtain a sweet/sour balance.

5. Heat a heavy sauté pan over medium-high heat and sauté the duck breasts, skin side down, for 4–5 minutes. Turn and sauté for three minutes more. Remove to a heat-proof plate and hold in a low oven while finishing the sauce. Pour the Calvados into the sauté pan and bring to a boil. Scrape the bottom of the sauté pan with a wooden spoon to pick up caramelized bits of flavor. Allow the Calvados to reduce to a bubbly glaze, then pour the reserved sauce into the sauté pan and stir to combine the flavors.

6. To slice the duck breasts, position a sharp knife at one o'clock to the duck breast, angle the knife, and carve into broad, diagonal, $1/4$" thick slices. Divide the cabbage among six warm plates and arrange the duck breast slices on top in a starburst pattern. In the center of each plate, place a small mound of julienned leek slivers. Sprinkle the apple cubes randomly around the outside perimeter of the cabbage. Ladle a circular band of sauce over the duck breast slices. Dust each serving with thyme leaves and serve immediately. Serves 6.

Creamy Mashed Potatoes with Garlic and Sage

2   pounds of Idaho potatoes

$^1/_2$ cup minced shallots

3   large cloves of garlic, peeled and minced

2   tablespoons unsalted butter

1   cup half-and-half

$^1/_2$ cup all-purpose stock

6   sage leaves cut into fine slivers

    salt and freshly ground black pepper

    freshly grated nutmeg

1. Cook the potatoes, whole and unpeeled, about 15 minutes in water to cover until they can be easily pierced through with a skewer. Drain the potatoes and allow them to cool.

2. In the same pot, melt one tablespoon of butter and sauté the shallots and the garlic over medium-low heat for one minute. Add the half-and-half and simmer gently for ten minutes.

3. Peel the potatoes and pass them through a ricer into the sauce pan with the cream, or mash in the cream with a potato masher until smooth. Add the stock, the remaining butter, and the sage leaves. Season with salt, pepper, and nutmeg to taste. Serves 6.

Apple-Pistachio Tarte with Calvados

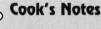

Cook's Notes

To make a flour mix for tender pastry, combine 3 cups all-purpose flour with one cup cake flour.

1 $^3/_4$ cups pastry flour mix

7   ounces cold unsalted butter cut into $^1/_4$" cubes (separate 6 ounces of butter for the pastry from 1 ounce for the tarte topping)

1   scant teaspoon salt

$^1/_2$ teaspoon sugar

2–3   tablespoons ice water

4   large Golden Delicious apples

$^1/_4$ cup shelled pistachios, finely minced

$^1/_4$ Demerara sugar

4   tablespoons Calvados

2   tablespoons unsalted butter cut into $^1/_4$" dice

$^1/_2$ cup apricot jam

Cook's Notes

Demerara sugar is natural, unrefined sugar. Health food stores are a good source for natural products. Granulated sugar can be substituted for demerara sugar.

1. To prepare the pastry, place the flour, 6 ounces of butter, the salt, and the sugar on a work surface or in a large bowl. Toss the butter bits with the flour. Using your fingertips, work the flour and butter together, pinching it into a crumbly mixture that resembles coarse meal. Drizzle one tablespoon of water over the mixture and toss to evenly dampen. If the mixture still feels dry, add a few more drops of water. Gather the pastry into a rough ball. With the heel of your hand, press a small portion of the dough down and away from the edge of the dough ball opposite you, smearing the flour and butter together against the work surface. Smear bit by bit. Using a pastry scraper, gather the dough together and repeat the process. Gather the dough into a ball and press into a slightly flattened disc. Wrap in film and chill 20 minutes before rolling.

2. On a lightly floured surface, roll the pastry dough $^1/_8$" thick. Transfer the pastry to a 10"–11" tarte pan with a removable bottom. Using a knuckle, gently work the pastry into the corners of the pan. With the overhang draping loosely over the edge of the pan, run the rolling pin over it to trim off. Gently press the extra dough on the sides of the tart pan level to the top of the edge (this gives the sides a little extra rein-forcement). Prick the sides, edges, and bottom of the tarte with a fork. Line the pastry with foil and fill with pie weights or dried beans.

3. Preheat the oven to 450°.

4. Bake the pastry shell on the lowest oven rack for 10 minutes. Remove the pie weights and return the pastry shell to the oven for 10 minutes or until light golden.

5. Peel the apples and remove the cores, stems, and blossom ends. Place the apples cut side down and slice paper thin.

6. Spread half the apple slices in an even layer on the baked tart shell. Sprinkle with half the sugar and half the pistachios. Spread the rest of the apple slices evenly on top and sprinkle with the rest of the sugar and the pistachios. Drizzle 2 tablespoons of the Calvados over the apples. Distribute the remaining one ounce of butter bits evenly over the top. Turn the oven down to 400° and bake the tart for 40 minutes.

7. To glaze the tarte, in a small pan combine the apricot jam and the Calvados. Place the pan over medium heat and melt the jam. Strain the jam into a small bowl. Brush the glaze evenly over the surface of the tarte. Serves 6–8.

Scallop Gratin with Caviar

4 ounces scallops (leave Bay scallops whole; slice sea scallops into two coins of equal thickness)

$1/4$ cup heavy cream

1 egg yolk

1 teaspoon sour cream

1–2 teaspoons lemon juice

2 tablespoons snipped chives

   salt and pepper

   a dash of cayenne pepper

1 small tin of caviar (30 grams)

1. Arrange the scallops on 2 small heat-proof plates or scallop shells. For sea scallops, slightly overlap the slices in a flower petal pattern.

2. In a small bowl, whisk the heavy cream, egg yolk, sour cream and lemon juice together until the mixture is slightly thickened. Season with salt, pepper, and a dash of cayenne.

3. Preheat the broiler.

4. Place the scallop plates on a baking tray and broil, 3–4 inches from the broiler element for 30 seconds (to achieve the proper distance from the broiler, elevate the

tray on an overturned cake pan). Remove the tray from the oven and spoon an equal portion of sauce and a sprinkling of chives over each portion. Return the tray to the broiler and cook for $^1/_2$ to 1 minute more or until the sauce is bubbly and flecked with golden brown.

5. Top each serving with a dollop of caviar and serve immediately. Serves 2.

Walnut-Crusted Rack of Lamb

1   8-rib rack of lamb

$^1/_2$ cup finely ground walnuts

$^1/_4$ cup fresh bread crumbs

1–2 tablespoons fresh thyme leaves

1   tablespoon snipped fresh chives

1   small garlic clove, crushed

    salt and freshly ground pepper to taste

    a tiny pinch of cayenne

2–3 tablespoons walnut oil

1. Have the butcher remove the backbone from the rack and "French" the ribs (scraping 3" of bone clean). Trim away the "fell," a thin, papery coating, and most of the fat. Lower oven rack to lowest setting.

2. Preheat the oven to 425°.

3. Combine the walnuts, crumbs, thyme, chives, and garlic in a medium bowl and season to taste with salt, pepper, and cayenne. Stir in just enough walnut oil to bind the mixture. Evenly coat the meat side of the lamb rack with the mixture. Place the rack in a small roasting pan and roast the meat on the lower oven rack for 20 minutes or to 125–130° for rare to medium rare meat. Use an instant-read meat thermometer inserted in the thickest part of the meat to test for doneness.

4. Remove the roast from the oven and loosely cover with foil. Rest the rack of lamb for 10 minutes before carving.

5. Carve the rack between the ribs and arrange 3–4 ribs on 2 warmed plates. Garnish each plate with a mound of sweet potato frites above the lamb and a bouquet of watercress on each side.

Cook's Notes

If you want a sauce with the lamb, the red wine sauce for the duck breasts in this chapter is equally good with lamb.

Sweet Potato Frites

1   extra large sweet potato

1   bottle vegetable or safflower oil

   fine sea salt

1. Peel the sweet potato and cut into fine slivers using a mandolin or vegetable cutter. Alternatively, cut them into fine julienne shreds by hand (see Appendix).

2. Place the sweet potato slivers in a bowl of ice water for 20 minutes (or until ready to cook).

3. Drain the potatoes and dry completely. Fill a high-sided frying pan (cast iron frying pans are ideal for frying potatoes) half full with oil and heat the oil to 385°. Or, test the temperature of the oil by frying one potato sliver. It should rise to the top of the oil and become crisp in about 30 seconds. Cook the potatoes in small batches. They should dance freely in the hot oil as they fry. They should be cooked and crispy in about 30–60 seconds.

4. With a slotted spoon or a skimmer, remove the cooked potatoes to paper towels to drain. Sprinkle them lightly with the salt. Hold the finished fries in a low oven while you prepare the remaining batches.

Watercress with Rose-Scented Vinaigrette

1   large or 2 small bunches of watercress (about 2 loose cups), rinsed and dried

$^1/_4$ teaspoon salt

   a grinding of fresh black pepper ($^1/_4$ teaspoon or to taste)

1   teaspoon whole pink peppercorns

1   tablespoon tarragon vinegar or champagne vinegar

2   tablespoons olive oil

$^1/_4$ –$^1/_2$ teaspoon rose flower water to taste (optional)

141

1. In a small bowl, combine the salt, pepper, and pink peppercorns. Using the back of a teaspoon, lightly crush the pink peppercorns. Whisk in the vinegar, then the olive oil and rose flower water to taste.

2. Keep the watercress sealed and well chilled until just before serving, then toss the watercress with just enough vinaigrette to lightly cover the leaves.

Chocolate-Dipped Strawberries

1 pint of large, ripe strawberries

1 recipe chocolate glaze (see Raspberry-Chocolate Cake in Chapter 8)

Fondue forks or wooden skewers

1. Rinse the strawberries and pat dry. Leave the stems and green hulls intact (if they are attractive) and pile the strawberries in a pretty bowl or basket.

2. In an attractive, heatproof bowl, prepare the chocolate glaze over a small pot of simmering water. Immediately bring the bowl of warm glaze to the table and place on a hot pad.

3. Spear and eat the strawberries fondue style.

Cook's Notes

Try the chocolate glaze with ripe, juicy pears or bananas.

Chapter 11

Right in Your Own Backyard

In This Chapter

➤ Outdoor celebrations

➤ A fiesta

➤ A tea party

➤ The recipes

When someone you care about reaches a milestone, it calls for a celebration. Outdoor parties have a definite cachet, because nothing is more pleasing than having Mother Nature as a backdrop for a happy fête. Your own backyard offers an opportunity for making magic with a special theme. When the mood is footloose and fancy-free, our fiesta fits the bill. Opt for hosting an elegant tea when the occasion calls for a bit more refinement. Both parties naturally lend themselves to an outdoor theme. Of course, not all milestones occur when weather permits outdoor festivities, so both party scenarios can be staged indoors or easily moved indoors. But when the sun or moon shines brightly and balmy breezes blow, revel in it!

Sage Advice

"Happy are those who sing with all their heart. To find joy in the sky, the trees, and the flowers."

—Henri Matisse

Whether you choose a festive fiesta or sophisticated tea, these party themes are a perfect complement for a special event. The occasion may be a birthday, anniversary, graduation, shower, or promotion. Or maybe you're just in the mood to lift your own spirits and those of your lucky guests. Why not invent a reason? Have a party to herald the anniversary of summer solstice; throw a fête to honor Carmen Miranda; consult a book of famous birthdays and celebrate the birthday of...perhaps Henri Matisse.

An Outdoor Celebration Beckons

When planning an outdoor celebration, add a few key considerations to your basic party checklist. Because you're dealing with Mother Nature, outdoor entertaining requires more advance planning than indoor parties. The following list describes some particulars, along with some ideas for outdoor decorations, that you can use to embellish a fiesta or a tea:

Tents: If you can't move a party quickly and efficiently indoors, don't second guess the weather; rent a tent. If your event is in the fickle early or late summer months, consider renting space heaters to cover unexpected temperature dips. Chapter 17 covers the details on party rentals. At many rental companies you also can find silver tea services, urns, large pitchers for sangria, extra serving accessories, etc.

Reality Bites

Don't have an outdoor party for more people than you can move indoors unless you know *beyond doubt* that the weather won't turn foul.

Traffic flow: Your company will be moving in and out of the house to use the guest bath. A chance always exists that the ground may be damp. Consider purchasing plastic runners from a hardware or discount outlet to protect rugs and wood floors.

Lawn: Of course, you want an impeccable lawn for the party. If you don't have regular lawn service or the time to spend on proper mowing, edging, and trimming, book a maintenance company well ahead. In busy summer months, a company needs advance notice to work an extra job into its schedule of regulars. Plant flowers or purchase hanging baskets well ahead of the occasion so flowers are lush.

Smart Move

Note on invitations that your party will be on the lawn and to wear appropriate shoes.

Bugs: Buy lots of inexpensive webbed citronella candles in a rainbow of colors, or focus on a single color theme. Massed on a wall or around the perimeter of a patio or garden, this stock item transforms into a special effect. Or hang paper lanterns from trees with a citronella candle affixed inside. The container holding the candle should be fairly deep and have some weight. Common sense dictates that if it's really windy, nix the paper lanterns. Catalogs and discount outlets offer a variety of outdoor lighting alternatives, although somewhat more costly.

Wind: Be prepared for a breezy or gusty day. Use weights to nail down anything that may blow away from a buffet table or set tables; pretty paperweights, polished stones, or small garden statuary attractively fit the bill. Roll flatware in napkins and tie with a pretty ribbon. Used paper plates take off like Frisbees, so station a clean, decorated trash can in a convenient spot.

The Extra Mile
Fill a pretty basket with travel-size bug repellent tubes or sprays as an extra party favor.

Good Spirits
Fill a big clay pot with ice and south-of-the-border beers, and have pitchers of Sangria and/or Margaritas. Recipes for both drinks are in Chapter 1.

A Fiesta

The menu:

Steve's Guacamole with Blue Corn Chips

Spicy Black Beans and Rice

Citrus-Marinated and Barbecued Pork Tenderloin Fajitas

Warm Tortillas (store bought)

Cherry Tomato Salsa

New Mex Hot Sauce

Jicama and Watercress Salad

Apricot-Lime Mousse Cake

The recipes for this menu can be found at the end of this chapter.

There's nothing demure about a fiesta. Give it plenty of pizzazz! Match the vibrant flavors of the menu with fanciful invitations, bright primary colors, and lively Mariachi music. Strew the buffet table with paper flowers. Roll flatware in two or three shades of green napkins and stand them upright in clay pots to resemble cacti. At discount stores you often can find inexpensive tin oil lanterns that suit the theme and chase the bugs. Use an array of mix-and-match colorful bowls and platters for presenting food on the buffet. By the way, car blankets are great for extra seating, and fit into the free-and-easy theme.

Smart Move

Will kids be at your fiesta? Entertain them by letting them decorate straw sombreros with crepe paper and paper flowers purchased at a craft shop. A pinata is also a festive and fun addition to your party.

Plan your food preparation around the make-ahead opportunities. Note that the salsa and salad are wet dishes, so if you're using paper plates, look for sturdy ones or buy enough so guests can double them up. Extra napkins are in order as well as plenty of non-alcoholic thirst quenchers—a must with spicy food. Remember to check your charcoal supply or the gas tank on your grill.

Tea for More Than Two

The menu:

> Oyster Mushroom Sandwiches on Walnut Bread
>
> Cured Ham, Arugula, and Mustard Butter on Orange-Fennel Rye
>
> Smoked Trout Mousse Sandwiches on White Bread
>
> Curried Crab and Asparagus Tartlets
>
> Salmon Gateau
>
> Fruit Kabobs
>
> A selection of cheeses
>
> Madelines

The recipes for this menu can be found at the end of this chapter.

The history of tea began 3,000–5,000 years ago in China, but the ritual of afternoon tea didn't begin until the 1840s. The English Duchess of Bedford, Anna, instituted "tea," finding the custom a greatly restorative interlude during the long wait for dinner at 8:00. The late afternoon pause for tea with all its accouterments and ceremony never infiltrated the American way of life except for an occasional renaissance in posh hotels. And what a pity that we rarely turn to a tea party for entertaining. Particularly for an outdoor party, nothing is nicer than tea in the garden. Just the fact that it's uncommon makes a tea party extra-special. To take a tea party over the top, set up croquet or bocci on the lawn.

Start your party early, at 4:00 or 5:00. Have two buffet tables: one for food and one for champagne (a perfect complement to the menu) and tea. You don't need to have set tables for this party, but definitely arrange seating areas here and there around the yard. In early summer or fall when the air is still a bit nippy, offer three different hot teas, each identified with a different colored ribbon on the pot. In the height of summer have a selection of several iced teas. A tea party calls for a kitchen/serving helper. To keep food looking fresh, arrange it on smaller platters and have your helper make sandwiches and refresh trays throughout the party.

A Buffet Table Design for Tea

A table set for tea should convey a sense of old-world charm and refinement.

Table linens: A buffet tablecloth in white or off-white is proper tea table attire and the best complement to garden flowers. Bold colors and patterns distract from the outdoor scene. If you set up other tables for seating, use the same color cloth and napkins.

On the buffet table: For a special presentation, arrange sandwiches on china or crystal cake stands. A three-tiered server or silver platter is perfect for the Madelines. Use rose petals, edible flowers, or candied violets for garnishing.

A table set for tea.

Flowers: Fill empty votives or tiny clay pots with oasis and rim the perimeter with rose leaves. Top with moistened moss and "plant" a single flower, such as a Gerber daisy, in the votive. Insert a florist's prong (used for greeting cards) in the pot. On a card, inscribe the name of one dish on the menu. Attach card to the prong and place arrangements next to the corresponding dishes, creating a random pattern the length of the table.

Votive planters.

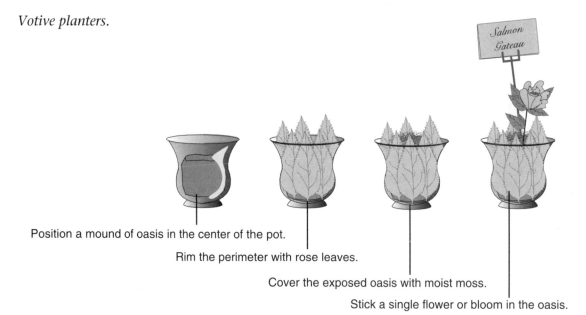

Position a mound of oasis in the center of the pot.

Rim the perimeter with rose leaves.

Cover the exposed oasis with moist moss.

Stick a single flower or bloom in the oasis.

Music: If you're going all out, hire a cello player or violinist. Otherwise use a portable CD player. If you're handy, buy extra speaker wire and bring your speakers outdoors. Play light-hearted waltzes or instrumental arrangements from movie scores.

Candles: If the party drifts into evening, bring out the webbed citronella candles mentioned earlier or outfit various sizes of glass hurricanes with citronella candles. If a croquet or bocci game is in progress, illuminate the area with citronella torches. Don't line your walk with votives in paper bags—this idea has become far too common.

The Least You Need To Know

➤ An outdoor party is the crowning touch for a celebration.

➤ Planning well ahead is essential to cooperate with mother nature's foibles.

➤ Whether the mood is festive or refined, go the extra mile with a special theme.

The Recipes

Steve's Guacamole

From good friend, great cooking pal, and restaurateur Steve Gillum, of Cafe d'Oro, *Cleveland Heights, Ohio.*

2 large shallots, peeled and finely minced

3 large cloves of garlic, peeled and finely minced

2 ripe avocados, peeled and cubed

the juice of two limes and one lemon

$1/2$ cup minced fresh cilantro

1 jalepeno pepper, seeds and membranes removed and very finely minced (optional)

$1/2$ cup peeled seeded and diced tomatoes

salt and freshly ground black pepper to taste

1. In a large bowl, combine the shallots, garlic, avocado, and citrus juices. Using a fork, mash the avocado and blend the ingredients. Fold in the diced tomato, cilantro, and minced jalepeno and season to taste with salt and pepper. Bury the avocado pit in the prepared guacamole to keep the color from turning. Cover and refrigerate until ready to serve. Makes about 4 cups. Serve the guacamole with blue corn chips or "bruschetta" style on grilled bread.

Cook's Notes

If friends are sensitive to garlic or hot peppers, omit them. The large amount of shallot and citrus make for a tasty guacamole without the extra punch. Use only ripe avocados. Ripe flesh yields to gentle pressure. Ripen avocados at room temperature then refrigerate.

Spicy Black Beans and Rice

1 pound black turtle beans

1 teaspoon baking soda

12 sun-dried tomatoes, cut into slivers

1 smoked ham hock (optional)

1 teaspoon dried thyme

2 teaspoon cumin seeds, lightly toasted in a dry pan

1 tablespoon salt

6 dried New Mexico chilies, soaked
   in hot water to cover till softened

1 small can natural apple juice (5 $\frac{1}{2}$ oz.)

   non-stick cooking spray

4 ancho chiles

4 chipolte chiles

1 large onion, peeled and chopped

2 cloves of garlic, peeled and chopped

2 tablespoons balsamic vinegar

2 teaspoons ground cumin

1 teaspoon cinnamon

1 teaspoon marjoram

   a few pinches of sugar or to taste

   salt to taste

3 cups plain cooked white rice

1 can miniature ears of corn, drained

5 radishes, diced

$\frac{1}{2}$ cup feta cheese, crumbled

$\frac{1}{2}$ cup minced cilantro

Cook's Notes

An ancho chile is a dried poblano; a chipolte is a smoked jalepeño.

Reality Bites

Protect your hands with rubber gloves when handling chiles. *Capsaicin*, the chemical that makes chiles hot, is easily absorbed into the skin. "Hunan hand" is known only too well to those who deal with chiles barehanded. Beware of touching your eyes or other sensitive body parts with tainted fingers. Capsaicin is most concentrated in the placenta, or the membrane, of a chile, not in the seeds.

1. Rinse and pick over the beans. Place the beans in a large pot, cover with 2" of water, and add the baking soda. Bring the water to a boil and boil for 5 minutes. Drain the beans and return them to the pot. Again, cover the beans with water by 3" and add the sun-dried tomatoes, smoked ham hock, dried thyme, cumin seeds, and salt to the pot. Over high heat, bring the beans to a boil, then reduce and adjust the heat to maintain a gentle simmer. Add extra water if necessary to keep beans submerged

as they cook. Cook the beans just until they are tender to the bite. Cooking time will vary depending on age of the beans. Begin checking the beans for doneness after 30 minutes. Remove the cooked beans from the heat and reserve in their pot. The beans may be prepared a day ahead to this point. Cool, cover, and refrigerate.

2. To make the sauce, remove the stems and seeds from the softened New Mexico chiles. Tear the chiles into small pieces and place them in the container of a blender jar. Add the apple juice and process the chiles to a smooth purée. Leave the purée in the blender jar.

3. Coat a small sauté pan with non-stick spray and over medium heat, turn the ancho and chipolte chiles in the warm pan until they soften. Remove the stems and seeds from the chiles and tear them into pieces. In the same sauté pan, sauté the onion and the garlic with the chile pieces until the onion is translucent. Scrape the mixture into the blender jar containing the purée. Add the vinegar, cumin, cinnamon, and marjoram to the blender and purée. The texture should be like a thick milkshake; thin with water if necessary. Add sugar and salt to taste. The sauce can be refrigerated for up to one week in a sealed container or it can be frozen for several months.

Cook's Notes

This sauce is a hot-food lover's delight. For a milder sauce, cut the heat by puréeing one 15-oz. can of diced tomatoes in the blender with the sauce.

4. Drain the beans, reserving their liquid. Place the beans in a heatproof casserole and stir in the one cup chile sauce and $1/2$ cup bean liquid. The beans should be well coated but not too soupy. Add more chile sauce and bean liquid to adjust the taste and texture. If you used a ham hock, shred the meat from the bone and add it to the beans. Reheat the beans, covered, in a 325° oven for 20–30 minutes before serving.

5. To serve, mound the beans in the center of a large warm serving platter. Surround the beans with hot rice. Arrange mini-corn ears between the beans and rice. Scatter the radishes and the feta cheese over the beans and dust the whole platter with minced cilantro. Serves 8–10.

Citrus-Marinated and Barbecued Pork Tenderloin Fajitas

juice of one orange

juice of one lemon

juice of one lime

$^1/_4$ cup safflower oil

$^1/_3$ cup Tequila

1 tablespoon ground cumin seed

2 teaspoons dried oregano

1 teaspoon ground coriander seed

$^1/_2$ teaspoon cinnamon

1 teaspoon salt

freshly ground black pepper

a healthy dash of cayenne pepper

4 pounds of pork tenderloin, trimmed of fat and tendons

4 large bell peppers (mix red, green, and yellow)

2 poblano peppers (or substitute more bell peppers)

4 Spanish or Vidalia onions, peeled and sliced

non-stick spray or vegetable oil

1 cup loosely packed fresh oregano leaves

salt and freshly ground black pepper

1 cup sour cream or plain yogurt

1 cup slivered scallions

1 cup minced cilantro leaf

cherry tomato salsa

New Mex hot sauce

30 flour fajita tortillas

1. In a glass, ceramic, or enameled dish large enough to hold the pork tenderloins, combine the citrus juices, oil, tequila, cumin seed, dried oregano, coriander seed, cinnamon, salt, black pepper, and cayenne pepper. Roll the pork tenderloins in the marinade. Cover the dish and marinate the pork in the refrigerator for 6–12 hours, turning occasionally. Remove the tenderloins from the marinade, pat them dry, and turn the "tail" of the tenderloin under to form a cylinder of equal width. Tie the tails with a piece of string.

2. Remove the stems, seeds, and membranes from the bell and poblano peppers and cut them into $^1/_2$" strips. Lightly coat a large sauté pan (cast iron is ideal) with non-stick cooking spray. Place the pan over high heat and when it is hot, sauté the peppers and the onions in batches until they are slightly charred (the peppers and onions will not char in an overcrowded pan).

3. Transfer the vegetables to a heatproof bowl, toss them with the oregano leaves, and add salt and pepper to taste. The vegetables can be prepared an hour or two ahead and reheated in a low oven.

4. Prepare a charcoal grill (when the charcoal has a layer of gray ash through which a red glow is visible, the fire is ready), or heat a gas grill on medium-high heat.

5. Brown the tenderloins on all sides, turning for two to three minutes. Cover the grill and cook the tenderloins, turning occasionally, to an internal temperature of 140°.

Begin checking the temperature after 15 minutes. Transfer the tenderloins to a warm platter and allow them to rest for a few minutes before carving.

6. Slice the pork on the diagonal into paper-thin slices. Transfer the slices to the center of a warm platter and surround them with the vegetables. Serve the fajita garnishes, sour cream or yogurt, slivered scallions, minced cilantro, cherry tomato salsa, New Mex hot sauce and any leftover guacamole, in separate bowls. Serves 8–10.

Cook's Notes

Warm the tortillas following manufacturer's instructions. Insulated hot/cold picnic carrier pouches are handy for keeping tortillas warm.

Cherry Tomato Salsa

2 quarts cherry tomatoes, washed, dried, and quartered

1 large onion, minced

3–4 cloves of garlic, minced

2 jalepeno or other small hot peppers, seeded, membranes removed, and finely minced

$^1/_2$ cup minced cilantro leaf

$^1/_2$ cup minced mint leaves

the juice of one or two limes

salt and pepper to taste

1. In a large mixing bowl, combine all the salsa ingredients. Adjust the seasoning, adding more garlic, herbs, lime juice, salt, and pepper to taste.

Cook's Notes

Vary the salsa ingredients depending on locally available produce. For instance, use tiny yellow pear tomatoes for half of the tomatoes. Experiment with different hot chiles instead of the jalepeno. Feature a flavored mint, such as pineapple or chocolate, and use all mint, no cilantro. Makes 2 $^1/_2$ quarts.

Jicama and Watercress Salad

4 tablespoons fresh lime juice

$^1/_2$ cup grapefruit juice

3 tablespoons rice wine vinegar

1 teaspoon honey mustard

$^1/_2$ cup vegetable oil

   salt and freshly ground black pepper to taste

1 small jicama (about one pound), peeled and julienned

3 small bunches of watercress

6 scallions, thinly sliced

1. In a flat ceramic, enameled, or glass dish, combine the citrus juices, rice wine vinegar, and honey mustard. Drizzle in the oil, whisking. Season to taste with salt and pepper. Stir in the jicama, cover, and refrigerate for several hours.

2. Just before serving (the jicama should be icy cold), drain the jicama, reserving the dressing. Place the jicama in a salad bowl. Toss the jicama with the watercress and scallions, adding more dressing to lightly coat the watercress and scallions. Serves 8–10.

Apricot-Lime Mousse Cake

Cook's Notes

Mousse cakes were popular during the heyday of nouvelle cuisine. Typically made with a buttery genoise, this cake is a much lighter version, *sans beurre*.

10" springform pan

   parchment paper to line the pan and make a collar

   non-stick cooking spray

6 large eggs, separated, plus 2 extra whites

$1^1/_2$ cups superfine sugar (reserve 2 tablespoons from the total amount for beating the egg whites) the zest of one lime

3 tablespoons lime juice

1 teaspoon vanilla

1 cup cake flour

$^1/_2$ cup corn starch

$^1/_8$ teaspoon cream of tartar

$^1/_2$ cup confectioners sugar

$^1/_2$ cup rum, plus 4 tablespoons

$^3/_4$ cup lime juice (about 4–5 limes)

2 packages unflavored gelatin

1 15 oz. can apricot halves in natural syrup

$^1/_2$ cup plus 2 tablespoons granulated sugar

1 $^1/_2$ cups heavy cream

4 tablespoons apricot jam

1 cup shredded coconut

1. Lightly spray the bottom of the spring form pan with non-stick cooking spray and line it with parchment. Cut a 3"×30" strip of parchment for the paper collar and set aside to use later.

2. Preheat the oven to 350°.

3. In an electric mixer, beat the eggs and the superfine sugar until the eggs lighten in color, double in volume, and fall from the whip in a ribbon when it is raised. Remove the work bowl from the machine and with a large rubber spatula, fold in the lime zest and juice and the vanilla.

4. Sift the cake flour and corn starch together and fold half into the batter. When it is thoroughly incorporated, fold in the other half.

5. In a clean bowl, whip the egg whites, adding the cream of tartar when they foam. When the egg whites begin to mount, gradually drizzle in the 2 tablespoons of reserved sugar. Beat the egg whites until soft peaks form. Whisk $^1/_4$ of the whites into the cake base to lighten it.

6. With a large rubber spatula, gently fold in the rest of the whites until well combined. Pour the batter into the cake pan, mounding slightly in the center.

7. Bake the cake on the center oven rack for 40–45 minutes or until a cake tester or toothpick comes clean when inserted into the center of the cake. Rest the cake on a rack for 10 minutes before unmolding.

155

8. Remove the cake from the pan and slice it in half horizontally (using a ruler as a guide, insert toothpicks into the center of the cake and around the perimeter for a knife guide).

9. In a small bowl, combine the confectioners sugar and $1/2$ cup of rum and stir until the sugar dissolves. Turn the cut sides of the cake up and dab an equal amount of rum syrup over each half with a pastry brush. Wash the springform pan and return the bottom cake half to the pan.

Cook's Notes

To properly fold, use a large rubber spatula and cut down through the center of the mixture. Bring the spatula up the side of the bowl, giving the bowl a $1/4$ turn as you scoop. Cut down through the center again and repeat, turning, until the ingredients are evenly combined.

10. To prepare the mousse filling, put the lime juice in a small heatproof cup and sprinkle the gelatin on top. Place the cup in a small pan of simmering water to melt the gelatin.

11. In a blender or food processor, purée the apricots with their liquid and the granulated sugar. Transfer the purée to a large bowl and whisk in the gelatin mixture. Set the bowl in a larger bowl filled with ice. Stir the purée until it becomes slightly thickened and syrupy, indicating that it is ready to set.

12. Whip the heavy cream to the soft peak stage and fold it into the purée. Pour half of the mousse over the cake bottom in the springform pan. Place the other half of the cake on top of the mousse. Assemble the paper collar around the inside perimeter of the cake pan and pour in the rest of the mousse. Chill until the mousse is set, about 6 hours.

13. To finish the cake, in a small sauce pan, melt the jam with the rum. Unmold the cake and brush the jam liberally on the sides of the cake. Press the coconut into the sides of the cake and chill until serving time. Serves 8–10.

Cook's Notes

If you don't have time to make a cake, just prepare the apricot mousse. Pour it into pretty crystal glasses, chill until set, and serve it with a sprinkling of coconut; or use parfait glasses, layering the mousse and coconut. Prepare the mousse with any puréed fruit.

Tea Sandwiches

1. Bread for tea sandwiches should be rich, moist, and densely textured. A boutique bread shop should offer a good selection. Choose three different breads with flavors complimentary to the sandwich fillings; the ones in the menu offer an example. Have the bread shop remove the crusts and slice the bread 1/4" thick (take the scraps home to make crumbs).

2. When preparing tea sandwiches, make one whole sandwich, then cut the sandwich into two smaller shapes such as triangles or finger sandwiches. A standard loaf should yield about 24 sandwiches. Although there is more waste and half the yield, you can cut out rounds with a 3"–4" biscuit cutter. Cut the rounds before assembling the sandwiches. Process the scraps for bread crumbs.

3. Assemble some sandwiches just before the party begins, then replenish the trays with freshly made sandwiches throughout the party.

Oyster Mushroom Filling

8 ounces oyster mushrooms, cleaned, tough bases removed and discarded, and very finely minced

1 large shallot, finely minced

2 tablespoons unsalted butter

2 tablespoons Amontillado sherry

$^1/_2$ cup heavy cream

$^1/_2$ cup flat leaf parsley, minced

4 ounces cream cheese, softened

salt, pepper, cayenne, and freshly grated nutmeg

$^1/_2$ lemon

1. In a medium sauté pan, heat the butter; when it foams, sauté the mushrooms and shallot until softened.

2. Add the sherry and allow it to evaporate.

3. Add the heavy cream and the cream cheese and turn the heat to low. Stir the mixture until thickened and season to taste with salt, pepper, cayenne, nutmeg, and drops of lemon juice. Makes 1 $^1/_2$ cups

For any tea sandwich, use only a thin layer of filling.

Mustard Butter

4   ounces unsalted butter, softened

2   tablespoons Dijon style mustard

    a generous grinding of fresh black pepper

$^1/_2$ pound smoked ham sliced paper thin

2   bunches arugula, washed and dried

1. In a food processor, process the butter, mustard, and black pepper until smooth. Alternatively, beat the mixture with a wooden spoon until smooth and blended.

2. To make the ham sandwiches, spread both slices of bread with the mustard butter. Use one layer of ham per sandwich, trimming the ham as necessary. Cover the ham with one layer of whole arugula leaves.

Smoked Trout Mousse

1   whole smoked trout

$^1/_4$ cup plus 2 tablespoons sour cream

4   tablespoons unsalted butter, softened

3   teaspoons horseradish

    salt, freshly ground black pepper, and drops of lemon juice to taste

$^1/_2$ cup snipped chives

1. Remove the skin from the trout and break the flesh into chunks.

2. In the work bowl of a food processor fitted with a knife blade, place the trout along with the sour cream, butter, and horseradish. Purée until the mixture is smooth. Add the salt, pepper, and lemon juice to taste.

3. Transfer the mixture to a mixing bowl and fold in the snipped chives. Makes 2 cups.

Cook's Notes

Trout Mousse may also be prepared with smoked salmon; a dollop nestled in a Belgian endive leaf is an attractive hors d'oeuvre.

Curried Crab and Asparagus Tartlets

12 pre-baked tart shells

4 ounces real crab meat, flaked (check for and discard any cartilage)

6 asparagus spears

4 egg yolks

$^3/_4$ cup heavy cream

1 teaspoon curry powder

salt and freshly ground black pepper to taste

Cook's Notes

Prepare one batch of the pastry dough following the recipe in Chapter 10, omitting the sugar. Chill. Roll the dough 1/8" thick and fill 12 2"–3" tart shells with the dough. Pre-bake the shells per recipe instructions.

1. Snap the tough ends off the asparagus spears and bring a skillet of water to a boil. Blanch the asparagus for 1–2 minutes. Drain and rinse under cold water until cool. Remove the asparagus tips and cut them in half lengthwise. Slice the stalks into $^1/_4$ " slivers.

2. Evenly divide the crab and the slivered asparagus stalks among the pre-baked pastry shells. Place the pastry shells on a baking sheet.

3. Preheat the oven to 400°.

4. In a small mixing bowl, whisk the egg yolks with the cream and curry powder until they are thoroughly combined. Fill the pastry shells with the custard mixture. Carefully slide the tray into the oven taking care not to slosh the custard out of the shells.

5. Bake the tarts for 15–20 minutes or until the custard is firm. Allow the tarts to cool. With the tip of a small, sharp knife, gently loosen the tarts from the molds, then lever out of the mold with a fork. Garnish each tart with a piece of asparagus tip. The tarts may be rewarmed on a heatproof platter in a low oven.

Salmon Gateau

An exchange student from St. Tropez, Peggy Cadel, loved to cook. Here's one of her favorites, a recipe from her mother.

2 quarts water

2 1/4 cups white wine
(reserve 1/4 cup for the sauce)

2 carrots, peeled and sliced

2 onions, peeled and sliced

2 teaspoons salt

1 bay leaf

10 black peppercorns

1 teaspoon dried thyme

1 whole salmon fillet (about 1 3/4 lbs.)

5 slices white sandwich bread

1 cup whole milk or enough to cover the bread

3 whole eggs

1/4 cup minced fresh tarragon leaves,
plus a few whole sprigs to garnish

1 1/2 cups heavy cream

2 tablespoons sour cream

1 lemon

salt and freshly ground black pepper

a few dashes of cayenne pepper

1 tablespoon unsalted butter

1 large shallot, minced

1/2 cup poaching liquid

1. Prepare a *court bouillon.* In a soup pot, combine the water, white wine, carrots, onions, salt, peppercorns, bay leaf, and thyme. Bring the liquid to a boil, then reduce the heat and simmer for 30 minutes. Strain the broth into a clean bowl and cool.

2. Remove any feathery bones from the salmon fillet with tweezers. Place the fillet in a large sauté pan (cut the fillet in half if necessary) and add enough court bouillon to cover the fish. Remove the fillet from the liquid and bring the court bouillon to a boil. Slip the salmon into the liquid. Turn the heat down and adjust the court bouillion to a gentle simmer. Poach the salmon for 10 minutes. Remove the salmon from the heat and allow the salmon to cool in the court bouillion.

3. Preheat the oven to 375°.

4. Place the bread in a pan or a bowl and cover it with milk.

5. Transfer the salmon fillets to a plate and remove and discard the skin and gray flesh. Flake the salmon into a large mixing bowl. Squeeze the milk from the bread and shred it over the salmon. Add the eggs, tarragon, 1/2 cup heavy cream, and sour cream to the mixing bowl and beat the mixture with a fork to combine. Season the mixture to taste with drops of lemon juice, salt, freshly ground pepper, and pinches of cayenne pepper.

6. Transfer the mixture to an oiled 5–6 cup mold (loaf pan, fish mold, soufflé mold, bundt pan, and so on) and lightly cover it with foil. Bake for 35–40 minutes or until a toothpick inserted in the center of the loaf comes clean.

7. Unmold the salmon loaf onto a platter. Cut the loaf into 12 slices (the slices may be cut in half lengthwise for smaller portions). Garnish the platter with a few whole tarragon sprigs. Serve warm or at room temperature.

8. To prepare the sauce, in a small sauce pan, melt the butter over medium-high heat. Add the shallot and cook just until it is translucent. Add $1/4$ cup dry white wine and reduce it to a glaze. Add the poaching liquid and reduce it by half. Whisk in one cup heavy cream and simmer until the sauce is slightly thickened. Season to taste with drops of lemon juice, salt, pepper, and cayenne. Cool the sauce and refrigerate until ready to serve.

Cook's Notes

For a quick meal on a hot night, poach salmon fillets, chill them, and serve with the sauce.

Fruit Kabobs

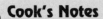

Cook's Notes

Make fruit kabobs with cubes of summer melons, pineapple chunks, and strawberries or grapes. Cut the fruit into 1" pieces and thread onto bamboo skewers (cut long skewers in half with scissors). Marinate the kabobs for an hour in the mixture described below.

8 ounces plain yogurt

3 tablespoons wildflower, clover, or orange blossom honey

the juice of one lime or to taste

$1/4$ cup fresh mint leaves, minced

1. In a flat, glass, enamel, or ceramic casserole or dish large enough to accommodate the fruit kabobs, combine the yogurt, honey, lime juice, and mint. Whisk vigorously to combine.

161

Madelines

2 madeline plaques (a tray with shell-shaped indentations)

4 ounces unsalted butter, melted

$^1/_2$ cup flour to prepare plaques

$^3/_4$ cup superfine sugar

2 eggs

4 ounces unsalted butter melted and cooled

$^3/_4$ cup sifted cake flour

   the grated zest of one large orange

1 tablespoon orange flower water

A madeline plaque.

1. Liberally coat the shell indentations in the madeline pans with melted butter. Put the pans in the freezer for five minutes. Butter the trays again and liberally dust them with flour. Lightly knock the excess flour out of the pans.

2. Preheat the oven to 400°.

3. In an electric mixer, beat the sugar and the eggs until light, fluffy, and doubled in volume.

4. Pour in the butter, beating until it is well combined.

5. Remove the work bowl from the machine and using a large rubber spatula, fold in the cake flour. Fold in the orange zest and orange flower water.

6. Fill each indentation in the madeline molds $^2/_3$ full. Place the trays on the center oven rack and bake them for 9–10 minutes. Remove the trays from the oven and allow them to cool for 10 minutes.

7. To unmold, carefully slide the tip of a small sharp knife around the edge of the madeline molds. Release the madelines from their molds by gently flicking them out with a fork. Makes 24–30 madelines.

Dinner at Eight

You just received a simple, polished little invitation in the mail. Without saying much, it says a lot: "Please come for dinner at eight." You know you're not joining friends to throw some steaks on the grill. And even if the time is really 7:30, you get the picture. "Dinner-at-eight" is the idea. It's a classic dinner-party agenda that calls for a little order, decorum, and formality. Of course, every party unfolds around food, drink, and conversation, but dinner-at-eight is more programmed than, say, a Sunday supper, a festive celebration, or a cocktail party. Your host will be especially attentive to the timing and flow of the evening. Flowers, table setting, and little details will be tasteful but subdued. Everything will be carefully planned but appear to transpire naturally. Contributing to interesting dinner conversation will be expected of you as a guest. It's a program that's evolved through the centuries and it's one more piece in the whole entertaining collage.

So what about the prospects of you hosting dinner-at-eight? Do you glow with anticipation? Shrink from intimidation? Find it just so much highfalutin la-de-da? A lot of history and hype has certainly branded an image on dinner-at-eight. Here's how it happened.

The Dinner-at-Eight Mystique

At the beginning of the eighteenth century, dinner parties were a High Society enterprise. The working man scraped together a humble, early-evening meal and the wealthy entertained, dining elaborately and late in the evening. Then, along came the Industrial Revolution and the gap began to close between workers and "society." An expanding and increasingly successful middle class entered the realm of entertaining while High Society and its sovereignty over dinner-party etiquette began to dwindle. Longer work hours and commutes, part and parcel of middle class financial success, contributed to eventually pegging eight o'clock as the fashionable hour to have a dinner party.

In essence, dinner-at-eight is a sociable process that transpires around a dinner table over a meal of several courses. The prelude is cocktails and the finale is coffee and cordials in the living room. Our modern rendition of dinner-at-eight sprang from another revolution; service à la francaise versus service a la russe. Up until the mid-eighteenth century in Europe, service à la francaise was the mode. A monumental number of dishes were served simultaneously on the dinner table or buffet for diners to pick and choose from, either serving themselves or having out-of-reach food brought by a footman.

It was a Russian ambassador to Paris who introduced a new manner of serving a meal. The Russians laid their table with a complete place setting for each dinner guest to whom each course was served separately. Warm food was the obvious bonus, and thus service à la russe won out. At the turn of the nineteenth century, dinners were elaborate affairs where guests were swept through up to eight courses that were served with a mind-boggling array of flatware, china, and crystal. Minding your manners according to a code of etiquette that dictated painstakingly faultless table manners and highly polished deportment was de rigeur. One false move and your desirability as a guest was likely to be on the ropes.

Lucky are we who can capture the sum and substance of dinner-at-eight and dispense with much of the superfluous excess and fanfare of those days. We don't have to buy out the floor at Tiffany's to host a dinner-at-eight. Conducting a meal with a little bit of glamour and refinement today is more about an order of things than how much and how it's presented. In other words, when the program is well planned, it is equally charming whether dinner is served with the simplest or the very finest entertaining accessories.

Thankfully, rigid social mores have relaxed too, but they haven't vanished. Life would be pretty ho-hum without a note of gentility to remind us what civilized creatures we are. In the heart of everyone who loves to entertain, there's a definite allure about hosting a dinner-at-eight no matter how casual most entertaining has become. Here are two up-to-date options for your dinner party: either put on the Ritz or throw a little impromptu pomp. Either way, dinner-at-eight is a simple matter of precise organization, discriminating details, and savvy timing.

> **Sage Advice**
> As told to Cesar Ritz by his first employer: "You'll never make anything of yourself in the hotel business...it takes a special knack, a special flair, and it's only right that I should tell you the truth: you haven't got it!"
>
> —from *Cesar Ritz: Host to the World*, by Mme. Marie Ritz

Puttin' on the Ritz

The menu:

A Melange of Fresh and Smoked Fish

Tenderloin Medallions with Portobello Mushrooms and Madeira

Rosemary Polenta

Rapini with Toasted Garlic

Mesclun and Belgian Endive with St. Andre Croutons

Raspberry Galettes

The recipes for this menu can be found at the end of this chapter.

It was a humble shepherd in the Alps named Cesar Ritz who made a name synonymous with luxury and style. Ritz and his colleague, master chef August Escoffier, began the process of transforming nineteenth-century extravagance into streamlined elegance. Their motto was simplicity; they were forward-thinking men. These two knew that attention to little details, rather than excess, was what counted. So, you may associate "putting on the Ritz" with going overboard, but that's not how the name gained renown. They just did the right things right.

Ritz focused his efforts on the genuine comfort and pleasure of his hotel guests with an aim to delight rather than overwhelm. He made a point of knowing the personal preferences of his clientele, the acme of hospitality. Escoffier simplified the outrageously opulent menus of the day. Bottom line, beyond their foresight and creativity, they were both organizational masterminds who focused on enhancing fundamentals and downplaying exorbitance. Herein is the key to hosting a perfectly splendid dinner-at-eight.

Go over Chapters 1 through 4 with a fine-toothed comb. Don't cut corners on any of the organization details, and allow yourself more time than you think you'll need for the planning to ensure you'll be cool as a cucumber at your party. The special details that distinguish an exceptional dinner-at-eight are always subtle. Review Chapters 5 through 7 for tips on etiquette and the art of being a gracious host. Let's discuss a few specific ways to approach this party to get your imagination going.

When putting together your guest list, think about people who will respond well to one another. Remember, they'll be seated at your table for several courses, and good conversation is an intrinsic element of this party. Don't be afraid to mix different groups, ages, or personalities; just avoid inviting people who may obviously rub each other the wrong way.

Never invite more guests than you can comfortably seat at your table. Make out place cards on good paper stock with a fountain pen and arrange a thoughtful seating plan. If cocktail food calls for plates, use the real thing. Real cocktail napkins instead of paper are also a special touch. Put a small bouquet of flowers and a scented candle in the guest bath and a vase of flowers and a few votives at the bar. Set your table with your best; everything should be spotless. For example, immaculately clean and pressed cotton passes the test, rumpled Irish linen does not; and sparkling clean, ordinary glassware takes precedence over water spotted Baccarat. Make sure your table setting is properly aligned, evenly spaced, and uncluttered. Water as well as wine glasses should always be used at a lengthy dinner. Buy good bottled spring water and float a paper-thin lemon slice in each glass. After dessert, have coffee and cordials waiting for your guests in the living room.

When you're putting on the Ritz, hiring someone to help out in the kitchen and with serving is a must. Consider yourself a maestro, conducting the sequence and tempo of the whole evening. Timing is very important at this type of party. When serving a multi-course meal, an extended cocktail hour isn't appropriate. Enjoying a meal served course-by-course is supposed to be a leisurely affair, but it should not drag on ad infinitum! Of course, don't march your company around like a drill sergeant or rush them through courses.

Hire a polished and professional server with whom you'll have a tacit understanding, because someone you have to coach, correct, or babysit is more work than help. One practical option for hiring serving help is to engage a catering outfit experienced in small dinners. They can supply your cocktail hors d'oeuvres or other dishes, if you so desire, as well as adeptly apply final touches and serve whatever food you have prepared. We'll supply you with a preparation plan and time schedule for serving dinner. Stick to it as closely as possible. Following the plan, the entire meal will be ready ahead except for warming and final touches. You should be able to relax and enjoy your party.

Your Schedule

A week before the party, carefully follow the guidelines in Chapter 4 and accordingly prepare your cards and inventory the bar and butler's pantry. If you're preparing all the food, here's how to go about it:

➤ A day before the party: Make the Madeira sauce, pastry cream, and vinaigrette. Wash and seal lettuce in zip bags. Make and chill the polenta. Set the table.

➤ The morning of the party: Make the galettes and the sauce for the fish. Blanch the rapini and cut the polenta. Arrange the first course on plates, seal with film, and refrigerate.

➤ An hour before the party: Sear tenderloin medallions, toast garlic for the rapini, and toast croutons for the salad.

Good Spirits
Serve a young Sancerre or Sauvignon Blanc with the appetizer, and a California Pinot Noir or Italian Amorone with the entree (plan on a little extra to finish with salad and cheese).

Serving Schedule for Your Helper

Preparing a written schedule for your helper puts them in charge.

➤ **8:45** Bring the first course to the table, fill the water glasses, and light the candles.

➤ **9:15** Check on the progress of the first course. Gently re-warm the tenderloin and rapini; slide polenta under the broiler. The host will come to the kitchen to begin plating the food as you clear the first course. Serve the entree. Slip first-course plates in the dishwasher.

➤ **9:40** Toast the salad croutons, and toss and plate salads. Check on progress at the dinner table. Clear the entree plates and serve the salads. Put the entree plates in the dishwasher.

➤ **10:00** Whip cream and assemble the desserts. Clear salads; serve dessert. Start the coffee and ready the coffee tray.

➤ **10:30** Bring the coffee to the living room. Clear the dinner table and finish tidying the kitchen.

Reality Bites

REALITY BITES

A host quietly signals a server to indicate when to clear a course. Plates are never stacked to clear. Remove only two at a time.

Impromptu Pomp

The menu:

> Mixed Lettuces with Chevre Baskets
>
> Golden Orecchiette with Porcini Mushrooms
>
> Herbed Foccacia
>
> Lemon Ice in Natural Lemon Shells

The recipes for this menu can be found at the end of this chapter.

Suppose a significant relative, friend, or colleague suddenly arrives in town and you'd love to host a special evening just for them. Or maybe you've been procrastinating about doing the same for someone nearby and life's been so hectic that now it's a "just do it" situation. If you're the sort who's perpetually caught in an impromptu whirlwind, it certainly proves the justice of a well-stocked butler's pantry and developing a personal scheme as outlined in Chapter 6. The basics of your entertaining setup are in place and ready to roll. Beyond this, we're going to give you a supply list for your freezer and larder, plus a last-minute grocery list for your impromptu menu. Since this menu has one less course than "putting on the Ritz," it's quite practical for weeknight entertaining. Arrive home at 5:30 p.m. and greet your guests at "eight." If you keep your bar, larder, and freezer stocked, an impromptu menu will be ready at your beck and call. Use the same principle to stock up for one or two other favorite simple menus. Let's see how it works.

An Impromptu Table Design

A butler's pantry is an absolute necessity for the occasional (or frequent) impromptu host. Since the ultra simple menu will become distinguished by presentation, we'll give you a few ideas for things to find and keep in your butler's pantry that will fit the bill. The following impromptu host has traditional tastes. If yours are contemporary, arts and crafts, or whatever, adapt accordingly.

➤ *Table linens*: A simple linen or natural fiber cloth or place mats in white, off white, or a neutral tone should be clean as a whistle, pressed, and waiting. Extra large napkins show you care about how you entertain.

➤ *Centerpiece*: Center a single candelabra in the middle of the table (a special glass hurricane may fit the bill for other tastes). Needless to say, there should be plenty of candles on supply in your butler's pantry.

➤ *Flowers*: Single flower blossoms (such as freesia) in small glass vases look elegant and they're usually available at grocery stores when there's no time for the florist. Use a tall glass vase for an arrangement at the bar and arrange your glassware for cocktails around it.

➤ *Serveware*: Attractive salad plates that are different from your other plates, or a collection of individual salad plates (use a different one to serve each chevre basket salad), will lend a note of panache to your first course. A glass cake stand makes an elegant presentation for dessert. Line the plate with lemon leaves and arrange the lemon shells on top. A collection of individual demitasse cups and freshly ground French roast or espresso makes a perfect finale.

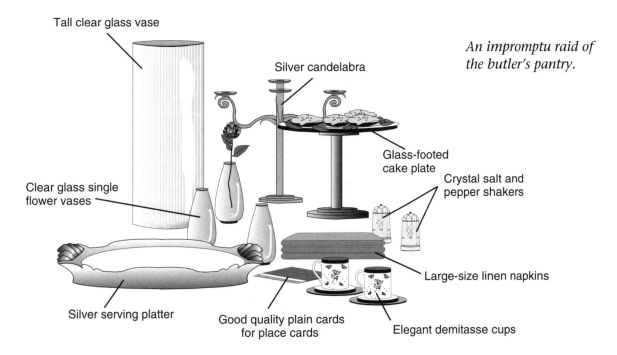

Tall clear glass vase

Silver candelabra

An impromptu raid of the butler's pantry.

Glass-footed cake plate

Crystal salt and pepper shakers

Clear glass single flower vases

Large-size linen napkins

Silver serving platter

Good quality plain cards for place cards

Elegant demitasse cups

Stocking Up for an Impromptu Party

In the larder:

>sherry vinegar
>
>Dijon mustard
>
>walnut oil
>
>dried porcini mushrooms
>
>orecchiette
>
>dried rosemary
>
>freeze-dried chives

In the freezer:

packaged winter squash purée

unsalted butter

bacon

good coffee

walnuts

optional: lemon ice

From the store:

tomatoes

lettuces

goat cheese

shallots

heavy cream

lemon ice

lemons

mint or lemon leaves

At the bar:

Limoncino or lemon-flavored vodka or rum

Manzanilla sherry

A case of wine designated to impromptus

Good Spirits

Serve a youthful and herbal domestic Sauvignon Blanc with the chevre basket salad and a Chateauneuf du Pape with the pasta.

Plan of Attack

➤ **5:30** Soak the mushrooms; prepare the bread baskets and hollow out the lemon shells.

➤ **6:15** Prepare the chevre filling for the bread baskets; prepare the pasta sauce and hold.

➤ **6:45** Cook the bacon, wash and dry the lettuces, prepare the vinaigrette, assemble the salad per the recipe, and refrigerate.

➤ **7:05** Set the table and set up the bar. Tidy the guest bath. Set up a coffee tray.

➤ **7:30** Heat a pot of water for the pasta and hold below a simmer so you can quickly bring it to a boil. Toast the chevre baskets and get the coffee ready to brew. Set up salad plates, pasta bowls, bread basket, and dessert plates where you can efficiently plate and serve the food.

You have the entire menu under control and with very few last-minute tasks to put dinner on the table, you can feasibly serve without help. When you assemble the salads, bring the pasta water to a boil and gently reheat the sauce. Put the bread and pasta bowls in a low oven to warm. Freshly made orecchiette will cook much faster than dried. Time accordingly. Cook fresh pasta after you clear the first course. Cook dried pasta when you serve the first course (set a timer, briefly excuse yourself to drain sauce and hold the pasta, covered, in a low oven). After you clear the entree, turn on the coffee and assemble dessert. With your serving thus organized, last-minute tasks for each course shouldn't keep you away from your guests for more than ten minutes.

Reality Bites
The preparation and serving schedules for both menus are guidelines based on the theoretical hour of "8:00." By all means, amend or relax the schedule to your liking.

The Least You Need To Know

➤ Organization, timing, and discriminating details are the savoir faire of a successful dinner-at-eight.

➤ Dinner-at-eight is more about an order of things and a tempo than excess and fanfare.

➤ Put together a guest list of people who will respond well to each other.

The Recipes

A Melange of Fresh and Smoked Fish

This is a "create as you go" first course to use for both menus. It's a cinch to put together and the epitome of a user-friendly first course for a sit-down dinner. Assemble the plates hours ahead if you like, wrap tightly in film, and store them in the refrigerator. The idea is to juxtapose 2–3 different fish and the composition depends entirely on what you happen to find at the market that day. What makes it special is an attractive presentation. Here is what you'll need:

➤ Bottled grape leaves

➤ Smoked, cured, or poached fish (2–3 ounces total per serving)

➤ Caviar or fish roe

➤ A mayonnaise-based sauce (prepare your own mayonnaise or use a quality store-bought brand)

Choose plates for the melange in a color complementary to the grape leaves and the types of fish you are using. Line each plate with one or two rinsed and dried grape leaves. Attractively arrange the fish on top of the grape leaves, then scatter a spoonful of fish roe over the fish. Either cup the mayonnaise sauce in tiny lettuce leaves to nestle on each plate, or use any petite container you may have that will fit on the plates. Garnish each serving with one or two lemon wedges and pass a basket of crisp toast points. Here are a few possibilities that we encountered on a given day at a local fish market:

➤ Alaska hot smoked salmon with cracked black pepper, poached salmon, salmon gravlax, salmon roe

➤ Hot-smoked trout or white fish, Norwegian cold-smoked salmon, trout mousse, white fish caviar

➤ Salmon mousse rolled in Norwegian cold smoked salmon, beluga caviar

➤ Smoked trout mousse and poached trout, flying fish roe

Cook's Notes

Sauce Andalouse, in Chapter 14, complements the melange. Using homemade mayonnaise makes it extra special. The recipe can be found in Chapter 9.

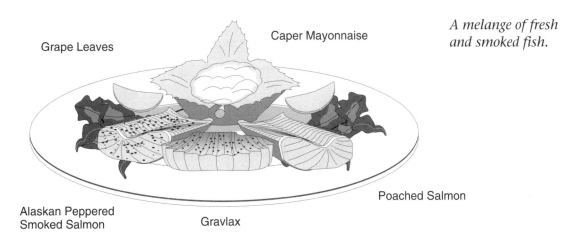

Grape Leaves

Caper Mayonnaise

A melange of fresh and smoked fish.

Poached Salmon

Alaskan Peppered
Smoked Salmon

Gravlax

Tenderloin Medallions with Portobello Mushrooms and Madeira

3 tablespoons unsalted butter

3 tablespoons vegetable oil

$^1/_2$ cup beef trimmings cut into small dice (from the tenderloin or from another cut of beef such a shin)

1 carrot, peeled and finely chopped

1 large shallot, peeled and minced

10 large portobello mushrooms, stems removed and reserved and caps sliced paper thin

5 pounds beef tenderloin cut into $^1/_2$"-thick coins (medallions)

salt and pepper to taste

$1^1/_2$ cups Rainwater Madeira

5 cups all-purpose stock

2 beef marrow bones

salt, freshly ground pepper, and Madeira to taste

1. To make the sauce, in a sauce pan, heat one tablespoon of butter and one table-spoon of oil over medium-high heat until the butter foams. Add the beef trimmings and brown them well. Add the carrot, shallot, and mushroom stems to the pot and sauté until the shallot is translucent. Pour the Madeira into the sauce pan, raise the heat, and reduce the Madeira almost to a glaze. Add two cups of all-purpose stock. Reduce the heat and slowly simmer the sauce to reduce by half.

2. Meanwhile, brown the marrow bones under the broiler. Add the rest of the stock and the marrow bones to the sauce pan and continue to simmer gently until the sauce is well flavored and it lightly coats a spoon. Strain the sauce, pushing on the

173

solids with the back of a spoon. Season the sauce to taste with salt, plenty of freshly ground black pepper, and a few more drops of Madeira, if desired. The sauce may be made a day or two ahead. Cool the sauce, cover, and refrigerate.

3. To prepare the medallions, in a large sauté pan, heat the remaining two tablespoons of butter and the remaining two tablespoons of oil over high heat until the butter foams. Lightly salt and pepper, the medallions and sear them in the hot pan for $1^1/_2$ minutes per side. They should be very rare (the medallions will cook to medium rare when they are warmed in the sauce). Transfer the medallions to a plate. Do not wash the sauté pan. If you are making the recipe early in the day, cool, cover, and refrigerate the medallions. Bring them to room temperature one hour before finishing the dish.

4. Reheat the sauté pan over medium heat (add a bit more butter and oil if necessary) and sauté the sliced portobello mushroom caps until they are wilted. Reserve the mushroom caps in the sauté pan. If you are preparing the mushrooms ahead, cool, cover, and refrigerate the sauté pan.

5. To finish the dish, bring everything to room temperature. Put the sauce in the pan with the mushrooms. Fifteen minutes before serving, warm the sauce until bubbly. Taste and correct the seasoning. Slip the medallions into the sauce and warm over low heat, turning for about 5–8 minutes.

6. On warm dinner plates, arrange three polenta triangles in an arch at the top of the plate. Overlap 5 medallions beneath the polenta. Place a spoonful of rapini on either side of the polenta. Ladle the warm sauce and mushrooms over the medallions. Serves 8–10.

Rosemary Polenta

6 cups water

2 cups yellow cornmeal

1 teaspoon salt

$^1/_2$ cup heavy cream

2 tablespoons minced rosemary leaves

non-stick cooking spray

3–4 tablespoons olive oil

1. Bring a large pot of water to a rolling boil. When the water boils, gently "shower" the cornmeal into the water in a thin stream, whisking rapidly as you pour (this prevents lumps from forming). Add the salt to the cornmeal and stir continuously

with a wooden spoon until the polenta forms a thick mass that pulls away from the bottom of the pot. Tilt the pot and mound the polenta on one side of the pot. It should be thick enough to hold a wooden spoon standing up. Stir in the cream and the rosemary.

2. Spray two 8"×8" baking pans with non-stick cooking spray and scrape half of the polenta into each pan. Evenly smooth the top with a wet spatula. Cool, cover, and refrigerate the polenta. The polenta can be made a day or two ahead.

3. Unmold the polenta onto a work surface. Cut each square block of polenta into three equal strips. Cut each strip into 5 triangles. Spray a baking sheet with non-stick cooking spray and transfer the polenta triangles to the tray. If you are preparing the recipe in advance, cover and refrigerate the tray. Bring the polenta to room temperature one hour before serving.

4. Just before serving, heat the broiler on high. Use overturned cake pans to elevate the baking sheet 3" below the broiler element. Brush the polenta with olive oil on both sides. Broil the polenta until light golden on both sides, turning the triangles once. Serves 8–10.

Rapini with Toasted Garlic

Cook's Notes

Rapini, also commonly known as broccoli raab, is a distant relative of the turnip. It has a pleasantly bitter twang that compliments the richness of the medallions and the smoothness of the polenta. You may substitute good old-fashioned broccoli, steamed spinach leaves, or Swiss chard.

4 bunches of rapini, heavy stalks trimmed off, rinsed, and coarsely chopped

1 tablespoon salt

6 cloves of garlic, peeled and finely minced

2 tablespoons olive oil

   salt and freshly ground black pepper to taste

1–2 tablespoons of balsamic vinegar to taste

1. Bring a large pot of water to a rolling boil. Add the tablespoon of salt and the rapini. Return the water to a boil and blanch the rapini for three to five minutes or until tender-crisp. Drain the rapini and rinse under ice-cold water until cooled. Shake off

the excess water and roll the rapini in several layers of paper towels. Seal the bundle in a zip bag and refrigerate. Bring the rapini to room temperature one hour before serving.

2. Just before serving, heat a pot or sauté pan large enough to hold the rapini over medium heat and film the bottom with the olive oil. Add the garlic to the pan and sauté just until it turns golden. Turn the heat to low and toss the rapini with the garlic in the pot to gently warm. Season the rapini with salt, pepper, and balsamic vinegar to taste. Serves 8–10.

Mesclun and Belgian Endive with St. Andre Croutons

10 cups of mesclun mix

4 Belgian endive

2 tablespoons good quality raspberry vinegar

$^1/_2$ teaspoon salt

a generous grinding of fresh black pepper

1 teaspoon grainy mustard

$^1/_2$ cup walnut oil

20 $^1/_4$" broad diagonal slices from a crusty baguette

$^1/_2$ cup olive oil

$^1/_2$ pound St. Andre cheese

$^1/_2$ cup toasted and finely chopped walnuts

Cook's Notes

Mesclun is a variety of young garden lettuces. If mesclun isn't available, substitute escarole and raddiccio torn into small pieces.

1. Wash and dry the lettuces. Core the Belgian endive and separate the leaves. Wipe away any grit from the leaves with a damp paper towel. Seal the lettuces in zip bags and refrigerate until you are ready to toss the salad.

2. To prepare the vinaigrette, in a small bowl, combine the raspberry vinegar, salt, pepper, and mustard. Whisking, drizzle in the walnut oil in a thin, steady stream. Taste and correct the seasoning.

3. Preheat the broiler.

4. Lightly brush the bread with olive oil on both sides and lightly toast the croutons under the broiler until they are golden on both sides. Spread the cheese on one side of each crouton. Run the cheese croutons under the broiler until the cheese is bubbly.

5. Combine the lettuces and the toasted walnuts in a salad bowl and toss them with just enough dressing to lightly coat the leaves.

6. Divide the lettuce among 8 or 10 salad plates, distributing the Belgian endive evenly among the salads. Garnish each salad with two cheese croutons and serve immediately. Serves 8–10.

Raspberry Galettes

10 ounces unsalted butter

  a pinch of salt

2 egg yolks

$^1/_2$ cup plus 2–3 tablespoons confectioners sugar

$^2/_3$ cup heavy cream

1 pound pastry mix (about 3 $^1/_2$–3 $^3/_4$ cups)

1 cup whole milk

1 vanilla bean

3 egg yolks

4 tablespoons granulated sugar

2 tablespoons flour

1 quart raspberries, rinsed and dried (substitute thinly sliced strawberries)

1 cup heavy cream whipped to firm peaks

1. To prepare the galettes, place the butter, 2 yolks, sugar, and cream in the work bowl of a food processor fitted with the knife blade. Process the ingredients with on/off bursts until the butter is in bits. Add half the flour to the work bowl and pulse again, just until blended. Add the rest of the flour to the work bowl and pulse just until the pastry comes together. Remove the pastry from the work bowl, flatten into a disc, wrap in film, and chill for 20 to 30 minutes.

2. Preheat the oven to 375°.

3. On a floured work surface, roll the dough $^1/_4$" thick. Cut the pastry into 20–24 rounds with a 3"–4" fluted biscuit cutter. Transfer the pastry to ungreased cookie sheets and lightly prick each round several times with a fork. Bake the pastry rounds for 10–12 minutes or until light golden. Turn the baking sheets every five minutes to ensure even browning. Transfer the pastry rounds to a rack to cool. The pastry can be made a day ahead and hermetically sealed in a container.

4. To prepare the pastry cream, in a saucepan combine the milk and the vanilla bean. Scald the milk by heating until small bubbles appear around the perimeter of the pan. Remove the pan from the heat and allow the vanilla to infuse in the milk for 10 minutes.

5. In a large mixing bowl, beat 3 egg yolks and the sugar until the mixture becomes thickened, pale yellow in color, and falls from a raised whip in a ribbon. Stir in the flour and thin the mixture with a spoonful or two of the milk.

6. Remove the vanilla bean from the milk and heat the milk to just below a boil. While whisking the egg mixture, pour in the hot milk. Return the mixture to the saucepan and place the pan over medium-high heat. With a wooden spoon, stir in a figure "8" pattern to reach into the corners of the pan. Bring the pastry cream to a boil. Boil, stirring for three minutes. Remove the pan from the heat and press a piece of film directly on top of the pastry cream to prevent a skin from forming. Cool and refrigerate until ready to assemble the desserts.

7. To assemble the galettes, spread a thin layer of pastry cream on the bottom sides of each galette. Place half of the galettes on dessert plates. Top the galettes on the dessert plates with a single layer of berries. Pipe rosettes of whipped cream over the berries (or spread a layer of whipped cream over each one with an off-set spatula). Top each one with a galette. Just before serving, dust the tops with confectioners sugar. Serves 8–10.

Chevre Baskets

6 round crusty hard rolls, about 4" in diameter

2 tablespoons unsalted butter, melted (or use walnut oil)

6 ounces of Montrachet or Bucheron goat cheese

1 medium tomato, peeled, seeded, and diced

2 tablespoons snipped chives

6 ounces of country style bacon in one piece, cut into $^1/_2$" dice

10 cups mesclun salad mix (a mixture of tender young lettuces), washed and dried

$^1/_4$ finely chopped walnuts, toasted

2 tablespoons sherry vinegar

1 generous teaspoon of dijon style mustard

   salt and freshly ground black pepper

5–6 tablespoons walnut oil

1. Preheat the oven to 325°.

2. To make baskets from the rolls, cut two parallel incisions, $^1/_2$" apart in the center of each roll, beginning one-half inch from the end of the roll. Do not pierce through the bottom of the rolls. Next, make a cut around the equator of the roll to remove a "v"-shaped section of the roll. Make an incision around the top of the roll to make a basket handle $^1/_4$" thick. Remove the remaining insides of the roll to make a basket with a $^1/_4$" thick shell. Lightly brush the insides of the baskets with the melted butter or the walnut oil and toast them in the warm oven until they are golden brown.

3. In a small bowl, lightly mash the goat cheese with a fork and toss with the diced tomato and snipped chives. Fill the bread basket with the cheese mixture and reserve.

4. In a small sauté pan, cook the bacon over medium heat until it is very crisp. Remove to paper towels to drain.

5. In a salad bowl, whisk together the sherry vinegar, mustard, and salt and pepper to taste. Drizzle in the oil, whisking. Put the mesclun and bacon cubes on top of the vinaigrette, cover the salad, and refrigerate until just before serving.

6. Just before serving, return the chevre baskets to the warm oven for about five minutes or until the cheese is warmed through. Toss the salad and arrange on six salad plates.

7. To serve, nestle a warm chevre basket in the center of the salads on each plate. Serve with a fork and knife. Serves 6.

Cook's Notes

Substitute two large, ripe pears, peeled, cored, and diced for the bacon in the salad.

Golden Orecchiette with Porcini Mushrooms

2   loose cups dried porcini mushrooms

2   tablespoons unsalted butter

1   cup minced shallots

2   cups heavy cream

1   package frozen winter squash puree, defrosted

$^1/_3$ cup Manzanilla or other dry sherry

1   teaspoon dried rosemary

   salt and freshly ground black pepper to taste

   a dash or two of cayenne pepper

   freshly grated nutmeg

1. Put the porcini mushrooms in a small bowl and add hot water just to cover to reconstitute the mushrooms.

2. In a medium sauce pan over low heat melt the butter. Add the shallots and gently sauté them until they are translucent but do not allow them to brown.

3. Remove the mushrooms from their liquid and reserve the liquid. Check the mushrooms for any grit and rinse them if necessary. Finely chop the mushrooms.

4. Add the mushrooms to the shallots and stir in the cream, squash, sherry, and the rosemary. Pour the reserved mushroom liquid through a cheesecloth-lined strainer into the sauce. Gently simmer the sauce for 5 minutes. Season to taste with salt, pepper, cayenne, and nutmeg.

5. Bring a large pot of water to a rolling boil. Add the orecchiette and cook according to the manufacturer's directions. Before draining the orecchiette, remove and reserve one cup of the pasta water. Drain the pasta, transfer to a warmed pasta serving bowl and toss with the sauce. The pasta should have a rich, silky-smooth texture. Add a little pasta water if the sauce is too thick. Adjust the seasoning to taste and serve immediately in warm pasta bowls. Serves 6–8.

Lemon Ice in Lemon Shells

6   large lemons

1   quart lemon ice

12 lemon leaves, or lemon verbena or lemon balm leaves

6   tablespoons Limoncino (see Chapter 1) or lemon-flavored vodka or rum

1. Cut a sliver from the stem ends of the lemons so they stand upright without rocking. Cut $1/3$ from the top of the lemon and with a small, sharp knife, cut around the inside perimeter of the lemon to loosen the flesh. Using a grapefruit spoon or other small spoon, scrape out all the lemon flesh. Scrape directly into a container (use the lemon juice to make lemonade the next day). Seal the lemon shells in zip bags and store in the refrigerator until ready to serve.

2. To serve, fill the lemon shells with lemon ice. Place the shells on dessert plates and decorate each plate with two lemon leaves. Drizzle one tablespoon of liquor over each serving and serve immediately. Serves 6.

Cook's Notes

If lemon leaves, lemon verbena, or lemon balm leaves aren't available, sprinkle each dessert plate with a dusting of grated zest from two whole lemons.

Chapter 13

A Casablanca-Inspired Cocktail Party

> **In This Chapter**
>
> ➤ Jazzing up the common cocktail party
>
> ➤ Cocktails Casablanca-style
>
> ➤ The recipes

Cocktail parties have been a popular form of entertaining for years. Probably because they generally aren't as lengthy and don't require the diligent preparation of a sit-down dinner or other more elaborate party scenarios. But frankly, cocktail parties can be pretty dull affairs. What's so fun about a bunch of people milling around jingling ice cubes in a glass, trying to remember the last decent joke they heard? And what about the perceived "ease" of a cocktail party? When the party is over you usually have one huge mess on your hands: glasses and balled-up napkins are everywhere; crumbs are ground into the rug; ravished hors d'oeuvre trays clutter the kitchen. Looks like a cocktail party isn't necessarily an entertaining "easy-way-out" after all.

But let's not focus on the downside because a cocktail party really can be a fun way to entertain and it's the perfect scenario for hosting a slew of guests. Maybe something more than just drinks and hors d'oeuvres, like a jazzy theme, is what's needed to revive the tired old cocktail party. How about a theme recalling the bygone era when cocktail parties were all-out *swanky* affairs? You just might be hosting the party of the year. *Casablanca* is the theme and you're going to host the quintessential bash: wonderfully nostalgic, showy, glamorous, and chic. Whether you choose to throw a cocktail-time only party or have an all-evening open house is up to you. The organizational details, design ideas, and menu will graciously accommodate either type of party.

A Perfectly Splendid Bash

Before getting into the specifics of the theme, let's address the big picture of hosting a cocktail buffet or open house for a crowd. First of all, because these types of parties are frequently held in the fall and winter months around holiday time, we'll deal with the reality of handling sheer numbers indoors. Enter your own front door and imagine the party in progress. Go through the party step-by-step, with a mental picture of your house teeming with guests:

➤ Who takes your coat and to where?

➤ Where do you find a drink?

➤ Is there an hors d'oeuvre buffet, or are trays strategically placed here and there and hot items passed by a server?

➤ Are there plenty of places to set drinks and hors d'oeuvre plates?

➤ Is everyone jammed into a noisy room, or are guests mingling freely through the house?

➤ Is the atmosphere close and stuffy or well ventilated?

In particular, pay attention to creating a traffic pattern that encourages movement, mixing, mingling, and convenience of food and drink. Don't tackle this kind of a party without a bartender and server; they too should have a little polish and panache for this affair. One good bartender can handle up to 50 people. If you have budget considerations, hard alcohol and stocking a full bar is not mandatory. It's perfectly acceptable to serve only champagne, white wine, and soft drinks.

In this case, once the party's underway, a bartender can circulate with a wine or champagne bottle, offering refills. If you decide to have a full bar, have the bartender mix drinks and pour champagne. Set up a separate self-serve bar for wine and soft drinks. Depending on your floor plan, having the full bar service away from the main party may be more practical. Then, servers take orders and pass drinks on a tray. This method eliminates guests queuing up at the bar.

Even if you opt to present all the food on a buffet at a large party, a server/helper is essential to keep clutter at bay and replenish food trays. Always plan on having two trays for each item; one on reserve in the kitchen ready to quickly replace a tired-looking hors d'oeuvre tray on the buffet. Napkins and hors d'oeuvre plates should be at both ends of the table. If you're hosting a very small cocktail party—say, ten people—you can get by without a server, but a bartender will definitely lend cachet to the event as well as help with clean-up when the party is over.

The other option for food presentation is to have one or two hors d'oeuvre trays with room temperature items in various rooms, and your server can pass hot hors d'oeuvres. Flank self-serve hors d'oeuvre trays with plenty of napkins. Each room should have convenient places to rest a drink or plate.

Reality Bites
Cocktail parties aren't for toddlers and pets. Hire a favorite baby sitter for little ones and secure your pets in a place where they don't feel trapped.

When you have a crowd and no air conditioning or fan system to promote air circulation, crack windows in each room before the party begins. Don't forget to turn the heat down a few degrees.

Cocktails at Rick's

The menu:

> Rick's Hill of Beans with Cucumber Chips
>
> Spicy Lamb Torpedoes en Brochette
>
> Asparagus Batons, Creme Fraiche, and Caviar
>
> Wings of War
>
> Checkerboard Sandwiches
>
> Eggplant-Tomato Fleet
>
> Teardrop Cookies with a Chocolate Kiss

The recipes for this menu can be found at the end of this chapter.

The pressures of this crazy world are why people love parties where they can let go and live a little. Casablanca has the tongue-in-cheek charm, nostalgia, and panache to make a marvelous cocktail party. Get into the spirit beginning with invitations. Movie stills are

Sage Advice
"The problems of three little people don't amount to a hill of beans in this crazy world."

—Humphrey Bogart as Rick in *Casablanca*

Good Spirits
Let the champagne flow. Look for recipes for kir royale and a nostalgic champagne cocktail in Chapter 1.

popular greeting card motifs, and Bogart is never hard to come by. Make small black-and-white reproductions to decorate plain white invitations. WWII fighter planes, poker chips, or big band memorabilia are other ideas for creating invitations appropriate to the theme.

To get your guests into the swing of things, recommend an attire: black and white to honor one of the world's best black-and-white films, '40s garb, hats from the era (a prize to the best), or black tie.

The invitation could read, "Here's looking at you, Clare and Louis. Deck yourselves out in black & white attire on December 1 at 7 p.m. for a festive holiday open house. A prize goes to the best *Casablanca* hat." Have some fun watching the film and come up with your own ideas.

You can prepare everything on the menu well ahead. Consult the recipes to organize a plan of attack. Note that the recipes serve around 10 people so you can easily use them for other smaller parties. Double, triple, or quadruple the amounts according to the size of your party.

Invitation ideas for cocktails at Rick's.

Airplane motif

Cocktail glass motif

Humphrey Bogart photo card

Creating an Atmosphere for Cocktails at Rick's

A Casablanca theme points to recreating a dramatic atmosphere with a touch of the exotic. Here are some ideas to get you going:

➤ *Table linens:* For a buffet table use a plain white cloth to emphasize the food. Use a card to identify each hors d'oeuvre.

➤ *Flowers:* Decorate the whole house with exotic flowers; gardenias, lilies, orchids, or hibiscus are perfect choices. A dramatic option is an all-white flower theme—lilies everywhere, for instance. Consult with a florist several weeks before the party to inquire about availability and place orders if necessary.

➤ *Candles:* Scented candles such as natural cypress tie into the theme. Place two or three around each room. Burning incense, if not too strong, ties into the exotic theme.

➤ *Music:* Play classic cocktail piano tunes or big band '40s favorites. If you have a piano, hire someone from a local music school to play. Tell the pianist what you're looking for so he or she understands the spirit of the party.

The Extra Mile
If your party is around the holidays, as guests arrive, gift the ladies with a pretty handkerchief and the gentlemen with a boutonniere.

The Least You Need To Know

➤ Organizing traffic flow and devising a practical serving strategy are essentials when entertaining a crowd indoors.

➤ Don't overlook coat storage and ventilation when you're having a crowd.

➤ A bartender and server with a bit of personal élan are an asset to a festive party.

➤ With the right theme, an ordinary cocktail party can become a perfectly splendid bash.

The Recipes

Rick's Hill of Beans with Cucumber Chips

1   19-ounce can of chick peas, drained and rinsed

1$^1/_4$ cups pitted cracked Moroccan or marinated green olives

3   large garlic cloves, peeled and minced

1   tablespoon dried thyme

2   rounded tablespoons plain yogurt

$^1/_2$ teaspoon salt

  freshly ground black pepper, to taste

2   tablespoons olive oil

3   tablespoons minced coriander leaf plus several sprigs for garnish

2   English cucumbers cut into $^1/_4$" slices

$^1/_2$ cup tiny black olives

1. In a food processor fitted with the knife blade, combine the chick peas, olives, garlic, thyme, yogurt, and salt until smooth. Taste and adjust the seasonings, adding freshly ground pepper and enough olive oil to achieve a highly seasoned, smooth mixture. Transfer the dip to a storage container. Cover and refrigerate for about one hour to allow the flavors to marry. (This can be made a day ahead.)

2. To serve, mound the chick pea mixture into a pyramid shape in the center of a large platter and dust the top of the mound with the minced coriander. Decorate around the base of the pyramid with coriander sprigs and black olives. Surround the dip with the cucumber slices. Alternatively, fit a pastry bag with a star tip and pipe the chick pea mixture onto the cucumber rounds, garnishing each round with a piece of black olive and a pinch of minced coriander leaf. Makes approximately 2 $^1/_2$ cups.

Spicy Lamb Torpedoes en Brochette

Cook's Notes

A brochette is a skewer with small pieces of meat threaded on it.

4   large cloves of garlic, peeled

$^1/_2$ cup firmly packed flat leaf parsley

1   pound ground lamb

2   rounded tablespoons sweet Hungarian paprika

1   teaspoon salt

    a generous grinding of black pepper

8   ounces plain yogurt

$^1/_4$ cup fresh mint leaves, minced

1   small bunch scallions, slivered

$^1/_2$ teaspoon ground coriander seed

3   tablespoons coarsely cracked black peppercorns

    non-stick cooking spray

32 miniature pita rounds or triangles cut from large pita

1. To prepare the torpedoes, chop the garlic by dropping the cloves through the feed tube of a food processor with the machine running. Add the parsley to the work bowl and pulse to chop. Distribute the lamb around the blade and add the paprika, salt, and pepper. Pulse the mixture until it is thoroughly combined.

2. With dampened hands, divide the lamb mixture into 32 equal portions and form them into inch-long logs.

3. Cut the skewers in half with scissors and thread two torpedoes on each skewer to make a brochette. Seal the brochettes in zip bags and freeze, if desired.

4. In a small bowl, prepare a yogurt sauce by combining the yogurt, mint, scallions, coriander seed, and salt and pepper to taste. Cover and refrigerate the sauce for 30 minutes to allow the flavors to marry.

5. (If you have frozen the brochettes, thaw and bring to room temperature before proceeding.) To finish the brochettes, spread the cracked pepper on waxed paper and lightly roll the brochettes in the pepper to sparsely coat. Prepare an outdoor grill, or heat a stove top grill or heavy skillet over medium-high heat. Grill or sear the torpedoes on one side for 2 minutes. Turn a quarter turn and cook 2 minutes more. Turn twice more to cook a total of 8 minutes on all sides.

6. Hold the torpedoes in a 140° oven, covered, for up to one hour. Transfer the torpedoes to a chafing dish or a warm platter. Serve accompanied with the yogurt dip and a basket of split pitas. Makes 16 brochettes.

Asparagus Batons, Creme Fraiche, and Caviar

3 dozen asparagus spears

1 tablespoon olive oil

   salt and freshly ground black pepper

$^1/_2$ cup creme fraiche (see "Neoclassic Cucumbers" in Chapter 9 for a creme fraiche recipe)

1 tin Beluga caviar (see Chapter 10 for more on caviar)

1. Snap and discard the tough ends of the asparagus stalks. Spread the asparagus spears in a large roasting pan in a single layer. Drizzle the asparagus with the olive oil and toss to coat. Lightly season the asparagus with salt and pepper.

2. Preheat the oven to 500°.

3. Roast the asparagus in the hot oven for 8–10 minutes. They should be tender-crisp; avoid overcooking. Immediately remove the asparagus from the oven and transfer to a platter to cool.

4. Make the creme fraiche a day or two ahead or purchase ready-made creme fraiche. Lightly whip the creme fraiche, then fold in the caviar. Spoon into a crystal bowl (caviar should not touch metal). Place the bowl in the center of a round platter and arrange the asparagus around the bowl, tips radiating away from the bowl.

   If your budget has no limits, here's the classic way to serve caviar straight up. (See Chapter 10, the section entitled "Just the Two of You," for notes on caviar.) Fill a crystal bowl with crushed ice and nestle the open tin of caviar into the ice. Traditionally, caviar is served with a horn spoon to prevent crushing or damaging the eggs. Buy a brioche-style bread (one rich with butter and eggs) from a good bakery. Trim the crusts off, slice, and cut into triangles. Heat a broiler and lightly toast the bread on both sides. Center the crystal bowl on a silver tray and surround with the toast points.

Wings of War

32 chicken wings, pinions removed and wings separated at the joint

    the grated zest of one orange

$^1/_2$ cup orange juice

$^1/_2$ cup lemon juice

$^1/_2$ cup lime juice

$^1/_2$ cup orange blossom honey at room temperature

$^1/_4$ cup olive oil

2   tablespoons fresh ginger, peeled and minced

3   scallions, thinly sliced

1   tablespoon cayenne pepper

1   teaspoon cumin

1   teaspoon cinnamon

$1^1/_2$ teaspoons salt

3   tablespoons black sesame seeds or white sesame seeds toasted until brown in a
     dry skillet

10–12 scallion flowers, to garnish (see below)

3   orange slices, to garnish

6   cinnamon sticks, to garnish

1. In a glass, ceramic, or enameled dish large enough to accommodate the wings in
   one layer, combine the orange zest, citrus juices, honey, oil, ginger, scallions,
   cayenne, cumin, cinnamon, and salt. Whisk until the honey dissolves. Taste and
   adjust the seasonings. The mixture should be spicy. Put the wings in the marinade,
   turning them to coat. Cover and refrigerate the chicken wings for 6–8 hours, turning 2–3 times.

2. Preheat the oven to 350°.

3. Arrange the chicken wings on a rack in a roasting pan in a single layer. Scatter the
   sesame seeds evenly over the wings. Reserve the marinade for basting the wings.
   Roast the wings on the center oven rack for 45 minutes to one hour, turning and
   basting with the marinade every 15 minutes or until they are golden brown. The
   wings may be made several hours ahead. Brush with the marinade and reheat in a
   low oven.

4. Pile the wings on a large platter and garnish the perimeter with orange slices,
   cinnamon sticks, and scallion flowers.

To make scallion flowers:

Clean the scallions and trim the root end, leaving enough root intact to hold the
scallion together. Trim the scallion 3" from the root end (reserve the tails for another use). With a small sharp knife, make parallel slits from the root end (but not
through it), down the length of the scallion, turning and making parallel slits as
closely together as possible all around the scallions. Place the scallion in a tightly
sealed container of ice water. Refrigerate for an hour or two until they "blossom."

Checkerboard Sandwiches

1   recipe blender mayonnaise (see Chapter 9) (or use good quality commercial mayonnaise)

1   tablespoon curry powder

1   small red apple, cored and minced

$1/4$ cup minced watercress leaves and tender stems

$1/4$ cup fresh dill weed, finely snipped

$1/2$ pound Norwegian smoked salmon

$1/2$ pound smoked turkey

1   loaf thinly sliced cocktail pumpernickel squares

1   loaf thinly sliced white cocktail squares

1. Divide the mayonnaise in half. Add the curry powder, minced apple, and watercress to one half. Season the other half with the snipped dill.

2. To make the sandwiches, cut the smoked salmon and the smoked turkey to fit the bread. Spread the white bread with a thin layer of the dill mayonnaise and top with one layer of smoked salmon. Spread the dark bread with the curry-apple mayonnaise and top with the smoked turkey and a second piece of bread.

3. On a large rectangular tray, arrange the sandwiches in the center, alternating light and dark to make a checkerboard pattern. Make one batch of sandwiches up to an hour ahead, arrange them on a tray, cover tightly with film, and top with a damp tea towel. Refrigerate.

4. Set up an assembly line of the mayonnaise, salmon, turkey, and more bread to quickly prepare more sandwiches.

Checkerboard
sandwiches.

Eggplant-Tomato Fleet

1   eggplant (about 1 pound)

30 small, ripe plum tomatoes

2   large cloves of garlic, finely minced

2   shallots, finely minced

     the juice of one half lemon or to taste

$^1/_2$ teaspoon ground cumin

2   tablespoons minced, flat leaf parsley

     salt and freshly ground black pepper to taste

1   head Boston lettuce, leaves separated, washed and dried

1. Preheat the oven to 500°.

2. Place the eggplant in a baking dish and roast the eggplant for 20–30 minutes or until a skewer slides through without resistance. Remove from the oven and cool.

3. Trim off the stem end of the tomatoes. Cut them in half lengthwise and, with a small spoon, scrape out the seeds and pulp. Finely mince two whole tomatoes. Lightly salt the insides of the rest of the tomatoes and turn them upside down on paper towels to drain.

4. Peel the eggplant and finely chop the flesh. In a mixing bowl, combine the eggplant, minced tomato, garlic, and shallot. Add the lemon juice, the rest of the olive oil, cumin, parsley, and salt and pepper to taste.

5. From eight of the tomato halves, cut small isosceles triangles about 1" tall. Fill the rest of the tomato shells with the eggplant mixture.

6. Stack the Boston lettuce leaves and roll them tightly like a cigar. With a sharp knife, cut the roll into fine slivers. Make a bed of the slivered lettuce on a serving platter. Align the eggplant-tomato shells "regatta-style" on top of the lettuce. Insert a tomato triangle into each little "boat" to make a sail.

The eggplant mixture can be made a day ahead. Seal tightly in a container and refrigerate. Prepare the tomato shells the day of the party. Fill them about an hour before the party begins. Cover the platter with film and refrigerate the platter until serving time.

Eggplant-tomato fleet.

Teardrop Cookies with a Chocolate Kiss

2   egg whites

$^3/_4$ cup confectioners sugar

$^1/_4$ cup flaked coconut

1   tablespoon grated lemon zest

$^1/_3$ cup cake flour, sifted

2   tablespoons unsalted butter, melted and cooled

2   tablespoons heavy cream

1   tablespoon rose water or orange flower water

3   tablespoons unsalted butter

$^1/_4$ pound good-quality bittersweet chocolate, chopped into bits

$^1/_2$ cup heavy cream

1. Preheat the oven to 400° and lightly grease a cookie sheet.

2. In a mixing bowl, whisk the egg whites and sugar together until thoroughly combined. Whisk the coconut, lemon zest, flour, melted butter, and the cream into the egg white/sugar mixture. The batter will be very liquid.

3. Drop $^1/_2$ teaspoons of the batter 2" apart onto the cookie sheet (9 per batch). Stir the batter frequently to keep the ingredients evenly distributed.

4. Bake the cookies for five minutes. Watch them closely, removing the cookies from the oven as soon as they brown around the edges. Quickly transfer the cookies to a rack.

5. Protecting your fingers with a dish towel, immediately begin pinching together one side of the cookie (about a $^1/_4$" pinch) to form a teardrop shape. The cookies harden as they cool and must be formed when they are warm; make only one batch at a time. If some cookies harden before they can be formed, briefly return them to the oven to soften again. Makes about 25–30 cookies. Teardrop cookies keep well, hermetically sealed in a container, for about a week.

6. To make the chocolate kiss, place the chocolate bits in a large heatproof bowl with the butter. Place the bowl over a pot of simmering water (the bottom of the bowl should not touch the simmering water). When the chocolate and butter are melted, remove the bowl from the heat and beat the mixture with a wooden spoon until it is cool and thickened.

7. In an electric mixer or in a bowl and using a balloon whisk, whip the heavy cream to the soft peak stage, then beat it into the chocolate mixture with a whisk.

8. Fit a pastry bag with a tiny star tip and pipe a miniature rosette of chocolate into the pinched side of each cookie. Chocolate kisses may be piped the morning of the party. Any leftover chocolate can be frozen for future use.

Part 4
Special Situations

This section discusses entertaining circumstances that sometimes require an extra push.

Perhaps you're starting out on your own and feeling at a loss when it comes to entertaining. Maybe you invited friends to dinner, then suddenly discovered they have special dietary needs. There's an uncomfortable first time for everyone when it comes to hosting a business event.

These chapters offer practical advice to speed your way through the particulars of these situations.

Suddenly Single

Suddenly you're single. Whether it happened abruptly or you knew it was coming, becoming single always feels "sudden." Certainly you're not sailing these waters alone. Maybe you have your first *real* job and apartment of your own—say good-bye to the comfortable camaraderie of college life and pals. Perhaps you lost a spouse or significant other through death, divorce, or a break-up. Even if you're living in the same abode, the four walls just aren't the same anymore and you feel somewhat "out of it" with your long-time circle of friends. Or perhaps a new job moves you to unfamiliar territory and a new life begins.

Entertaining is one of the most significant ways to initiate your new life. Preparing for a party, you engage in homey rituals that christen your new habitat. You add pleasant amenities to your environment that, without a party pending, may not seem important. An old hand at party-giving probably needs a new stream-lined format to suit a new lifestyle. For a rookie in the kitchen, learning to cook becomes a pleasant, self-nurturing activity as well as a practical necessity. Don't be intimidated. Entertaining at home has a charm that forms friendships faster than any other social outlet. The game plan to ease you into the swing of things is foolproof. And remember, an invitation to a dinner party is always a special treat for the lucky guest.

Meeting New People

Becoming single doesn't mean former friends and couples are out of your social picture. But meeting other singles certainly brings a comfort level to your new situation by learning how they live their lives. If your pre-single companions were primarily from your same walk of life, you have entered a greatly expanded social spectrum. As a single person, you have a common ground with a vast age group from diverse walks of life. Tapping this resource, extending invitations to new acquaintances, and mixing old friends with new makes for lively parties.

Smart Move

A few tips for meeting new people:

➤ Invest in a new interest.

➤ Take an art, music, or film class or lecture series.

➤ Join a club likely to draw people from various professions.

➤ Volunteer for an organization where you interact with others toward a common goal.

"Singles" resources often prove disappointing. For the sophisticated individual, taking a class, joining a club, or volunteering for an organization is generally more socially enriching and provides you with a basis for an interesting guest list. For example, invite your art class to dinner. Most likely, your classmates will welcome the opportunity to learn more about one another in a casual setting. The instructor can be your guest of honor. If you're getting new acquaintances together with long-time pals, don't fuss over balancing men and women and don't limit the party to your own generation. A diverse mix of guests makes for the best parties. When your guests are meeting for the first time, proposing a toast is a welcome ice breaker. Go around the table and say something special or unique about each person:

"Kurt is an atypical wine merchant whose sense of humor allows him to share his extensive knowledge without being the least bit intimidating."

"How wonderful to have Julie, who has mastered the art of making everyone feel terrific."

It's much easier for your guests to initiate conversation when they know something about one another.

Another way to ease new people together is to have a party with a stimulating theme. For instance, have you, a friend, or an acquaintance just returned from an exciting trip? Choose an international variation of the menu in this chapter for your party and take your guests on a vicarious voyage. Focus on conversation, not slide shows.

Sometimes you click with people who cross your path on a routine basis but you neglect to consider a potentially engaging guest, such as your florist, wine merchant, barber, or any friendly shopkeeper. People who deal with the public have a wealth of experience with others and plenty of winning stories about their specialties and clientele. All it takes to get a party going nicely is someone who has something interesting to say. The gregarious nature of people in service businesses sparks stimulating conversation.

For singles who are having a big party, it's always a good idea to invite a close friend or favorite relative to act as cohost. Also, many people don't realize that restaurant waiters often freelance. Hire a personable waiter from a favorite restaurant who can serve drinks and get things going while you take coats and make introductions.

The Extra Mile
Enlisting your wine merchant to conduct a dinner tasting of wines selected for your menu can effortlessly get your party rolling.

Smart Move
An old college pal who was admittedly lousy with desserts used to invite friends to her apartment for dinner, then everyone walked to a local restaurant for dessert and coffee.

Party-Poopers

Beware of situations that can cast a pall on the life of a party. Suddenly you have a guest on your hands who is a full-time project—rarely to the delight of other guests.

➤ Don't invite the guy or gal who insists on catching the game's score during the party—unless, of course, you are hosting a party to watch a sporting event.

➤ Don't invite someone who needs to be a "star." It's your party, after all.

➤ Don't choose a cohost who needs training during the party. Your cohost should know you and your home well enough to be a silent helpmate, picking up where you leave off.

➤ Don't invite a know-it-all who can pick away at your confidence as a host.

➤ Don't invite someone who has a reputation for having one too many and becoming obnoxious.

Restocking Your Cabinets Without Breaking the Budget

Whether starting out cold or beginning anew, "suddenly singles" are often short on the basic accouterments of entertaining. Focus your first parties on a bistro theme. This motif is pleasantly in vogue these days, and the menu requires a minimum of equipment and serving pieces—ideal if you're building or restocking the larder. Although the cookware may warrant spending a few extra dollars, you'll have these key pieces forever and use them time and again. The rest of our mix-and-match recommendations are very sympathetic to a budget as well as being stylish, cheerful, and classic—you won't be purchasing throwaways.

Cookware

Consult Chapter 2 for specifics on cooking equipment. We recommend having these essential pieces:

➤ Heavy-duty oven-proof 5–6 quart casserole with a lid, preferably cast iron enameled in a cheerful primary color in which you can cook and serve

➤ 8"×3" sauce pan with a lid in which you can blanch vegetables or prepare rice pilaf, polenta, potatoes, etc. This pan also is practical for single-serving pan sautés—chicken breast, pork chop, etc.

➤ 8"–10" chef's knife and a utility knife

➤ Cutting board

Serveware

Consult Chapter 6, "Schemes, Themes, and Dreams," for places to find these items:

➤ Painted tin or lacquered tray for assembling hors d'oeuvres

➤ Bread basket

➤ Salad bowl and salad servers

➤ Fiesta ware in single, jewel-tone colors or mix of colors; or white bistro earthenware, shiny or dull with a dark green or navy border that translates as "neutral"

➤ Glass tumblers in bottle green or cobalt blue with hand-blown imperfections—you can use the tumblers for wine, water, or drinks

➤ Galvanized bucket or large clay pot to use as a wine cooler

Serve drinks in all-purpose tumblers.

Improvise a wine cooler using a bowl, vase, or clay pot.

Designer Notes

If you're purchasing flatware, consider bistro, hotel, or classic styles. These simple designs are smart with just about any table setting. Avoid trendy styles that become dated.

Classic flatware styles.

Hotel Pistol Shell Moderne

A Bistro Party

The menu:

    Marinated Shrimp with Crudités and Sauce Andalouse

    Spanish Fricassee of Chicken with Amontillado Sherry and Olives

    Saffron Risotto

    Romaine and Escarole Salad with Fennel and Manchego Cheese

    Crusty Bread

    Custard Tart or Nut Cake

The recipes for this menu can be found at the end of this chapter.

Bueno Appetito! This party scheme features a minimum of food preparation and a relaxed and cheerful ambiance to gradually ease a "suddenly single" intimidated by entertaining into party-giving. The appetizer spruces up store-bought cooked shrimp and commercial mayonnaise. Fill in around the central make-ahead entree with a good-quality packaged risotto mix, and a bread and dessert from your favorite bakery. The salad is simple to prepare, but if you're pinched for time, buy pre-cleaned, salad-ready mixed lettuces. Always make your own vinaigrette—it's so easy. Don't ever serve your guests bottled salad dressing. This menu serves well as an informal sit-down dinner for six or can be expanded to serve a buffet for a crowd. Feature Spanish Rioja wines with your menu—white for cocktails and red with chicken fricassee. The international variations on the entree offer different party themes based on the same menu and design ideas. With a few minor changes you can stage repeat performances and no one will be the wiser!

Good Spirits

Rioja wines vary in style depending upon the aging process. Younger Riojas are fresh and fruity; older ones are much more complex. *Con crianza* on a Rioja label means "with aging." Look for a young red Rioja to complement the fricassee.

Rioja: aged 1 year in oak, 2–3 years in the bottle

Rioja Reserva: aged 2 years in oak, 3 years in the bottle

Rioja Gran Reserva: aged 3 years in oak, 4 years in the bottle

Your Table Design

Primary colors and natural textures create a cheerful bistro ambiance and are easy on the budget.

➤ *Mats:* Raffia or straw woven mats do double duty as placemats and as trivets for warm casseroles, damp ice buckets, or wine coolers. A bare table is also an acceptable bistro look.

➤ *Linens:* Brightly colored bandannas from outlets or discount stores make great napkins, or look for solid-color napkins in primary colors. Avoid pastels, which are too seasonal, and patterned napkins, which tend to grow tiresome. You also can use bandannas as placemats with solid-color napkins.

➤ *Flowers:* Fill a big woven basket with loosely arranged flowers, or collect inexpensive clear glass containers with interesting shapes. Empty pottery mustard jars also make great vases. Arrange jars randomly on the dinner table or buffet. Or buy small pots of herbs for your table, then after the party, keep them in a sunny kitchen window.

➤ *Candles:* Chunky candles placed in small clay pot trays eliminate the need for candlesticks.

➤ *Music:* Play Aster Piazzola's native Spanish folk themes, tangos, fandangos, and flamencos.

Designer Notes

Keep your decor subtle. Play music like an elegant woman applies perfume—softly.

Designer Notes

Tie bandanna napkins in a loose knot and center on each plate. For a buffet, wrap flatware in the bandannas and arrange next to the stack of dinner plates.

Glass containers as vases.

Clear glass laboratory beakers

Bottled water containers as vases

Take a Side Trip

Bueno Appetito, from Italy:

Fill empty wine bottles with colorful, drippy candles for a nostalgic and relaxed '50s retro look. Tie a few bread sticks and a sprig of fresh oregano or rosemary in the knot of the napkins to treat your guests to a hint of aromatherapy. For an hors d'oeuvre, brush slices of Italian bread with olive oil, broil until toasted, and arrange in a basket. Combine chopped tomatoes with lots of chopped garlic, torn fresh basil leaves, a drizzle of olive oil, and salt and pepper to taste. Put the tomatoes in a colorful bowl and serve with a plate of sliced rounds of fresh mozzarella. Let everyone prepare their own bruschetta. For dessert, pick up Italian ice and cookies from an Italian bakery. How about some Pavarotti for a dinnertime serenade? Consult the master recipe for variations.

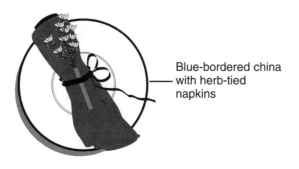

Bandanna napkins with herbs or bread sticks.

Blue-bordered china with herb-tied napkins

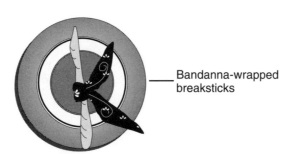

Bandanna-wrapped breaksticks

Bon Appetit, from Provence:

Empty pottery mustard jars make great containers for fresh or dried lavender. Use several smaller jars arranged around the table or one big jar in the center. Purchase a paté, crunchy corncihons, and cured olives to serve with cocktails. Select Châteauneuf-du-Pape or Côte du Rhône wines to complement the stew, and feature a rustic fruit tart for dessert. Treat your guests to Steffan Grapelli's jazz violin or the uplifting score from *My Father's Glory, My Mother's Castle.*

The Least You Need To Know

➤ Entertaining is your vehicle for opening new doors and enhancing your life.

➤ You can be creative within a budget. Focus on makes-sense, not make-shift.

➤ Low-key parties are the best for mixing and mingling, and you are a relaxed and happy host.

The Recipes

Marinated Shrimp and Crudités with Sauce Andalouse

1 large clove garlic, peeled and crushed

the juice of one lime

the juice of one half lemon

1 teaspoon extra virgin olive oil

$^1/_4$ cup fresh thyme leaves or dill

salt and freshly ground black pepper to taste

1 pound large cooked shrimp with tails on

1 bunch broccoli, trimmed and cut into bite-sized florets

1 small head cauliflower, trimmed and cut into bite-sized florets

1 large sweet red pepper, seeds and membranes removed and cut into bite-sized triangles

$^1/_2$ cup good quality store-bought mayonnaise

1 tablespoon tomato puree

1 small shallot, minced

$^1/_4$ teaspoon sweet paprika

2 tablespoons minced fresh thyme or dill weed

$^1/_4$ cup heavy cream, whipped to the soft peak stage

$^1/_2$ lemon juice

a few drops of Tabasco sauce

1. In a flat glass, ceramic, or enameled dish, whisk together the garlic, citrus juices, olive oil, herbs, and salt and pepper to taste. Toss the shrimp in the marinade, cover, and refrigerate for a few hours to imbibe with the flavors.

2. Bring a large pot of water to a boil. Blanch the cauliflower for one to two minutes or until tender/crisp, and with a slotted spoon, transfer to a colander and run under cold water to chill. Plunge the broccoli into the boiling water and blanch for 1–2 minutes. Drain and rinse under cold water to chill. Wrap the vegetables in paper towels, seal in a zip bag, and refrigerate. Seal and store the red peppers in the refrigerator until ready to use.

The Extra Mile Refer to Chapter 9 to make your own homemade blender mayonnaise.

3. In a mixing bowl, combine the mayonnaise, tomato purée, shallot, paprika, and herbs. Gently fold the whipped cream into the mixture until thoroughly combined. Season to taste with drops of lemon juice, Tabasco, salt, and pepper. Transfer the sauce to an attractive serving bowl, cover, and chill.

4. To serve, drain the shrimp and arrange in the center of a colorful platter. Alternate the red, white, and green vegetables around the shrimp. Serve accompanied by sauce Andalouse. Serves 6–8.

Spanish Fricassee of Chicken with Amontillado Sherry and Olives

2 3 $^1/_2$ pound chickens, each cut into 8 sections

   salt and freshly ground black pepper

2 tablespoons olive oil

1 small carrot, minced

1 small onion, minced

2 large cloves of garlic, minced

5 sun dried tomatoes cut into slivers

$^1/_4$ cup sherry vinegar

1 cup Amontillado sherry

2 cups all-purpose stock (see Chapter 17 for a stock recipe)

1 tablespoon tomato paste

1 strip of orange peel, $^1/_2$"×3"

1 bay leaf

$^1/_2$ teaspoon dried thyme

8 ounces pearl onions

2 tablespoons unsalted butter

2 tablespoons vegetable oil

$^1/_2$ teaspoon sugar

$^1/_2$ cup water or stock

   salt and freshly ground pepper

1 pound crimini or shiitake mushrooms, wiped clean and quartered

$^1/_2$ cup imported green olives, pitted and minced, to garnish

How to section a chicken.

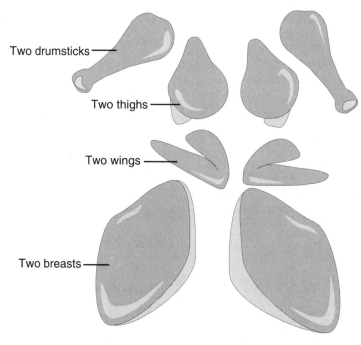

Two drumsticks

Two thighs

Two wings

Two breasts

1. Lightly salt and pepper the chicken pieces. Heat a large, heavy sauté pan or a heatproof casserole dish over medium-high heat. Glaze the pan with the olive oil, add the chicken pieces, being careful not to overcrowd the pan, and brown them on all sides. Repeat until all the chicken is cooked. Remove the chicken to a plate, pour off the fat in the pan, and return the pan to the heat.

2. In the same pan, sauté the onion, garlic, and sun dried tomatoes until the onion is translucent (about 3–5 minutes). Add the sherry and the sherry vinegar to the pan and bring them to a boil. Deglaze the pan, scraping the bottom with a wooden spoon to dislodge clinging bits of flavor. Reduce the sherry until it becomes syrupy. Stir in the stock, tomato paste, orange peel, and the herbs. Reduce the heat to low and return the chicken to the pan. Cover the pan with a lid placed slightly ajar and simmer the chicken for 30–40 minutes or until juices run clear when a thigh is pricked.

3. When the chicken is done, the sauce should lightly coat a spoon. If necessary, thin the sauce with more stock or thicken the sauce by combining one teaspoon of cornstarch and one teaspoon of water and stirring it into the simmering sauce. Discard the orange peel. Taste and adjust the seasonings, adding more Amontillado sherry, sherry vinegar, salt, and pepper to taste. Arrange the chicken in a clean casserole and cover it with the sauce.

4. Bring a medium-sized pot of water to a boil. Add the onions, return the water to a boil, and boil for one minute. Drain the onions and run them under cold water until cool. Trim the root end of the onions, leaving enough root to keep the onions intact. Slip off the onion skins.

> **Smart Move**
> To eliminate the need for supplying a dinner knife at a buffet, substitute 18 boneless and skinless chicken thighs for the chicken pieces. Cut the thighs into stew-sized pieces before browning.

5. Heat a medium-sized sauté pan with one tablespoon of butter and one tablespoon of oil. Sauté the onions, sprinkling them with the sugar, salt, and pepper, until they are flecked with brown. Add the water to the sauté pan, turn the heat to low, cover, and simmer the onions for 3–5 minutes or just until they can be pierced through with a toothpick. Add the onions to the chicken casserole.

6. In the same pan, heat the remaining butter and oil over medium-high heat. Sauté the mushrooms until they are lightly browned, seasoning with salt and pepper. Scatter the mushrooms over the chicken in the casserole.

continues

continued

7. The fricassee can be made a day ahead. Allow the casserole to cool completely. Cover the casserole and refrigerate. Bring the casserole to room temperature, then reheat for 30 minutes in a 325° oven. Before serving, sprinkle the casserole with the chopped olives. Serves 6–8.

Cook's Notes

Consult Chapter 1 for information about Amontillado sherry.

Romaine and Escarole Salad with Fennel and Manchego Cheese

8 cups romaine lettuce leaves and escarole, torn into bite-size pieces

1 small fennel bulb

$^1/_4$ pound Manchego cheese

1 tablespoon good quality red wine vinegar or sherry vinegar

1 generous teaspoon imported Dijon-style mustard

1 small clove garlic, crushed

$^1/_4$ teaspoon salt and a generous grinding of black pepper

4 tablespoons extra virgin olive oil or walnut oil

1. Wash and dry the lettuces. Remove the fronds (the delicate, feathery leaves of the plant) from the fennel bulb and finely mince them. Seal the fronds in plastic and reserve. Cut the tough green stalk from the fennel and discard. Cut the bulb in half through the root. Place the fennel cut side down and slice it into thin slivers. Seal the fennel in plastic and reserve.

2. Using a cheese plane or the wide cutter on a box grater, sliver the Manchego (the pieces do not have to be even). Seal the cheese in plastic and reserve.

3. In a small bowl, whisk together the vinegar, mustard, garlic, salt, and pepper. Slowly dribble in the oil, whisking continuously. Taste and adjust the seasoning. Just before serving, toss the lettuces and the fennel slivers in a large salad bowl. Toss with half the vinaigrette, adding more as necessary, just to coat the lettuce leaves. Scatter the Manchego cheese and the fennel fronds on top of the salad and serve. Serves 6–8.

Cook's Notes

Fennel has a fleshy, bulbous base and a leaf stalk with sprouting, feathery, dark green fronds. The texture is similar to but denser than celery. Fennel has a refreshing, mild anise flavor and is sometimes called "anise" in the U.S. It is popular both in Italy, as *finoccio*, and France, as *fenouil*.

Fennel bulb.

Cook's Notes

Manchego cheese is one of the most widely available cheeses in Spain. It is produced from sheep's milk and, depending on the cure, it can range in texture and taste from semi-soft and mild to hard and sharp. For this salad, look for the hardest texture—like an Italian parmesan.

Recipe Variations for a Side Trip to Italy

Substitute:

4 pounds of boneless, trimmed veal shoulder cut into stew-sized pieces for the chicken.

Add $1/4$ pound finely chopped pancetta when you sauté the carrot, onion, and celery.

Use 1 $1/2$ cups dry, white wine in place of the sherry and sherry vinegar.

Add $1/2$ cup porcini mushrooms reconstituted in hot water to cover, then minced, to the simmering stew.

Replace the olive garnish with 1 tablespoon minced lemon peel, 4 large cloves of garlic peeled and minced, and $1/2$ cup flat leaf parsley leaves, minced. Toss the lemon, parsley, and garlic together and strew them over the stew before serving.

Accompany the stew with a packaged polenta mix.

For a variation on the salad, simply serve a platter of paper-thin fennel slivers topped with shaved Parmigiano-Reggiano or Asiago cheese and plenty of freshly ground black pepper. Pass extra virgin olive oil and balsamic vinegar and allow guests to serve themselves.

Cook's Notes

Pancetta is a spiced, cured Italian "bacon." Some varieties are smoked. Look for pancetta in Italian markets. You may substitute a good quality bacon.

Recipe Variations for a Side Trip to Provence

Substitute:

3 pounds lean, boneless beef chuck cut into stew-sized pieces for the chicken.

Add 2 ounces of diced country bacon or ham when sautéing the carrot, onion, and garlic.

Use one cup of cognac instead of the sherry and the sherry vinegar.

Replace the stock with 2 cups of a light, fruity red wine.

Just before serving, scatter a handful of fresh thyme leaves over the stew.

Accompany the stew with boiled new potatoes tossed with extra virgin olive oil, salt, and freshly ground pepper and plenty of minced garlic and flat leaf parsley.

Chapter 15

Diet Dilemmas

In This Chapter

➤ Today's eating habits

➤ Diet fads versus reality

➤ Hosting guests with a variety of diets

➤ A savvy, '90s menu

Let's propose a hypothetical dinner party. Dean Ornish, Susan Powter, Colonel Sanders, and Mary Tyler Moore are going to be your dinner guests. Of course this guest list is a wild stretch of the imagination, but realistically, if issues of diet haven't influenced your entertaining yet, they certainly will eventually.

For many of us, a party is the time to loosen up and enjoy a few indulgences. But this may not be true for someone who just had by-pass surgery or someone with a food sensitivity who could be miserable for days because of an indiscretion. Even if you're sure

Sage Advice
At one time, Benjamin Franklin was a vegetarian and proponent of animal rights. He resumed eating fish when he witnessed a cod being cleaned and several smaller fish popped out of its belly. "…if you eat one another, I don't see why we mayn't eat you," he observed.

that every one of your guests is fit as a fiddle, you may be taking a risk. Someone's preoccupation with healthy eating can most certainly cast a pall on a yearning for Beef Wellington. Then, beyond medically prescribed and self-prescribed eating lurks a score of ominous allergies and intolerances to further challenge your dinner party plans. Just plain old healthy eating is hazardous—for every dietary dictum proclaimed, we soon hear a contradiction. The food blessed by the media today is declared the bane of our existence tomorrow. In a flash, last month's perfect party menu is hopelessly out of vogue.

Truth and Consequences

Sure, we've dramatically changed some unhealthy eating habits over the last few decades, but pursuit of dietary perfection is nothing new to the American palate. Over 100 years ago, hopeful purists hopped on the band wagons of diet evangelists who are now household names. Sylvester Graham, James Salisbury, and John Kellogg were all nutritional gurus. A quest for the ultimate diet regimen seems to be a hallmark of our society. But how can we believe government-endorsed dietary guidelines when best-selling diet and fitness books refute them? Most amazing of all, Americans are heavier than ever despite all this dietary preoccupation and fuss. Is the food pyramid the eighth wonder of the world, or will we soon discover it's pure folly? Should you entertain like you live on the Mediterranean coast or next door to a rice paddy, or is your style more of a French Paradox die-hard?

Hosting a dinner party in the '90s can certainly make an ordeal out of menu planning. Here are some general realities to sink your teeth into:

➤ Many people with heart disease abide by diets far less in fat than the recommended 30 percent of daily calorie intake. Your idea of a lean meal may be 20 percent off the mark.

➤ Our vegetarian population is on a rapid rise.

➤ Americans are more aware of food allergies, sensitivities, and intolerances than ever before.

➤ As our older population increases, they will require some very specific dietary needs.

Fads or Facts of Life

So what does all this food censorship mean? Maybe you could care less about political correctness when it comes to a party. Rest assured, we don't believe it's the responsibility of a host to cater to persnickety eaters. If you have a dinner party and invite friends who adhere to every popular diet that's published, they don't have the right to dominate your party plans. Frankly, a guest who balks at the au gratin potatoes or pokes at a pork tenderloin like it's a stick of dynamite is quite simply guilty of bad manners. An occasional indulgence won't send a health fanatic booking to the cardiologist or confessional.

On the other hand, we believe it *is* a host's responsibility to accommodate a guest who is on a restricted diet for medical reasons. It's thoughtless to ignore these needs, and we seem to encounter these realities more than ever before. Finally, respect vegetarians for their lifestyle choice.

Reality Bites
A *vegetarian* abstains from meat, poultry, and fish. *Lacto-ovo vegetarians* eat egg and dairy products. A *vegan* abstains from all animal products, including eggs, dairy, and cheese. Someone who abstains from just red meat and fowl is not a vegetarian.

Entertaining the Impossible

Let's say you're hosting a birthday bash for a friend. Among your invited guests is one with a heart condition who eats practically zero fat, one who has a gluten intolerance and can't consume any wheat products, and a vegetarian. Or perhaps you're in charge of a family gathering whose roster includes an elective dieter, someone who doesn't eat red meat, someone who prefers red meat, a lactose intolerance, and a renal diet. These situations are not hypothetical. They're true stories, friends.

Smart Move
For difficult or intricate dietary requirements, contact national or regional organizations or foundations established to provide information on specific diseases. Your local library should be able to direct you to the address and phone number of the appropriate group.

When you're facing what seems like an utterly impossible menu challenge for the first time, here's a common trap: If you focus on what people can't eat rather than the many things they *can*, you'll drive yourself crazy. The best approach is to sit down with a pen and paper and begin making a list of every diet-friendly food. Before you know it, a menu starts falling into place. Look for the best and freshest produce in the market to use as a menu feature. The best way to accent quality is with simplicity. When food choices are limited, let mother nature come to the rescue. Even though the market is glutted with surrogate products to assuage yearnings for fats, sugars, and the like, real food is always the best food. No-fat "ice-cream" can't hold a candle to a pyramid of plump, ripe strawberries for dessert.

Reality Bites
Gluten intolerance is called Celiac disease. Eating any food containing gluten, such as wheat, barley, or rye, causes bowel damage.

Making the Extra Effort

Because dietary restrictions are becoming commonplace, a gracious host should always inquire when entertaining someone for the first time. Just casually say, "Oh, by the way, do you have any food restrictions or allergies I should know about?" Believe it or not, many people are shy about taking the initiative to inform their host of a dietary restriction or problem. Always ask for the specifics of a diet; don't assume. For instance, you may prepare a yummy no-salt tomato-basil sauce for a guest on a renal diet and then find out the guest can't eat tomatoes. If you plan a Chinese meal for someone who is gluten intolerant, did you know that many soy sauces contain wheat?

Try not to make something different for the diet-bound eater—it singles them out. The extra effort that goes into planning a meal that everyone can enjoy makes for a successful party and a very appreciative guest. Here are a few general pointers:

➤ When entertaining vegetarians and non-vegetarians, stick with a vegetarian menu or accompany a meat dish with substantial pastas, grains, or legumes and several vegetable choices. Remember, a vegan won't eat fresh egg fettuccine.

➤ Aim for a variety of color, texture, and attractive garnishes for a low-fat menu.

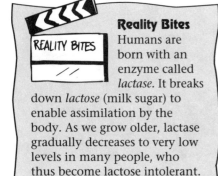

Reality Bites

Humans are born with an enzyme called *lactase*. It breaks down *lactose* (milk sugar) to enable assimilation by the body. As we grow older, lactase gradually decreases to very low levels in many people, who thus become lactose intolerant.

➤ Herbs, spices, and a judicious use of hot pepper compensate for the richness of fats and oils and add extra pep to low-salt food.

➤ Mustards are great flavor enhancers and also natural emulsifiers that can bring body to a weak sauce. Beware! Mustards are high in salt except for some honey mustards.

➤ You can skim all the fat off of homemade meat and vegetable stocks. They add marvelous texture to sauces and provide flavor and nutrients.

A Brief Lesson in Fats

Just in case you missed the low-down on the nature of fats, review this brief lesson:

➤ *Saturated fats* are the artery-clogging bad guys. Except for coconut and palm oil, these fats are solid at room temperature.

➤ *Hydrogenated oils* are chemically transformed fats that change a fat that is normally liquid at room temperature into a solid (for example, margarine). Recent studies are casting a bad light on these fats.

➤ *Polyunsaturated fats* are a healthier choice than saturated fats. These fats are liquid at room temperature. Safflower oil is the highest in polyunsaturates, followed by soybean, corn, and sesame oil in descending order.

➤ *Monounsaturated fats* are the superstars, known to reduce bad (LDL) cholesterol. They are olive oil, canola oil, and peanut oil.

➤ *Omega-3's* are highly beneficial fish oils that lower bad cholesterol and elevate good (HDL) cholesterol. Bluefish, salmon, tuna, sardines, and herring are all excellent sources of omega-3's.

A Politically Correct Menu

The menu:

Salad of Cucumber Gems and Haricots Verts

Sea Bass in Saffron Broth

Jasmine Rice

Garlic Croutons

Cassis Poached Pears with Star Anise

The recipes for this menu can be found at the end of this chapter.

Hopefully, you'll never encounter the mindboggling task of planning a menu for several conflicting diets. But good luck trying to avoid the low-fat brigade. You may as well get into practice with low-fat fare because this trend is here to stay. Here's a Mediterranean menu of lively, satisfying flavors that trim the fat way down and combine pleasing colors and textures with heady aromas—hardly a sacrifice for anyone. The popularity of a Mediterranean diet has much more going for it than just healthy food. You have the opportunity to go all the way, creating a joyful, uplifting mood to complement your menu.

Your Table Design

To set a Mediterranean-inspired table, focus on using cheery colors and natural accessories that convey a relaxed and happy mood.

➤ *Table linens and serveware:* Use colors and patterns that convey an easygoing *joie de vivre* on your table, or leave a rustic table bare and mix and match bright, cheerful napkins. Chunky tumblers and earthenware or "everyday" dishes go along with the mood.

➤ *Table decoration:* A cornucopia of vegetables or fruits piled into an earthenware tureen or rustic bowl go well with a pastoral setting. Arrange trailing ivy among the fruits and vegetables or on the table. A crockery jug or pitcher loosely filled with blooming branches also suits the theme.

➤ *Candles:* Use chunky candles of different heights arranged at random on the table.

➤ *Music:* Musical scores from a French or Italian film are a perfect complement to the relaxed and joyful ambiance. *My Father's Glory & My Mother's Castle* happens to be one of our favorites.

A Mediterranean table.

Other Low-Fat Recipes in This Book

Use the following list of other low-fat recipes to help create more politically correct menus:

➤ Vegetarian Cassoulet (bake garlic in foil at 350° for 1 hour instead of cooking in oil) (Chapter 8)

➤ Gertie's Baked Beans (prepare with 1 cup sun-dried tomatoes rather than bacon) (Chapter 9)

➤ Tom's Greens (Chapter 9)

➤ Sautéed Duck Breasts on Warm Red Cabbage Salad (skin the duck and use 1 tablespoon olive oil rather than duck fat or substitute boneless, skinned chicken breasts) (Chapter 10)

➤ Spicy Black Beans and Rice (Chapter 11)

➤ Fajitas (made with skinless chicken breasts rather than pork) (Chapter 11)

➤ Jicama Salad (Chapter 11)

➤ Cherry Tomato Salsa (Chapter 11)

➤ Fruit Kabobs (Chapter 11)

➤ Rick's Hill of Beans with Cucumber Chips (Chapter 13)

➤ Spicy Lamb Torpedoes (made with ground chicken or turkey) (Chapter 13)

➤ Tomato-Pepper Compote (Chapter 14)

➤ Eggplant-Vidalia Onion Purée (use 1 tablespoon olive oil rather than the butter) (Chapter 16)

➤ Liz's Chicken Salad (Chapter 16)

➤ Country Garden Soup (Chapter 17)

➤ Bay Scallop Sauté (with lemon only—no sauce Andalouse) (Chapter 17)

The Least You Need To Know

➤ When you entertain, inquire ahead about diet restrictions.

➤ Focus on diet-friendly rather than forbidden foods when planning a menu for a restricted diet.

➤ Show off natural, seasonal food and avoid artificial products.

➤ Even if you aren't a low-fat eater, learning a few techniques is a must for today's entertaining.

The Recipes

Salad of Boston Lettuce, Cucumber Gems, and Haricots Verts

> **Cook's Notes**
>
> Haricots verts are the slender, wispy green beans of open-air French market fame. With the popularity of specialty produce, they're now making an appearance in our markets. Substitute regular green beans only if they're fresh and tender. Alternatively, substitute julienned zucchini, asparagus tips, or whatever happens to be in season.

$^1/_2$ pound haricots verts

2   European cucumbers

3   medium-size heads of Boston lettuce

2   cups arugula

8   scallions

2   cups of spicy sprouts

$^1/_2$ cup loosely packed fresh mint leaves, minced

2   tablespoons lemon juice

1   clove of garlic, crushed

1   teaspoon Dijon style mustard

   salt and freshly ground black pepper

4–6   tablespoons light olive oil

1. Snap the stem ends off the beans. Bring a pot of water to a rolling boil. Add the beans, return to a boil, and blanch the beans for 30 seconds to one minute. Drain immediately and rinse under cold running water to cool. Drain on paper towels and reserve.

2. Peel the cucumbers (slice lengthwise) and scrape out the seeds with a small spoon. Using a small melon ball scoop, cut out as many balls of cucumber as possible. Bring a pot of water to a rolling boil and immerse the cucumber balls. As soon as the water returns to a boil, drain the cucumbers and run under cold water until completely cool. Drain on paper towels and reserve.

3. Wash and dry the lettuces and tear into bite-sized pieces. Trim the roots from the scallions. Sliver the white part into thin rounds. Sliver the greens lengthwise into fine shreds.

4. To prepare the vinaigrette, in a small bowl, whisk the lemon juice, garlic, mustard to blend with salt and pepper to taste. Drizzle in the oil in a thin stream, whisking constantly. Taste and correct the seasoning.

5. Place the lettuce leaves in a salad bowl and add half of the vinaigrette; toss to coat. In another bowl, toss the haricot vert and cucumber gems with the remaining vinaigrette.

6. Arrange the lettuce on salad plates and scatter the haricot vert, cucumber, scallions, sprouts, and mint leaves on top. Serves 6.

Sea Bass in Saffron Broth

1	tablespoon olive oil
1	onion, sliced
2	large cloves of garlic, sliced
1	small carrot, peeled and sliced
$^1/_2$	fennel bulb, sliced
1	large pinch of saffron (about $^1/_2$ teaspoon)
2	bay leaves
1	teaspoon dried thyme
$^1/_2$	cup dry vermouth
1 $^1/_2$	pounds tomatoes
2	cups clam broth
1	cup water
	a pinch of hot pepper flakes
6	6-ounce sea bass or halibut fillets
	the grated rind of one orange
	salt and freshly ground black pepper
12	Nicoise olives
1	cup basil leaves (when opal basil is available use $^1/_2$ cup opal basil and $^1/_2$ cup regular) sauce *rouille* (recipe follows)

continues

continued

garlic croutons (recipe follows)

extra virgin olive oil and hot pepper flakes

Jasmine rice pilaf

Cook's Notes

Make a double batch of broth and freeze for a future, extra quick meal.

1. Heat the oil in a soup pot over medium high heat and cook the onion, garlic, carrot, fennel, and saffron until the vegetables soften, about 5–10 minutes. Add the bay leaf, thyme, and vermouth and allow the vermouth to reduce until almost evaporated.

2. Cut the tomatoes in half, squeeze out the seeds, and coarsely chop the tomatoes.

3. Add the tomatoes, clam broth, water, and hot pepper flakes to the onion mixture. Bring the mixture to a boil over high heat. Reduce the heat to low. Simmer partly covered for 30 minutes. Remove from the heat.

4. Purée 2 cups of the vegetables with 2 cups of broth in a blender or food processor. Strain the rest of the broth into a bowl, pressing hard on the vegetables to extract as much liquid as possible. Discard the solids. Return the broth and the purée to the pot and season to taste with salt and pepper. Reserve. You should have 3 $1/2$ to 4 cups broth.

5. Preheat the oven to 400°.

6. Remove the skin from the fillets by making a small slit to separate the skin from the flesh at one corner of the fillet. Hold the skin down with a finger and glide a sharp knife, angled toward the work surface, the length of the fillet. Discard the skin.

7. Place the fillets in a single layer in an ovenproof baking dish. Sprinkle the fish with the orange rind, salt, and pepper. Bring the saffron broth to a simmer and pour it over the fish. Loosely cover the baking dish with a piece of foil and bake the fish for ten minutes.

8. Warm 6 wide, flat soup plates. Transfer the fillets to the soup plates and ladle the saffron broth over each serving to fill the bowls. Place a small mound of jasmine rice to the side of each fillet. Garnish each serving with snipped basil leaves and three

Nicoise olives. At the table, pass a basket of garlic croutons and a bowl of *rouille*, a cruet of extra virgin olive oil, and a small bowl of hot pepper flakes. Have a warm terrine of the remaining saffron broth ready for second helpings. Serves 6.

Cook's Notes

Rouille is a provençal red pepper mayonnaise fortified with plenty of garlic and a healthy jolt of hot pepper. Rouille is stirred into fish soups and stews, such as bouillabaisse. Here's a trimmed-down version. Either roast and peel your own peppers or use a store-bought roasted pepper not packed in oil or with other seasonings. The rouille should be very spicy.

Rouille

1 $1/2$ cups roasted red pepper, cut into 1" chunks

3–4 large garlic cloves, peeled

1–2 tablespoons of olive oil

cayenne pepper to taste

salt to taste

1. In a blender or food processor, combine the pepper with the garlic, adding just enough oil to achieve a smooth mixture. Season to taste with cayenne pepper and salt.

Garlic Croutons

1 French baguette cut into $1/4$" broad diagonal slices

non-stick olive oil cooking spray

1 large clove of garlic, bruised

1. Very lightly spray the bread slices with olive oil on both sides and rub vigorously with the bruised garlic. Place the bread slices on a baking sheet.

2. Preheat a broiler.

3. Toast them under the broiler, turning once, until golden on both sides.

Jasmine Rice

Cook's Notes

Jasmine rice is a long-grained, aromatic rice from Thailand. It is similar to but less expensive than Basmati rice, and is so flavorful that it requires no seasoning.

1 cup Jasmine rice

1 $^3/_4$ cups water

1. Bring water to a rolling boil in a medium sauce pan. Sprinkle in the rice, stir, then turn the heat down to low.

2. Cover and cook the rice over very low heat for 15–20 minutes. Fluff the rice with a fork and serve. Makes about 3 $^1/_2$ cups cooked rice.

Cassis Poached Pears

6 pears (firm, not overly ripe)

3 cups young, fruity red wine such as a Côtes du Rhône or light Merlot

3 cups creme de cassis

the grated zest of one half orange

several sprigs of mint

1. Peel the pears, cut them in half, and remove the cores. Place them in a deep skillet or other heatproof baking dish that will hold the pears in one layer, but as tight a fit as possible. Pour in the wine and the cassis and scatter the orange zest on top, submerging the pears.

2. Bring the liquid to a boil; reduce the heat to low. Simmer the pears for about 30 minutes or until they can be easily pierced with a skewer. Remove the pan from the heat and cool the pears in the poaching liquid.

3. To serve, place the pears cut side down on a work surface. Angle a sharp knife against the pear and slice $^1/_4$" thick slices from stem to blossom end, keeping the stem intact. Transfer the pears to dessert plates and press lightly on the pear halves to fan the slices. Spoon some of the poaching liquid over and around the pears and place a star anise and a few mint leaves on each serving.

Cook's Notes

Freeze the poaching liquid for poaching pears or other fruit in the future.

Chapter 16

It's Strictly Business

In This Chapter

➤ Business entertaining is a good will gesture

➤ Guess who's coming to dinner?

➤ Hosting a reception for a close colleague

➤ The working lunch

➤ Entertaining in a restaurant

Business entertaining today is a far cry from the notorious three-martini lunches and expense account extravaganzas lurking in our recent past. The bottom line still hasn't changed, though. Business entertaining is a goodwill gesture. It's not meant to cajole or curry favor. Keep this in mind and all your business entertaining will be successful.

In this chapter we'll cover several situations you may be likely to encounter. The tried-and-true organization and timing principles of any important party planning, as always, hold true. When you entertain for professional purposes, simply apply your own first-rate approach to business itself. Essentially, you are enhancing your professional deportment with an element of hospitality.

Although a certain amount of protocol pertains to any business function, don't confuse it with stuffiness. Being relaxed and natural is the most admirable asset a host can bring to any party, particularly a business occasion. In our casual day and age, many different kinds of parties are perfectly acceptable for business entertaining. Granted, if you're entertaining a distinguished person or highly valued client, dinner-at-eight is probably more what you're looking for than a Sunday supper. But for an office party a more relaxed fiesta may be an appropriate and refreshing change of venue.

Business Entertaining Is a Goodwill Gesture

New York's restaurant "21" opened its doors as a speakeasy. From the very beginning, "21" has been a haven for world-wide heavy-hitters of business, politics, publishing, and Hollywood. Their reputation rests on and continues with unaffected goodwill and unflappable service. And these qualities, bar none, are the most important elements in business entertaining.

> ### Sage Advice
>
> "...In spite of its aura of elegance and its steady stream of celebrities, "21" is anything but stodgy..."21" is as friendly as its service is impeccable. From chairman to doorman to dishwasher, the people who work at "21" have a genuine, unrehearsed affection for people."
>
> —from *The "21" Cookbook*

When it comes to hosting a business event, however, you may feel uncomfortable in the limelight and become distracted from the all-important bottom line. In this chapter, we'll advise you about how to stay on track with several different business entertaining situations. We'll cover hosting a business dinner or a reception to honor a colleague's accomplishment; having your committee for a working lunch; and restaurant entertaining (a frequent choice as a means for many ends). Although a working lunch and restaurant meetings have business on the agenda as opposed to the other two scenarios, these engagements still serve as a courtesy to promote communication on a less structured level away from the hectic office environment—i.e., goodwill.

It's only natural to feel uneasy the first few times around with business entertaining. Particularly if you're entertaining superiors, you may find your usual confidence has unfortunately taken leave. It's pretty hard to extend goodwill when the focal point is your own potential shortcomings. Put your anxieties under lock and key and concentrate on scrupulously organizing the details, adhering to a time frame, being politically correct when it comes to the guest list and menu, and resisting the urge to overdo. Confidence breeds graciousness, and with everything under control, that's exactly what you'll be.

Guess Who's Coming To Dinner?

Choose a simple, classic menu when entertaining someone important.

The menu:

> Asparagus Soup
>
> Veal Rib Chops with Tomato-Pepper Compote
>
> Eggplant and Vidalia Onion Purée
>
> Mesclun Salad
>
> Flan Renverse à l'Orange

The recipes for this menu can be found at the end of this chapter.

Of course you're on edge when called upon to entertain someone important. It's a given that everything has to be just so. Carefully follow the planning guidelines throughout this book and don't allow yourself to become distracted by unrealistic expectations. Let's get right down to the business of the glitches that could trip you up and the intangible elements that will take your dinner over the top.

First and foremost this occasion calls for hiring help, and the high school bulletin board isn't an option unless the respondent is someone you've engaged enough times to know they're polished to a "T." They should have enough cooking and serving experience to ready and serve the meal with unobtrusive efficiency. Whenever time constraints threaten to take you beyond outer limits, have part or all of your menu catered. Choosing the right outfit is of utmost importance. Consult Chapter 18 for full details.

If you are in charge of the guest list, don't include someone who would be out of place, and never overlook anyone who should be invited. Consult with someone in-the-know. Also, it's likely you'll be entertaining spouses that you haven't met. Devote some extra time to reviewing the guest list, making sure that titles and name usage (is it James, Jim, or Jamie; Katherine, Kate, or Katie?) are correct. Give special consideration to proper introductions, initiating conversations, and directing seating. A seating plan and place cards are *de rigeur* for this type of occasion. If you are single, enlist a trustworthy friend or associate to give you a hand when guests arrive to get cocktails and conversation underway.

Reality Bites
Don't ostentatiously fuss over a guest of honor. You will look foolish and they will feel uncomfortable.

Conservative is the right approach to decor, table setting, and menu. Lavish floral arrangements or going overboard with candles may be fun for other occasions, but for an important business dinner it's a superfluous display. Likewise, showing off a hobby or leaving promotional literature for your new venture on the coffee table is not in good taste.

The Extra Mile
If there are singles invited, ask them to bring a guest. This is especially important when a group is mainly composed of couples.

When you're planning a menu for business entertaining, it's particularly important to find out if any guests have serious dietary restrictions. The low-fat Mediterranean menu in Chapter 15 is a good alternative to serve guests who don't eat red meat or have dietary restrictions. Also note that the veal chop can be replaced by a grilled chicken paillard, tuna, or salmon steak. If there will be vegetarians at your table, accompany the entree with angel's hair pasta that they can have tossed with the tomato compote and a portion of the eggplant purée nestled in the center of the pasta.

Reality Bites
Abide by the 24-inch rule for each place setting. It's not the time to cram guests around a table *en famille*. Set up or rent a second table if necessary.

For a business occasion, a menu also requires thinking about what *isn't* appropriate to serve. For instance, "Chicken with 40 Cloves of Garlic" will follow your guests to tomorrow's business meeting, and even if your bouillabaisse is fabulous, it isn't compatible with dressy attire. Finally, review the timing details in Chapter 12 ("Dinner At Eight") to organize the flow of the evening and to direct the serving of the meal with quiet, polished efficiency.

24 inches per place setting gives elbow room.

A Simple and Sophisticated Table

Aim for setting a low-key, refined table for an important business dinner.

➤ *Table linens and serveware*: Real linens in white, ecru, or other soft, neutral tones. Use matching napkins in a napkin ring or folded in a simple rectangle or triangle. Avoid fancy napkin folds.

➤ *Table decoration*: Seasonal garden flowers or "garden" type flowers from a florist. Avoid suggestive flowers such as roses (except the tea rose variety) and the ubiquitous grocery store "bouquet."

➤ *Candles*: White or ecru candles in simple candlesticks (four to five at the most on a long table), or one or two clear glass hurricanes.

Don't clutter the table with any unnecessary ornaments or huge flower arrangements that make carrying on a conversation an exercise in the absurd.

➤ *Music*: Music should be a subtle, instrumental backdrop of a classical nature; nothing to induce sleep or, conversely, command too much attention.

Smart Move
Hire someone to direct parking for your guests' convenience if your driveway or neighborhood streets pose a problem.

A simple yet sophisticated table setting for a business dinner.

Hosting a Reception for a Colleague

When a friend or close colleague receives special recognition, hosting a reception in their honor is a thoughtful and significant gesture. When planning this sort of an occasion, always defer to your friend's wishes and convenience. Confer with your friend regarding the guest list. You hardly want to forget someone important to them. The date and time of day should also appropriately fit your friend's and guest's schedules. For a weekday event, late afternoon into early evening, perhaps 4:00 to 7:00, allows ample time for the honoree's colleagues, associates, and friends to attend between work and going home or before going on to a meeting. Alternatively, consider a Sunday afternoon reception from 2:00 to 5:00. Whether you host the event at home or elsewhere, consider traveling time and make convenience a priority for those attending.

Engaging or Using a Room Without Catering Facilities

Following are some important considerations if you are using a room for a reception that has no kitchen facilities.

➤ Is the location convenient and parking adequate?

➤ Are tables available for bar and food?

➤ Are there facilities for warming and chilling food? If not, settle for a room-temperature menu.

➤ How will clean-up and trash removal be handled?

➤ Do you need a cooler for ice?

➤ Is there a coat check or coat rack?

➤ Send directions or a map with the invitation.

A reception in someone's honor is a celebration that calls for appropriately festive touches. Focus on the nature of your friend's accomplishment, their favorite flowers, ethnic food, or anything that would be particularly pleasing to them. No Mylar balloons or silly party paraphernalia; the occasion does warrant a dignified approach. For an at-home reception in late February, a host hurried spring along and decorated the entire house with displays of spring bulbs in bloom. Balance a menu between cocktail-type food and more substantial fare that could constitute a light meal. Create a buffet that doesn't require last-minute attention so that trays can be easily replenished. Set up a self-serve bar at one end of the buffet table using a copper or tin bin filled with wine, beer, and soda on ice. Hire a helper (which can certainly be your high-school neighbor this time) to keep the buffet table neat and attractive and to clear used plates and cups as guests come and go. Here's a sample menu using recipes from the other chapters plus store-bought items:

Marinated Shrimp with Crudités and Sauce Andalouse

Belgian Endive Leaves with Smoked Salmon Mousse

Steve's Guacamole "Bruschetta"

Curried Crab Tartlets

A Locally Smoked Turkey Breast

A Selection of Fresh Bakery Breads

Mustards and Chutneys

Fruit Kabobs

Madelines

The Working Lunch

A working lunch at home for your committee or task group allows you to enhance compatibility and respect among coworkers. Relieved of the distractions and pressures of the workplace, business can transpire with renewed energy and focus. When you're setting a date, be sure to inquire about your colleague's afternoon commitments so you can plan a realistic agenda. Allow yourself time to set up for the meeting either the evening or morning before so that you can get right down to business when your committee arrives. Provide an uncluttered workspace with plenty of elbow room for everyone. Make copies of your agenda and supply extra pencils, note paper, and paper clips. On a separate, nearby table, set up beverages—pitchers of water or juice and pots of coffee or tea. Be considerate of your coworkers when it comes to lunch. Steer clear of highly spiced or heavy food that may induce late afternoon rumbles or nods.

Here is a simple menu that fits the bill. If it's an evening meeting, you may wish to begin with a soup such as the Asparagus soup in this chapter or the Tomato-Pepper Bisque in Chapter 10. For a lunch meeting, the salad and rolls should be sufficient. Accompany the salad with crusty store-bought rolls and an interesting herbal iced tea.

The menu:

Asparagus Soup *or* Tomato-Pepper Bisque

Liz's Chicken Salad, *or* Tenderloin, Tomato and Roquefort Salad with Basil

Crusty Rolls

Herbal Iced Tea

The recipes for this menu can be found at the end of this chapter.

Entertaining in a Restaurant

We turn to restaurants to satisfy entertaining needs not only for the convenience but because they're neutral territory. Perhaps you'll be working with a new subordinate and want to get to know them better. Maybe you're taking a perspective employee to dinner to gain insight outside the interview process. What if, out-of-the-blue, you're asked to entertain out-of-town clients? For the many occasions that we turn to restaurants for business entertaining, choosing an appropriate setting can make or break the outcome of your lunch or dinner. Whether you frequently use restaurants for entertaining or seldom have the need, don't get caught in a frantic last-minute search. Have two or three familiar establishments lined up.

The Extra Mile

Learn the art of balancing eating and conversation. Firing questions that demand an ongoing response will leave your guest sitting before a full (and probably cold) plate of food when you have finished.

Calling the Shots

Here are some things to take into account that will help you put your best foot forward when you entertain in a restaurant.

➤ A restaurant that you frequent is most likely to cater to your needs. When you know the maitre d' or manager and the restaurant floor plan, you can request a favorite table.

➤ Choose a restaurant with a broad-based menu. Finding out your new client has a wheat allergy when you pull up at "Pasta Paradise" is an unlucky situation.

➤ Look for a low-key, comfortable atmosphere and unobtrusive service. A sudden assault by loud music halfway through the meal, or a wait staff that carries on like old pals, is not a professional choice for business purposes.

Smart Move
In a restaurant, conduct yourself as though you were a host at home—gracious and in charge.

➤ If you are booking a private room and selecting a pre-set menu, make sure the room is appropriate to your needs and be democratic about the food choices.

➤ If you're taking clients out for pure entertainment, a more flamboyant scene may be in order, such as one representative of the locale or with top-notch entertainment. Always visit and try out new places beforehand.

The Least You Need To Know

➤ Choose an entertaining theme appropriate to the occasion.

➤ Don't allow unrealistic expectations to interfere with organizing details.

➤ Diligently review the guest list before a business affair.

➤ Establish and follow a schedule when entertaining for professional purposes.

The Recipes

Asparagus Soup

3   shallots, minced

1   stalk celery, minced

2^1/$_2$ pounds asparagus

3   tablespoons unsalted butter

6   cups chicken or vegetable stock (see Chapter 17 for a stock recipe or use canned)

1   tablespoon fresh thyme leaves

^{3}/$_4$ cup heavy cream

^{1}/$_2$ cup snipped chives

1. Snap the tough ends off the asparagus spears. Remove the tips from half the aspara-gus spears and reserve. Cut the remaining asparagus into ^{1}/$_2$" pieces. Bring a small pot of water to a boil and add the asparagus tips. Cook until they are tender and crisp. Drain and run under cold water until cool. Drain on paper towels and reserve.

2. In a large pot, melt the butter, add the shallot and the celery, and cook over me-dium heat until they begin to wilt. Add the asparagus and the chicken stock and bring to a boil. Skim away any foam; reduce the heat to low. Simmer just until the asparagus is tender.

3. Purée the mixture in a food processor in two batches. Return the purée to the pot. Season with salt, freshly ground black pepper, and grated nutmeg to taste. Stir in the thyme leaves and cream. Remove from the heat. Cool, cover, and refrigerate.

4. One hour before serving, bring the soup to room temperature. Gently reheat the soup over low heat. Do not allow it to come to a boil. Ladle the soup into warm soup bowls. Garnish each serving with snipped chives and the reserved asparagus tips. Serves 8.

Veal Rib Chops with Tomato-Pepper Compote

12 ripe plum tomatoes

1   red bell pepper

1   yellow bell pepper

2   cloves of garlic, peeled and minced

1 large shallot, peeled and minced

$^1/_2$ cup chicken or vegetable stock (see Chapter 17 for a stock recipe or use canned)

$^1/_2$ cup thyme leaves (lemon thyme is particularly good)

1–2 tablespoons Amontillado sherry

  salt and freshly ground black pepper to taste

8 veal rib chops $^3/_4$ " to 1" thick

3 tablespoons olive oil

  salt and pepper

1. Bring a large pot of water to a boil over high heat. Cut an "x" on the bottom of each tomato and plunge them into the boiling water. As soon as the skins split, remove the tomatoes and run them under cold water. Peel the tomatoes, cut them in half lengthwise, and gently squeeze out the seeds. Dice and return them to the pot.

2. Roast the peppers over an open gas flame or close to a broiler element, turning them, until they are evenly charred. Transfer the peppers to a paper bag and seal tightly for 5 minutes to steam the skins loose. Peel, seed, and trim the membranes from the peppers. Dice the peppers and add to the tomatoes in the pot.

3. Combine the garlic, shallot, stock, and thyme leaves with the tomatoes and the peppers. Bring the mixture to a simmer over low heat and cook for 20 minutes. Make sure all the liquid does not evaporate.

4. Add the sherry, and salt and pepper to taste. Set aside.

5. Meanwhile, prepare a grill or heat a stove-top grill or heavy skillet over medium-high heat.

6. Rub the veal chops with a few drops of olive oil and lightly season with salt and pepper. When the coals have a thin, even layer of white ash and a red glow beneath, or just before the pan begins to smoke, cook the chops for 3–4 minutes per side or until the internal temperature reaches 140–145°. Remove the chops to a warm platter, cover loosely with foil, and allow them to rest for 5 minutes before serving.

7. Serve the chops with the arc of the bone facing the rim of the plate. Pour any juices from the veal over the chops and ladle about $^1/_4$ cup of the warm compote (including some broth) over the chops. Border the chops with a portion of eggplant purée. Serves 8.

> ### Cook's Notes
>
> Serve the compote warm in the winter and chilled in the summer. It's also excellent with a grilled chicken paillard (a chicken breast pounded very thinly), grilled tuna or salmon steaks, or over a plain omelet or pasta. You may also accompany the veal chop with fresh angel's hair pasta, simply tossed with excellent extra virgin olive oil and fresh herbs.

Eggplant and Vidalia Onion Purée

2   small eggplants (about $3/4$–1 lb. each)

2   tablespoons unsalted butter

2   medium sized Vidalia onions, peeled and finely chopped

$1/2$ teaspoon dried thyme

$1/2$ cup dry white wine

salt and freshly ground black pepper to taste

a drop or two of Tabasco

1. Preheat the oven to 500°.

2. Place the eggplants in a baking dish and bake them whole for 15–20 minutes, until tender. Remove from the oven and cool.

3. In a small pot, melt the butter over medium heat; add the onions and the thyme, and cook for 3 minutes or until they begin to soften. Add the wine and continue cooking for 15 to 20 minutes until the wine has reduced by about half and the onions are very soft. Remove from the heat and set aside.

4. Peel and coarsely chop the eggplants. Combine the onions and the eggplant in a food processor and process until smooth. Return the purée to the pot and season to taste with salt, pepper, and a drop or two of Tabasco sauce. Gently warm over low heat before serving. Serves 8.

Flan Renverse à l'Orange

2   cups whole milk

$1/2$ cup heavy cream

1   small orange, washed and peeled (peel the skin (zest) only, not the pith (white part))

$^1/_2$ cup granulated sugar

$^1/_4$ cup water

3 eggs

3 egg yolks

$^1/_2$ cup of sugar

$^1/_4$ cup Triple Sec or Grand Marnier

1. Preheat the oven to 300°. Bring a tea kettle of water to a boil.

2. In a medium saucepan over medium-high heat, heat the milk and the cream to just below a simmer. Remove the milk from the heat and add the orange rind. Cover the pot and set aside, allowing the orange to infuse with the milk.

3. Meanwhile, warm 8 half-cup glass or porcelain ramekins in the oven.

4. In a small pot, mix the sugar and the water over medium heat until the sugar melts. Raise the heat to high and bring the sugar and water to a boil. Boil, without stirring, until the mixture is a light brown caramel color. Remove from the heat and immediately pour evenly into the ramekins.

5. In a clean mixing bowl, whisk the eggs and the yolks together until thoroughly incorporated. Remove the orange rind from the milk and bring the milk to a boil. Pour the milk into the egg mixture, whisking vigorously. Stir in the Triple Sec, then fill each ramekin with custard.

6. To prepare a water bath (*bain marie*), place a folded towel on the bottom of a roasting pan or deep gratin pan. Position the oven rack in the bottom third of the oven and place the pan on the oven rack. Transfer the ramekins to the water bath. Very carefully, pour boiling water around the ramekins until it reaches halfway up the sides of the ramekins. Cover the baking pan with foil and gently push the rack into the oven, taking care not to slosh water into the custards.

7. Cook the custards for 20–25 minutes or until a skewer inserted into the custard comes clean. The custards may still be wobbly. Remove from the oven and cool them in the water bath. When they are cool, remove from the water bath and cover and thoroughly chill in the refrigerator.

8. To serve, dip the bottoms of the ramekins into hot water. Run a small, sharp knife around the perimeter of the custards, then place a dessert plate on top of the ramekins and flip them over onto the plate. Serve immediately. Serves 8.

Liz's Chicken Salad

1   medium onion, sliced

$^1/_2$ cup cilantro, minced

2   tablespoons rice wine vinegar

$^1/_4$ cup dry white wine

    the juice of 6 lemons

    the juice of 3 limes

1   small jalepeño pepper, thinly sliced freshly ground black pepper and a large pinch of salt

1   1"-thick slice of orange

4   large, skinless and boneless chicken breast halves

    the juice of one large orange

4   tablespoons honey mustard

1   teaspoon ground cumin

    salt and pepper to taste

2–3 tablespoons olive oil

1   head of romaine lettuce, washed, dried, and broken into bite-sized pieces

1   head of red leaf lettuce, washed, dried, and broken into bite-sized pieces

1   small head radicchio, washed, dried, and leaves separated

1   cup cooked spaghetti squash

1   cup frozen peas, defrosted

1   cup of carrots cut into julienne matchsticks and blanched in boiling water until tender/crisp

1   cup of asparagus tips, blanched in boiling water until tender/crisp

$^1/_4$ cup toasted pumpkin seeds or pine nuts

1. To prepare the chicken: In a ceramic, enamel, or glass pan large enough to hold the chicken breasts in one layer, combine the onion, $^1/_4$ cup cilantro, rice wine vinegar, dry white wine, half of the lemon juice and half of the lime juice, the jalepeño pepper and the pepper and salt. Add the orange slice to the marinade and lightly crush it to release the juices and bruise the peel. Turn the chicken breasts in the marinade. Cover, refrigerate, and marinate for one or two hours.

Cook's Notes

To cook spaghetti squash, prick the whole squash several times with a knife and bake whole in a 350° oven for 40–45 minutes or until it can be pierced through or yields to pressure when poked. Cool, cut in half, and remove seeds. Pull the strands from the squash shell with a fork. Or, buy packaged pre-cooked spaghetti squash.

2. To prepare the vinaigrette: Whisk the orange juice and the remaining lemon and lime juice with the honey mustard and cumin. Season with salt and pepper to taste. Drizzle in the oil, whisking until the vinaigrette is well combined. Taste and correct the seasoning.

3. Remove the chicken from the marinade, and wipe dry. Heat a stove-top grill or heavy skillet over medium-high heat. Cook the chicken breasts for 5–6 minutes per side. Remove them to a plate and cool. When cool, cut the chicken breasts in broad, diagonal slices.

4. To assemble the salad: Stack the radicchio leaves, roll them tightly like a cigar, and cut the roll into thin slivers. In a large salad bowl, toss all the lettuces together with just enough dressing to coat. In another bowl, toss the vegetables lightly with dressing. Divide lettuce evenly on four dinner plates. Place a mound of the vegetables in the center. Surround the vegetables with slices of chicken breast. Garnish each salad with a dusting of the remaining cilantro and the pumpkin seeds. Pass the rest of the dressing and a basket of crusty rolls. Serves 4. (12–16 ounces of smoked turkey may be substituted for the chicken.)

Tenderloin, Tomato, and Roquefort Salad with Basil

2 tablespoons white wine vinegar

1 large shallot, minced

$1/2$ teaspoon dry mustard

$1/2$ cup extra virgin olive oil

salt and freshly ground black pepper

2 pounds new potatoes, unpeeled and cooked

1 head of leaf lettuce, washed and dried

1 pound rare roast tenderloin, sliced $1/4$" thick

2 pounds large ripe tomatoes, sliced $1/4$" thick

$1/4$ pound Roquefort cheese, crumbled

$1/4$ cup toasted pine nuts

1 small bunch of fresh basil

1. In a small bowl, whisk together the vinegar, shallot, mustard, and salt and pepper. Drizzle in the oil, whisking until thoroughly combined. Taste and adjust the seasoning.

2. Peel the potatoes and cut them into $1/4$" thick slices. In a large bowl, toss the potatoes with just enough vinaigrette dressing to coat and season with salt and pepper.

3. Line a platter with the lettuce leaves. Down the center of the platter, alternate overlapping slices of tenderloin and tomato. Leave a space at the top and the bottom of the platter to mound the potato mixture. Lightly salt and pepper the tenderloin and the tomatoes.

4. Scatter the Roquefort and pine nuts over the tomatoes and the tenderloin, and snip the fresh basil over the whole platter. Serves 4.

Chapter 17

Weekend Guests

In This Chapter

➤ Plan an easy-going itinerary

➤ Accommodations that accommodate

➤ On the menu for the weekend

➤ The recipes

Lots of times a weekend visit from out-of-town friends is motivated by a special event they're attending. The occasion dictates a busy weekend filled with activities, and the job of hosting requires little more than clean sheets and towels and a friendly welcome.

But what about the real business of inviting friends to your home when the agenda is their visit alone? It's a special time to deepen or renew friendships, and it's entertaining's most intimate form. A common folly is to get carried away with the role of tour guide/ social director that can make the prospects of Monday morning sound pretty good for guest and host alike. Not that an itinerary shouldn't be part of the picture; it definitely is an important element of any successful weekend sojourn. However, allow for enough unstructured in-between time for restful leisure or confidential *tête-à-tête* should the relationship warrant.

When you're entertaining more than one person or couple who will be meeting one another for the first time, it's important to give some serious thought to compatibility. Nothing is worse than friction in close quarters.

In Chapter 5 we discuss properly extending invitations to weekend guests. Chapter 7 offers advice about special courtesies to make a house guest feel comfortable, and niceties for the guest room that show extra consideration. In this chapter we'll dig below the surface, elaborate on some finer points, and finally, make sure no one goes hungry.

Plan an Easy-Going Itinerary

First of all, let's talk about the aesthetics of weekend guest hosting. How can "make yourself at home" seem heartfelt rather than trite? Well, actions speak louder than words in this case. Even though a familial ambiance is what makes weekend entertaining memorable, consideration for your guest's privacy, personal routines, and need for a little time alone is what makes a top-notch weekend host. After all, it is your turf, and often a house guest may attempt to conform to your *modus operandi* and feel awkward about your expectations of them. Put them at ease by letting them carry on without your tutelage.

Reality Bites

Some people are sensitive to heavily perfumed soaps. It's a good idea to have a supply of natural, unscented soaps for guest use.

For example, if you have your oatmeal every morning at 6:00 a.m., respect someone who delights in snoozing till ten on Saturdays. Let it be known that "I'm up with the birds every morning but you certainly don't have to be. Please relax and unwind. Coffee and breakfast breads will be on the counter for you to help yourself." Along the same lines, point out where to find glasses and cold drinks, and have a fruit basket on a table or counter for snacking.

Your house guest shouldn't have to anxiously wait for a bathroom occupied by teenagers or have to use one that looks like the aftermath of Waterloo. Make sure to adequately stock the guest bath with supplies such as paper products and soaps. There should be enough uncluttered counter space for a guest to spread out their own toiletries. Show your guests exactly where they can find everything they need and be prepared to fill in essential items they may have forgotten: toothbrush, toothpaste, shampoo, and so on.

The Extra Mile

When you're entertaining a couple, one of whom is a long-time dear friend, arrange an activity for the spouses, so you and your friend can have an hour or two alone.

Don't hover over a house guest. Everyone breathes easier with a little space. It's a nice gesture to supplement "alone time" by having pleasant options available. Offer the use of a bicycle and recommend a route. Map out a favorite walk on a little card or jot down directions to a specialty coffee shop or street of boutique shopping. Include notations about the shops or points of interest. Your guest may simply enjoy a rest or nap, so keep the guest room supplied with a selection of current, quality magazines.

As discussed in Chapter 5, it's a good idea to have your itinerary mapped out before the weekend for practical purposes of planning for a special excursion or event, packing and the like. Take into consideration your guest's personal tastes when making plans. If you happen to love antiques, don't drag someone off to a 17th-century exhibit when they couldn't care less about them. Don't make reservations for dinner at Pig Heaven if your friend doesn't eat red meat (even if you know there's a barbecued tuna steak on the menu, it's not exactly putting them first).

Inviting a pal who's a film buff for the weekend of a special film premier or festival is the right idea. Of course, if you have tickets to a Cleveland Indians game, obviously you have it made.

Our idea of an easy-going itinerary definitely begins with a relaxed Friday arrival. Capping off a busy week with the hassles of travel calls for the leisure to unwind, share stories, or catch up on old times. A carefree, friendly meal provides the opportunity to do just that. Plan a Saturday excursion for late morning or early afternoon, and let a light lunch fall in where it may. Everyone should have some time off in the early evening before cocktails and dinner out Saturday night. On Sunday, an unrushed farewell brunch timed around your guest's departure is a thoughtful send-off.

> **Smart Move**
> Realize that your guests are looking forward to a change of venue and an opportunity to unwind. A host who puts their own schedules aside can relax with their weekend company and enjoy a little "holiday" at home.

Accommodations That Accommodate

When you're readying a guest room or setting up a space for weekend guests to use, the most thoughtful thing you can do is ask yourself how you would feel after sleeping there. If you've never slept in your guest accommodations, the acid test is overdue. Obviously an ancient, lumpy mattress and battered pillow are less than comfortable, but remember to think beyond physical comfort. If a pull-out sofa in an office is where you direct overnighters, the room should be immaculately clean, neat, and uncluttered. The same goes for any make-shift set-up or children's room that's turned over to a guest. Anyone plopped among your business matters or personal or private effects of household members is bound to feel like an intruder.

As much as is humanly possible, space for a guest should be private and uninterrupted during their stay. Next to the bed, have a table where your guest can set a glass of water or tea and an adequate reading light. Another little extra that's appreciated is an alarm clock. If a guest wants to take a nap before a dinner or event, they can drift off peacefully knowing they'll awake on time without bothering you for a wake up call. It's always a good idea to check light bulbs and provide night-time illumination leading to the bathroom. Don't forget to adjust the heat or ventilation according to the weather and add or remove blankets as the season dictates. Consult the list of guest room specifics in Chapter 7 and the following illustration that features a guest room that truly says "Welcome." It provides good pointers to keep in mind when you outfit a guest room. The ottoman, for instance, can do double duty as a foot rest or luggage rack. Proper window covering allows for a restful sleep. If you don't have a water carafe, a bottle or two of good water is a thoughtful touch.

The Extra Mile
Frame a small photograph of a time you shared with your guest. Put it in the guest room with a card inviting them to take the photo home.

Very accommodating accommodations.

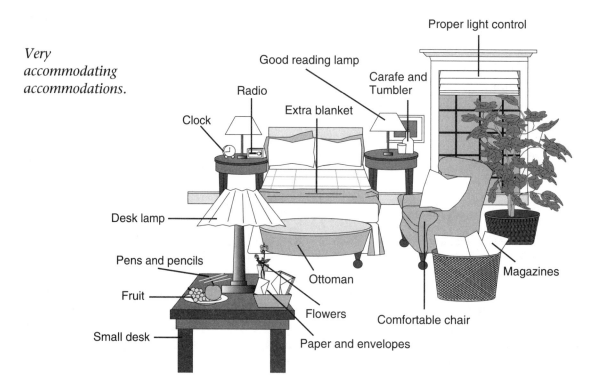

On the Menu for the Weekend

A menu plan for weekend guests should feature make-ahead or easily prepared dishes that allow hosts and guests to enjoy one another's company.

Designer Notes

Set a cheerful Mediterranean table like the one in Chapter 15 for your Friday supper.

Friday Evening

    Country Garden Soup

    Crusty Flat Bread

    Fresh Apricots, Blue Cheese, and Wildflower Honey

Or

    Celery Vichyssoise

    Bay Scallop Sauté

    Vegetable Slaw

    Homemade Ice Cream

Saturday's Lunch

    Swiss Chard Gratin

    Herbal Iced Tea

    Bakery Cookies

Sunday Brunch

    Olive and Proscuitto Cake with Tomato-Pepper Compote

    Fruit Kabobs

Or

    Norwegian Smoked Salmon

    Trout Mousse

Slivered Onions, Capers and Lemon Wedges

Flavored and Plain Cream Cheese

A Basket of Bakery Bagels

Specialty Jams and Jellies

Coffee and Tea

These menus set the tone for an unruffled, effortless ambiance. They'll get your weekend off on the right foot, from Friday suppers that convey a relaxed bonhomie, to Sunday brunches that fortify a traveler for their journey home. The first Friday menu is appropriate any time of year except the dog days of summer. We cover the steamy days with a cool and crisp alternative. A light make-ahead lunch suits the schedule when plans are to have a special dinner out. Pick a brunch option that favors your guest's proclivities; either the all-out indulgence of a rich, bready olive and proscuitto cake or low-fat smoked salmon and bagels to assuage the health-conscious. When you're pressed for time, the second brunch is completely store-bought and quickly assembled, unless you decide to make the trout mousse from Chapter 11.

Read the recipes through for variations and make-ahead advice. Arrange the smoked salmon and trout mousse on lettuce leaves in the center of a large tray with a small bowl of capers in between. Flank the fish with sliced onions on one side and lemon wedges on the other. Surround the tray with the cream cheeses and jams in attractive bowls. Serve as a brunch buffet with a napkin-lined basket of fresh bagels.

The Least You Need To Know

➤ Avoid the urge to overdo when you have weekend company.

➤ Being considerate of your guest's privacy and personal routines is the hallmark of an excellent weekend host.

➤ Thoughtful details in the guest room and bath are a hallmark of a gracious weekend host.

➤ Plan simple weekend menus ahead that encourage a relaxed and casual mood for both host and guest.

The Recipes

Country Garden Soup

2   tablespoons olive oil

1   large onion, peeled and chopped

1   leek, cleaned and sliced (see Chapter 20)

6   garlic cloves, peeled and chopped

1   small carrot, peeled and minced

$^1/_2$ teaspoon saffron threads

2   bay leaves

5   quarts chicken stock, fresh or canned

$^1/_2$ cup Arborio rice

3   boneless chicken breasts, sliced paper thin

3   large carrots, peeled and thinly sliced on the diagonal

3   stalks of celery, sliced on the diagonal

1   small head of escarole, cleaned and chopped (about 3 cups)

$^1/_2$ cup green peas or sugar snap peas

1   bunch Italian flat leaf parsley, leaves plucked from stems (about 1 cup loosely packed)

$^1/_2$ cup loosely packed basil leaves, snipped into slivers

    salt and freshly ground black pepper, to taste

    the juice of one half lemon, or to taste

$^1/_4$ pound whole fresh parmesan cheese (not grated)

$^1/_4$ cup hot red pepper flakes

1. In a large stock pot, heat the olive oil over medium heat. Add the onion, leek, garlic, carrot, saffron and bay leaves; gently cook the vegetables until they begin to soften. Reduce the heat to low and press a piece of foil directly over the vegetables. Cover the pot and let the vegetables "sweat" for 10 minutes (do not allow them to brown).

2. Remove the lid and discard the foil. Add the chicken stock; raise the heat to high and bring the soup to a boil. Add the arborio rice and reduce heat to low. Simmer the soup for 15–20 minutes, tasting the rice occasionally, until the rice is almost tender but not completely cooked. The soup can be made ahead to this point.

3. To finish the soup, increase the heat to medium-high. Add the chicken. Cook, stirring occasionally, at a rapid simmer for five minutes. Add the carrots, celery, and peas; simmer for five minutes, until the chicken is cooked and the vegetables are just tender.

4. Just before serving, stir the escarole, parsley, and the basil into the soup. Taste and correct the seasoning with salt, freshly ground pepper, and a few drops of lemon juice. Serve the soup as soon as the escarole wilts and the vegetables are still bright green. Ladle the soup into deep bowls. Pass a cheese grater with fresh parmesan cheese and a small bowl of pepper flakes. Serves 6–8.

Cook's Notes

As the soup sits, the vegetables will loose their bright green color but there will be no loss of flavor. For a vegetarian version, prepare the soup with vegetable stock. (At the end of the recipe section, you'll find recipes for vegetable stock and for an all-purpose stock.) In place of the chicken, use 1 pound of peeled, seeded, and diced tomatoes, and 1 pound of fresh shell beans (such as cranberry), or 1 $1/2$ cups cooked dried beans if shell beans aren't in season.

Fresh Apricots, Blue Cheese and Wildflower Honey

12 fresh, ripe apricots, rinsed and dried

4 ounces blue cheese

4 ounces cream cheese

$1/4$ cup finely chopped toasted walnuts or pine nuts

$1/2$ cup wildflower honey

a few nasturtium blossoms or mint leaves to garnish

Cook's Notes

A friend was a house guest in Venice. Her host served this exquisite combination with champagne. The apricots can be served either as an hors d'oeuvre or a dessert.

1. With a small, sharp knife, cut the apricots in half and remove the stones. Beat the cheeses with a wooden spoon until well combined and smooth or process them in a food processor.

2. Fit a pastry bag with a star tip and fill the bag with the cheese mixture. Pipe small rosettes into the apricot halves. If you don't have a pastry bag, spoon a large teaspoon into each half.

3. Arrange the apricots on a platter and dust them with the nuts. Drizzle a band of honey over the apricots. Garnish the platter with a few nasturtium blossoms or mint leaves.

Cook's Notes

Use small Seckle pears, or larger peach or pear halves instead of the apricots. Serve smaller fruits, as finger food. Serve the larger fruits on dessert plates with a fork and knife.

Celery Vichyssoise

1 tablespoon vegetable oil

2 large leeks, cleaned and thinly sliced

2 bunches of celery (about 1 pound), separate stalks, peeled and thinly sliced

1 pound of Idaho potatoes, peeled and diced

6 cups vegetable stock

3/4 cup heavy cream

salt and freshly ground black pepper, to taste

drops of lemon juice and 4–5 drops Tabasco, or to taste

6–8 Nasturtium blossoms, to garnish

1. In a Dutch oven or stock pot, heat the oil over medium heat and cook the leeks until they begin to soften. Add the celery and press a piece of foil directly over the vegetables. Cover the pot with a lid; reduce the heat to low and "sweat" the vegetables for 5 minutes. Do not allow them to brown.

2. Remove the lid and discard the foil. Add the potatoes and the stock. Bring the liquid to a boil, then reduce the heat to low and simmer gently for 15–20 minutes until the vegetables are very tender. Remove from the heat.

3. Remove the vegetables with a slotted spoon to a food processor or blender and process the vegetables until smooth. Transfer the puree to a large bowl or container. Stir in the broth in which the vegetables cooked and the cream. Chill the soup until cold. Season with salt, pepper, lemon juice, and Tabasco, to taste. Garnish each bowl with a nasturtium blossom before serving. Serves 6–8.

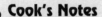

Cook's Notes

The herb gardener can try this soup with loveage instead of celery for an exotic summer cooler. It's especially good made with homemade vegetable stock, but canned chicken and vegetable broth are acceptable substitutes. When seasoning your soup, remember that cold food generally requires more seasoning than hot food.

Bay Scallop Sauté

1 1/2 pounds bay scallops

1 cup skim milk or buttermilk

1/2 cup cornmeal

1/4 cup flour

1 teaspoon paprika

salt (1/2 teaspoon or to taste)

freshly ground black pepper (1/4 teaspoon or to taste)

1. Place the scallops and milk in a large bowl. Cover the bowl and refrigerate for 30–60 minutes.

2. Meanwhile, spread a sheet of waxed paper or foil on a work surface and mix the cornmeal, flour, and paprika with salt and pepper until thoroughly combined.

3. Drain the scallops. Toss them with the cornmeal mixture until they are lightly coated. Remove the scallops to a clean piece of waxed paper or foil to dry for 20–30 minutes.

4. Heat a heavy 12" skillet over medium-high heat and thoroughly coat the pan with non-stick cooking spray or 1 tablespoon of vegetable oil.

5. When the pan is hot, cook the scallops in a single layer (do not overcrowd the pan), evenly browning them on all sides. Cook the scallops in batches if necessary, transferring the cooked scallops to a warm plate and holding them in a low oven. Serve immediately. Serves 6.

Cook's Notes

Serve the scallops with Sauce Andalouse from Chapter 8 or a good store-bought tartar sauce. Accompany this dish with a pre-cut vegetable slaw mixture tossed with your favorite vinaigrette and chilled until icy cold.

Swiss Chard Gratin

4   tablespoons olive oil

2 1/2   pounds Swiss chard, stems and leaves separated,
    stems sliced and leaves coarsely chopped

2   large leeks, cleaned and sliced

4–5   garlic cloves, peeled and chopped

1   teaspoon dried thyme leaves

1/4   pound proscuitto, chopped

1/2   cup water

1   large Idaho potato, peeled, quartered lengthwise and thinly sliced

1/2   cup grated parmesan cheese

    salt

    freshly ground pepper

    freshly ground nutmeg

3   eggs

1 1/2   cups toasted bread crumbs

1   teaspoon herbes de Provence

Cook's Notes

To clean Swiss chard, put the Swiss chard in a sink full of water and vigorously swish to expel any grit clinging to the leaves. Remove the stems by folding each leaf like a book and slicing off the stem. Chop the stems into halves and coarsely chop the leaves.

1. Heat two tablespoons of the olive oil in a large skillet. Cook the Swiss chard stems, leeks, garlic, thyme, and proscuitto over high heat until the vegetables begin to wilt. Reduce the heat to low, and continue to cook the vegetables, covered, for five minutes, until they soften.

2. Meanwhile, heat a large pot over medium-high heat. Add the Swiss chard leaves and one-half cup water. Cover the pot and steam the chard just until the leaves wilt (about 3–5 minutes).

3. With a slotted spoon, transfer the Swiss chard leaves to the skillet with the vegetables. Stir the potato into the vegetable mixture. Add the parmesan cheese and toss, seasoning with salt and plenty of freshly ground black pepper and nutmeg.

4. Break the eggs into a small bowl and beat them with a fork until blended. Mix the eggs with the vegetables until thoroughly combined.

5. Preheat the oven to 350°.

6. Oil a 9"×13" au gratin pan. Transfer the vegetables to the pan and smooth the top. Combine the bread crumbs and herbes de Provence and sprinkle over the gratin. Drizzle the remaining olive oil over the top. The recipe can be prepared a day ahead to this point. Allow the gratin to cool. Cover tightly with plastic film and refrigerate. Bring to room temperature before baking. Bake for 40 minutes. Serves 6.

Olive and Proscuitto Cake

$1/4$ cup lukewarm milk

1 package active dry yeast

5 large eggs, at room temperature

$1 1/4$ cups flour

6 tablespoons unsalted butter, softened

$1/4$ pound gruyere cheese, grated

1 cup cured green olives, pitted and sliced

$^1/_4$ pound proscuitto, whole and cut into dices

$^1/_2$ cup loosely packed flatleaf parsley leaves, minced

    freshly ground black pepper to taste

1. Preheat the oven to 325°.

2. In a large bowl, sprinkle the yeast over the milk. Let it rest for five minutes. When the yeast is foamy, add the eggs into the bowl and beat until well combined. Beat in the remaining ingredients with a large wooden spoon. Knead the dough for five to ten minutes, either by hand or with a mixer with the dough hook attachment, until a smooth, loose dough forms.

3. Transfer the dough to a 5–6 cup loaf pan and bake for 35 to 40 minutes or until well browned. Let the loaf cool for 10 minutes before cutting.

4. Slice the loaf into 1" thick slices and arrange the slices on a serving platter. Serve warm or at room temperature. Serves 6–8.

Cook's Notes

Serve the Olive and Proscuitto Cake with a sauceboat of warm Tomato-Pepper Compote. Look for the recipe in Chapter 16.

All-Purpose Stock

3–4 pounds chicken backs and necks

1 pound veal knuckle or neck bones

1 large carrot, peeled

1 large onion, peeled and stuck with 2 cloves

2 celery ribs with leaves

1 bouquet garni

> ### Cook's Notes
>
> Never salt a homemade stock. When using stock in a recipe, salt to taste after the dish is finished or a sauce is reduced. To make a bouquet garni, combine 1 bay leaf, 1 teaspoon dried thyme, 10 black peppercorns, 5 allspice berries, and several parsley sprigs and tie them in a small piece of cheesecloth.

1. In a large stock pot, place the meat bones and add water to cover the bones by two to three inches. Bring the liquid to a rapid boil over high heat. Skim off the foam as it rises to the surface. Foam will continue to form for about 20–30 minutes.

2. After the foam stops rising, reduce the heat to low and add the remaining ingredients. Simmer the stock for 4–6 hours, skimming occasionally.

3. Remove the pot from the heat and cool.

4. Using a fine mesh strainer, strain the stock into a clean bowl and discard the solids. Refrigerate the stock overnight.

5. Remove the accumulated fat from the top of the stock and discard. The stock can be refrigerated for two days or frozen for up to two to three months. Makes 8–10 cups.

> ### Cook's Notes
>
> For a brown stock, broil the bones and the unpeeled onion, cut in half, until they are well browned. Transfer the bones and onion to the stock pot along with any drippings in the broiler pan and proceed with the recipe.

Vegetable Stock

1 tablespoon olive oil

2 onions, peeled and sliced

2 leeks, cleaned and sliced

2 garlic cloves, peeled and sliced

3 carrots, peeled and sliced

1 fennel bulb, sliced

3 leafy celery stalks, roughly broken

2 cups of parsley, leaves and stems

1 cup mushroom stems

3 tomatoes, coarsely chopped

1 bouquet garni

2 cups dry white wine

3 quarts water

1. Heat the olive oil in a large stock pot and cook the onions, leeks, garlic, carrot, and fennel over high heat until they begin to soften. Add the remaining ingredients and bring the liquid to a boil. Reduce the heat to low and cook the stock for 40 minutes.

2. Remove from the heat and cool.

3. Strain the vegetable stock through a fine mesh strainer, pressing on the vegetables to extract as much liquid as possible. Stock can be refrigerated for 2–3 days or frozen for 2–3 months. Makes about 12 cups.

Part 5
Knowing What It Takes

One of the most common entertaining faux pas is not hiring help when you need it. This section will clue you in on when, why, and how to hire help for a party, and when you need a full-fledged catering outfit to take over the details.

People who like to entertain are generally top-notch guests themselves. However, let's reexamine the basics of good old-fashioned manners, because everyone needs a little brushing up now and then. Included are some extra little courtesies that will take you to the top of anyone's guest list.

I CAN THROW YOU ONE HECK OF A HOEDOWN!

Chapter 18

Letting Someone Else Do the Job

In This Chapter

➤ Off-premise catering

➤ Hiring bartenders, servers, and kitchen help

➤ Rentals

➤ It's the big one

Probably the first time you consider hiring a caterer for some or all of your party needs is when you've come close to pushing yourself over the edge with your last party. Take a realistic look at your party plans. Whenever an occasion exceeds your time constraints, cooking capabilities, or kitchen facilities, it's time to relegate part of the undertaking to someone else. It's impossible to be host, bartender, and kitchen staff when your guest list inches beyond ten people (of course, this doesn't apply to casual picnics, or potluck gatherings). Even if you're planning a completely make-ahead menu, hiring just one helper to act as bartender and server and clean up the kitchen makes a great difference. There are many options for hiring assistance for your party.

Off-Premise Catering

Off-premise catering describes food service operations that prepare all food off premise from where it is served. Within this realm we're blessed with a multitude of possibilities for tailoring party service to your needs. This segment of the food industry ranges from the self-employed cook, to small specialty businesses that will help plan, prepare, and deliver your party menu, to large firms that provide everything (tables, chairs, linens, decorations, flowers, food, liquor, bartenders, and servers).

This gives you, the buyer, plenty of latitude depending on the type of event you're hosting, how involved you'd like to be in the execution, and how much you want to spend. For catered events away from home, one generally engages a club, banquet hall, or hotel or restaurant party room. It's unlikely in this case that you can bring in an outside caterer. Ordinarily, you choose from a list of pre-set menus, and provide your own flowers and music. Beyond deciding upon a reliable operation that suits your style and price range, there's not much to do except write the check.

Smart Move
Some restaurants cater off premise, and skilled waiters often welcome an outside job now and then—as do some chefs.

Here, we'll focus on off-premise catering to explore the many different arrangements you can devise to suit your particular situation, party, and budget. It's even possible to cater your own party by seeking out the best carry-outs in your vicinity, planning a menu around their specialties, and hiring your own help. Check out these scenarios:

➤ *At a party for 10,* the hosts prepared their specialty main dish item. They bought an antipasto assortment from an Italian market for hors d'oeuvres and hired one kitchen helper. The helper had a dessert business (she provided desserts) and worked parties on the side.

➤ *At a party for 16,* the hostess prepared a risotto, salad, and dessert. The caterer provided hors d'oeuvres and sent one competent server who bartended, passed hors d'oeuvres, grilled the rack of lamb entree, helped serve and clear, and kept the kitchen under control.

➤ *At a larger event for 30,* the host prepared half the food and hired a chef to prepare the rest and manage all last-minute food preparation. A bartender and one clean-up person were also hired. The host rented extra tables and linens independently and booked a valet from a local restaurant.

➤ *For an al fresco summer fête for 50,* the caterer supplied everything: food, liquor, wine, service, tables, chairs, linens, tableware—even the tent and torchères.

There are as many caterers as there are options for their hire. How do you find the one right for you? Either a personal recommendation or a catered party that impressed you is far preferable to the telephone directory or other ads. Always, always ask for references. When asking friends or references about the caterer's competence, explore the process they experienced:

➤ How did the caterer work out the menu?

➤ What did your friend supply on her own?

➤ What were the caterer's or helper's strengths and weaknesses?

➤ How did your friend prepare for the caterer's arrival?

➤ Was the caterer pleasant to work with and did he take direction well?

➤ When and how was the caterer paid?

Lacking a recommendation, inquire at a favorite restaurant, or ask your boss or a business associate for the name of a caterer who's popular in town. When forced to use the yellow pages, conduct a personal interview with a caterer before hiring him. Seeing his operation says a lot about how he does business. Ask him to tell you about a party similar to the event you're hosting that he recently catered. Don't be shy. You're the customer. If you're put off by a snooty attitude, cross him off your list. Who needs a condescending ego pervading their party?

Reality Bites
Larger caterers usually add a surcharge for liquor they provide. When you buy your own wine, there is often a corkage fee (an extra charge per bottle beyond the cost of the wine). Be sure to inquire about surcharges and corkage fees when interviewing a caterer.

When you're hosting a large event, it's not uncommon to stage a run-through of the menu so you can sample your choices. Considering the cost, this is a courtesy that you should expect, not a favor. For smaller parties, if you frequent a quality carry-out, they're an excellent candidate for rounding out the menu. You know what they can do and what to expect.

Finally, what does a caterer need to know to establish a good relationship with her client and meet her client's expectations? Here are a few pointers from one of our favorite catering/specialty carry-out operations, *Paula's Pantry*, in Shaker Heights, Ohio, regarding important details a client is likely to overlook.

➤ What is your budget?

➤ Does the party have a theme?

➤ What time of day is the party and how long will it be?

➤ Is it formal or informal?

➤ Do you require servers, bartenders, or rentals?

➤ Are there favorite foods you want to incorporate into the menu?

➤ Are there foods you don't like?

➤ Will there be vegetarians at the party?

➤ Are you aware of any food allergies or medical restrictions?

➤ If this is a cocktail party, will the guests be eating dinner elsewhere?

The first step before calling a caterer is to zero in on how much you want to spend. It's not uncommon for an enthusiastic host to devote considerable time to planning an event, then faint dead away at the price tag. A competent caterer can propose alternatives to guide you as close to your ideal as possible.

It's important to provide as much information as possible about your party, personal likes and dislikes, and your style of entertaining before embarking on menu planning or deciding how much help you'll require. A menu and how it is served determines party staffing needs and influences cost. This can call for flexibility and compromises on your part to stay within a budget. When a caterer is in charge of the entire party, she will know what time to have her staff arrive. If you're hiring helpers on your own, make sure you allow them enough time to familiarize themselves with the kitchen, the bar, and how you want the meal served and cleaned up. You can't provide much guidance if you're dressing or arranging flowers when they arrive. Sometimes it's prudent to have helpers stop by a day or two before the party for a dry run, depending on the size of the event.

Reality Bites
Tipping etiquette. Tip 20 percent of the total bill. Give the tip to the head server to distribute among other staff, or divide and distribute the tip to each individual. Accordingly, tip helpers you have hired independently based on their bill.

Hiring Your Own Bartender, Servers, and Kitchen Help

Staffing your own party requires a little homework on your part. Think about some of the party scenarios we described. In the first one, the kitchen helper supplemented her dessert business income by working parties. At the second, the bartender worked for a caterer and also had cooking and serving expertise. If you are hiring one person for a sit-down dinner, this is the ideal. At the third party, the chef worked at a local restaurant. The bartender was a waiter from another restaurant and the valet came from a third restaurant.

There are many qualified individuals who freelance from other jobs or provide in-home party assistance as their primary occupation. Here's a list of possible sources for seeking them out:

➤ Restaurant waiters and kitchen staff

➤ Cooking schools

➤ Community colleges that offer a hospitality degree

➤ Job bulletin boards at any college or high school

Don't forget about employing your own children, nieces, or nephews. It provides them with a great job opportunity.

A given in the service industry is that anyone worth their salt is in demand. Plan ahead. Have the person to your home for an interview. Her conduct, bearing, and grooming will tell you a lot about her work habits. Ask her to describe several parties she serviced and ask for a few references. Be very specific about what you expect of her at your party. Her response should indicate confidence or a lack of it.

Once you have hired someone, don't forget to tell him where to park his car and what to wear. Have everything organized before he arrives. Use sticky notes to identify serving pieces. Provide lists that detail the sequence of serving, passing extra helpings, and clearing, complete with a time schedule. To spare time away from your guests, have the caterer's check and tip prepared and in an envelope. When you find someone good, hang on to him. Be sure to ask how far in advance you should call for future parties.

Rentals

Both nationwide and local outfits service the needs of the party-giver. Some focus exclusively on party equipment, and these are the operations where you will find everything right down to candlesticks, silver serving pieces, large coffeemakers, and barbecues. Consult your telephone directory for a complete listing or ask friends who they rent from.

When using a rental company for the first time, stop by their facility and inspect the condition of their equipment. Acquire a price list and ask about delivery and pick-up, and whether they charge for this service. How are the items delivered? Since you will be packing them up, this is an important consideration. For instance, do you want to make two runs before and after your party with 15 loose folding chairs jammed in your car? Or would you rather have them delivered and picked up, neatly packed in a canvas carrier that holds six chairs each and has a carrying strap for easy transport to the garage? Plates and glassware are inexpensive rentals with the added advantage of being easy to return— you simply scrape, rinse, and pack them up. The rental company does the dish washing. The same goes for linens—they do the laundry, not you.

Of course, it's entirely possible to borrow items from friends or relatives to round out your party needs. This calls for extra care on your part—polishing silver, laundering linens, and returning the borrowed fare at a time convenient for the lender. What if you break a friend's favorite platter? The convenience of using a rental company spares time and aggravation.

It's the Big One

So far, we've advised how to dive in and take charge of your entertaining needs for just about every conceivable kind of party. Not this time. When you decide to go for the big one and host a huge gala, be it a wedding, golden anniversary party, dinner dance or grand reception, hire an expert. Not just any caterer, but an established business experienced in managing large events. This isn't to say you can't celebrate a beautiful wedding, anniversary, or other special occasion on a smaller scale. But when you decide to go over the top with the details and guest list, it's a job for a professional.

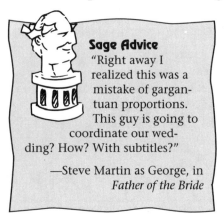

Sage Advice

"Right away I realized this was a mistake of gargantuan proportions. This guy is going to coordinate our wedding? How? With subtitles?"

—Steve Martin as George, in *Father of the Bride*

Bigger numbers call for bigger strategy and a facility capable of executing the details with utmost efficiency. The independent people you hired to help out with smaller parties and found so competent probably aren't the right choice for a big event. Let's say you hire Liz as the chef, Sarah for desserts, Kate to do table design, Charles and Ed for flowers, Steve to tend bar, and entrust Bill, Scott, and Holly to organize servers. You're asking for trouble, because when something goes wrong, who's in charge? You. What if someone falls ill the day of the big event? That's *your* problem. Who coordinates people who have never worked together before? You do. This is the time to entrust your party to a management expert.

Follow these guidelines:

➤ Start researching appropriate companies as soon as you have determined a date for your event.

➤ Rely on personal recommendations or a personal experience at a party for leads.

➤ Set up interviews and check out the company's place of business.

➤ You should *like* the caterer. You'll be working closely together on your party plans.

➤ Who will be in charge at the party? Meet them and establish a rapport before the event.

➤ Ask for a detailed breakdown of everything included in the cost.

➤ If you are signing a contract, read it carefully, don't skim. Look specifically for any details that relate to the type of occasion you're having.

If your heart is set on a grand occasion, we'll assume that you're willing to spend the money to do it right.

The Least You Need To Know

➤ Be realistic about your party plans and hire help when you need it.

➤ Off-premise catering offers many options for the entertainer.

➤ Freelance individuals can effectively meet many of your service needs.

➤ Renting rather than borrowing party equipment saves time and aggravation.

➤ Always hire a professional to manage a big event.

Many Happy Returns

Originally the word *hospitality* meant that one opened their house to any stranger who happened along, providing them with a meal and a bed. Somewhere along the way these drop-in guests must have worn out their welcome, because during the 1600s, bishops in England began limiting hospitality to friends and relatives. During the next few centuries manners became so well defined that one step out of line and the sorry guest was a social outcast.

Thank goodness we're no longer bound by the strict confines of Victorian etiquette. Today the casual mode reigns. But sometimes it seems we've thrown good old-fashioned manners completely out the window. Face it—an anything-goes attitude as a guest won't make for an embraceable you. A stuffy, contrived stance doesn't cut it either. There is a happy medium. Think of an invitation as a request for the pleasure of your company. Being yourself and encouraging good fellowship among other guests is the value you bring to a party. Here's the clincher: what constitutes agreeable companionship seems to be getting stretched beyond bounds these days—an invitation to someone's home is not an invitation to appear on The Oprah Winfrey Show. Leave your stress, issues, and baggage at home. Don't be a dysfunctional guest.

Another aspect of our casual modern culture that's to a guest's disadvantage is the predominance of hand-to-mouth feeding. It's entirely possible to receive adequate nourishment without ever touching a fork, knife, or spoon. Therefore, facing an array of flatware at a formal dinner can pose quite a dilemma. Good manners really haven't gone out of style; only the superfluous formulas. Welcome guests are always conscious of their deportment, keeping conduct, table manners, and conversations in good taste. Extending a few extra courtesies beyond this is the best compliment you can pay a host. Those invitations are sure to keep right on rolling in.

Sage Advice

"Behavior is a mirror in which everyone shows his image."

—Johann Wolfgang Von Goethe

Being a Good Guest Starts with the Invitation

Your responsibility as a guest begins with the invitation. Always respond promptly. Tossing an invitation into a mail pile is an opportunity for procrastination. Put it in a spot you can't ignore and reply within a week. If you can't commit to a telephone invitation then and there, also make a point to return the call within a week. Hopefully, your invitation supplies all the party details. If not, ask about attire, parking, and so forth well before the party to avoid plaguing your host with last-minute interruptions.

This is also the time to tell your host if you have any dietary restrictions. Maybe you feel uncomfortable about doing so, but what a terrible mistake not to! Dropping this little bomb as you sit down to the table, or picking around on your plate, really puts a host on the spot. Certainly you can't expect special treatment at a large gala event, but for more intimate occasions, always allow your host to respond appropriately. Offer to bring something you can eat if your host's menu poses a problem. If you're bringing a dish to a party for whatever reason, come equipped with everything to serve it. For instance, if you're supplying bread, cut it just before leaving for the party. Arrange it in a basket with a cloth napkin and bring butter or seasoned oil in a serving container. The basket and napkin can double as a host gift.

Arrivals

Two things are guaranteed to annoy a host right off the bat: arriving too early or arriving too late. *Never* come early to a party; these few moments before guests arrive are precious moments for a host. Fifteen to twenty minutes late is acceptable but a delay of thirty minutes or more requires a phone call. Of course, this doesn't apply to an open house or casual picnic, but it's particularly important at sit-down dinners. And—horror of horrors—should you forget a party, send a beautiful bouquet of flowers and a sincere note of apology with a brief explanation.

Conversation

Good conversation creates the synergy for a successful party. Make an effort to talk to new people. Draw them out by asking about their interests, or broach an interesting subject of positive substance. Even more important, be a good listener. Steer clear of intimate or depressing topics, and above all, never use a party as a soapbox opportunity for expressing strongly held views or for passionately pleading a cause.

What if you arrive at a party and there across the room is You-Know-Who—the last person in the world you want to see. Don't do the hokey-pokey around the perimeter of the room or hide out behind other guests to avoid them. Don't drag a friend off to wail your discomfort. The only sophisticated response is to make the first move. Approach the antagonist with a genuine smile and extended hand. There's no need to converse at length, but when you move on, you'll feel great.

Reality Bites

When your children are included in an invitation, don't assume that another guest is enamored by your little one's endless chatter or game of tic-tac-toe while you are socializing out of reach. Look after your kids when they're invited to a party.

Table Manners

Table etiquette is a courtesy rooted in practicality: You look civilized while eating; it keeps the table from resembling a Roman orgy; it allows servers to unobtrusively and efficiently do their job. Here's a review of the two accepted modes of managing fork, knife and spoon: American and European.

First, always wait for your host to commence the meal or for them to signal you to begin before picking up flatware or taking a sip of water or wine. In the American method, hold the fork in your left hand and the knife in your right hand for cutting. After cutting, rest the knife on the rim of your plate with the blade positioned toward the center of the plate. Transfer the fork to your right hand to eat. Point fork tines down for cutting and up for eating. Don't cut more than one or two bites at a time.

For the European method, the fork remains in the left hand for eating. Also, you may hold your knife while eating or rest it on the plate. When holding both knife and fork while eating, the knife negotiates morsels of food onto the fork.

Reality Bites

After a drink or two, expressive hands can swiftly topple a row of glasses like a stack of dominoes—at someone else's expense.

If you rest your fork during a meal, place it tines down on the left side of the plate. When you put down both fork and knife to pause for conversation (but haven't finished a course), place fork (tines down) and knife on opposite sides of the plate, tip pointing toward the center and handles slightly flared out. This indicates that you don't want your plate cleared. When you finish eating, place the knife and fork side-by-side, handles pointing toward your right shoulder and tips positioned toward the center of the plate. This tells a server to clear your plate and deters the possibility of utensils falling off the plate when it's removed.

Tines down pointing center for pause.

Tines down at right side of plate when finished.

If you use a spoon with the entree, place it to the right of the knife on your plate when you're finished. Never rest used flatware on the table. A used soup or dessert spoon rests on the underplate or in the center of the bowl. When you're served a multi-course dinner and face a mystifying array of flatware, use the utensils from the outside in for each successive course. When in doubt, observe your host and follow their lead. Sometimes a dessert fork and spoon or a soup spoon are placed above the dinner plate. If a bread and butter plate or salad plate are used, they will be to the left of your dinner plate.

At a sit-down dinner where courses are passed on a tray, or when helping yourself from a buffet, refrain from piling mounds of food on your plate. You're not chowing down in a mess hall, and it looks vulgar to others at the table. At the end of the meal, leave all dinnerware as is—*don't* push an empty plate away from you.

Now for the napkin: put it in your lap when you sit down. If you leave the table during dinner, it goes to the left of your plate. At the end of the meal, put the napkin on the table where the dinner plate was, or to the right of the plate. Last but not least, don't use your dining chair as a lounge chair.

A few archaic rules of the table that many people don't realize are perfectly acceptable today are:

The Extra Mile
The best dinner table is a friendly forum. Try to balance conversation with dinner partners on both sides of you and feel free to chat or banter across the table.

➤ If you are served bone-in chicken or other fowl, or a bone-in pork or lamb chop, it's perfectly acceptable to pick up the bone and nibble.

➤ It's okay to lightly rest your elbows on the table between courses.

➤ A piece of bread may be used to dab up sauce on your plate—just don't scour the plate.

Smart Move

If you encounter the uncomfortable situation where the persons on either side of you are engaged in conversation with someone else, briefly excuse yourself for the lavatory. Your return to the table will present the opportunity to rejoin a conversation.

Little Courtesies That Count

A host always remembers considerate gestures from a guest and makes the effort to include them in future parties. Besides, good words have a way of getting around. Here are a few tips for becoming a sought-after guest.

➤ Come armed with some fresh or amusing subjects for discussion.

➤ Bring a small, thoughtful gift.

➤ Be courteous to all guests.

➤ When a guest's conversation becomes argumentative or is leading into off-color subjects, attempt to redirect the topic.

➤ If an offer to help has been turned down, don't relentlessly persist.

➤ Never wear out your welcome.

➤ Send a thank-you note the next day.

Host Gifts

Two things about gifts: they should be thoughtful on your part and pleasing to the recipient. Guests aren't *expected* to bring host gifts. You're better off empty-handed than bringing any old thing you snatched in a rush or stuff from around the house that's impossible to ditch (like a fruitcake). To evaluate a gift, ask yourself if you would use it.

Then, for the acid test, ask yourself whether your host will use it. Never bring food meant to be served unless you were specifically asked to bring it. Of course, homemade preserves or pickles for the larder are always welcome.

As for wine, if your host appreciates fine wines, by all means bring a bottle. Seek out one you think he would particularly enjoy. However, wine is becoming a rather ubiquitous host gift. Take some time to think of a more personal token. If you don't know your host well, everyone loves flowers and they're always special. The rule of thumb to follow is send them ahead so your host has time to arrange cut flowers or work an arrangement into her scheme. A host's favorite flower (a single bloom) or seasonal potted bulbs or plants, such as narcissus in December, are fine to bring rather than send. Following are a few ideas for appropriate host gifts:

➤ Beeswax or hand-dipped candles or quality scented candles

➤ An interesting aperitif or cordial for the bar

➤ Seasoned oils or vinegars

➤ Fine candies

➤ Exotic teas or coffees and biscotti

➤ An ornament during the holidays

➤ A natural hand cream for the kitchen or guest bath

➤ Soaps for the kitchen or guest bath

➤ Fireplace matches

Etiquette for the Weekend Guest

Nothing beats spending one or two days relaxing with good friends. An awkward hour here or there just doesn't happen. Without offering or being asked, you just know what to do. But what about the overnight stay with an acquaintance who's less than intimate? Feel just a little bit uncomfortable? Start off on the right foot by offering to make all your own transportation arrangements. If you receive a genuine offer of assistance, accept. Always ask about an appropriate time to arrive, and inquire about weekend plans so you'll know what clothing to bring. It's also a good idea to throw a travel clock and a good book in your bag.

If you want to do something special for your host, don't spring any surprise that could intrude on his arrangements. Propose your gesture ahead of time: "Larry, a new carry-out

Smart Move
Allow yourself and your host some "time-out." Excuse yourself for an hour or so to nap or enjoy a good read.

in my neighborhood has fabulous canapés. Let me be in charge of cocktail time on Friday or Saturday," or "Sharon, pick a spot for us to take you and Lew for dinner in the city on Saturday." In any case, if a host refuses, *don't* argue or whine. Contrary to party etiquette, a weekend guest should always pitch in. Help with dishes, keep the bath tidy, don't leave your things lying around the house, and make the bed or strip it when you leave.

Gifts for the Weekend Host

Put some extra thought into a gift to bring to a weekend host. It can be in tune with a hobby or passion of your host, or perhaps something they would use and appreciate for future entertaining:

➤ Imported lavender sachets

➤ Coffee-table book

➤ Flowers

➤ A unique antique, china, or silver serving piece for the antique collector

➤ A clear crystal bedside carafe and tumbler

➤ A CD set for the music lover

➤ A serving tray, if you're bringing canapés or breakfast breads

➤ Linen hand towels for the guest bath or kitchen

➤ Regional specialties from your home town in an attractive basket

➤ Hand-dipped chocolates in a crystal or porcelain dish

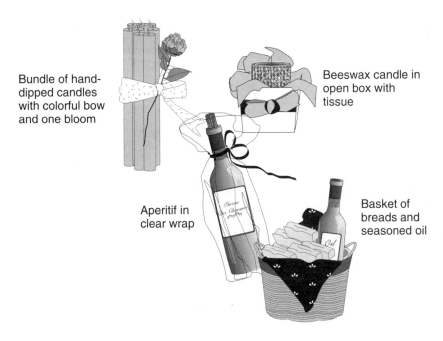

Use open gift wrap for host gifts.

Bundle of hand-dipped candles with colorful bow and one bloom

Beeswax candle in open box with tissue

Aperitif in clear wrap

Basket of breads and seasoned oil

The Least You Need To Know

➤ Thoughtfulness and good manners distinguish a good guest.

➤ Keep your conversations light and entertaining at parties.

➤ Adhere to appropriate etiquette at the dinner table.

➤ Bring a gift that will please rather than impose upon your host.

➤ A weekend stay calls for extra consideration.

The ABCs of Entertaining

Appetizers are a prelude to a meal. Serve appetizers that will enhance the appetite for the enjoyment of the rest of the meal. Never serve overly rich or heavy appetizers, and keep serving sizes small.

Burning the cut ends of stems of poppies, poinsettias, and hollyhocks and dissolving one tablespoon of salt in the water in the vase will keep the bouquet longer lasting.

Cooking terms and techniques you're likely to encounter when entertaining:

Blanching vegetables by immersing them in rapidly boiling water then quickly chilling them under cold water stops enzymatic action and sets the color of the vegetable.

Deglazing means lifting flavorful caramelized meat juices from the bottom of a sauté pan by adding a liquid, raising the heat, and stirring to capture and concentrate flavors.

Julienne is a method of cutting meats or vegetables into thin slivers. Using zucchini as an example, cut it in half lengthwise, place cut side down, and slice lengthwise into ¹/₄" slices. Stack several slices and cut into slivers.

Leeks often harbor sandy soil and should be thoroughly cleaned. Remove and discard the tough dark green leaves. Cut the leek in half lengthwise, keeping the root intact. Rinse the leek halves under cool running water, separating the leaves to flush out any sand. Shake dry and proceed to prepare them according to the recipe.

Sautéing means quickly cooking smaller pieces of meat, fish, or vegetables, uncovered, in a hot pan with a small amount of fat.

Stock (meat, fish, or vegetable broth) for making sauces must be homemade. Having some in your freezer is a valuable investment for the entertainer. Canned stocks are acceptable for soups but they cannot be reduced; it only concentrates salt and preservatives.

Decorative elements for a party should be in keeping with the theme or style of your event. Let them enhance your surroundings but never command your guest's attention.

Everyone responds to a thoughtful compliment. Take the time to speak to each of your guests and say something meaningful.

For **flower arrangements** follow these basic rules:

➤ Always cut flowers before arranging. The cell at the bottom of the stem is dead and will prevent water absorption. To cut stems, hold the flower in one hand and in the other hand position a small sharp knife at a 45° angle to the stem. Quickly pull the stem away to make the cut.

➤ Use tepid water and a floral preservative.

➤ Strip off any foliage below the water line.

➤ Flowers should be double the height of the vase.

➤ Mix form flowers (biggest) and fillers flowers (smallest) at a ratio of 30/70 percent.

Guestbooks provide enjoyable memories of wonderful parties and are helpful for documenting menus and guest lists for future reference.

Hosts should always "host" with a keen awareness of their guests and act as a guide to the flow of the party and the conversation.

Introduce new arrivals to everyone as soon as they enter a room to ensure that a warm and welcoming ambiance prevails.

Juniper branches on a white table, studded with tiny white flowers, make an elegant and festive wintertime dinner table.

The **key** to any successful party is your attention to detail. Another card to add to your index card party file is one with notes about guest's interests, preferences, job titles, and so forth. You'll never be at a loss generating spirited conversation.

Lighting has a definite impact on the mood of your party. Keep it soft and relaxing but remember that diners should be able to see what they are eating. A lampshade lined in peach-colored silk casts a flattering glow throughout any room and on your guests.

Master a few basic cooking techniques and use menus and recipes based on them when you entertain. Timing for cooking and serving will be under your command. Trying out new dishes and unfamiliar techniques for the first time at a party is asking for trouble.

Notepaper for invitations, place cards, and thank you notes in white or ivory double-weight card stock goes the extra mile, especially when written with a fountain pen. The simplicity is more impressive than elaborately embossed or designed cards.

Oasis is a dense material used for flower arranging and helps to adapt flower size and vase size. Keep some on hand in your butler's pantry.

Place cards are a courtesy at seated dinners when entertaining a large group. They spare a guest the discomfort of finding a seat when they aren't well acquainted with all of the company.

Quality, not quantity, is always the focus of a good party menu, table design, and other party decorations. Spend your dollars wisely on the freshest food, and buy only those entertaining accouterments that you'll use and love for years to come.

Roses will last longer when you cut the stems (at a 45° angle) under running water. Remove thorns and leaves below the water line and add 2 tablespoons of salt to the water in the vase.

Store pressed linens and napkins by rolling them on cardboard tubes. They'll stay smooth and wrinkle free. A hanger for large tablecloths should also have a broad cardboard roll to prevent creasing the cloth.

Temperature for doneness in meats should always be taken with an instant-read thermometer inserted into the thickest part of the meat. Bring meat to room temperature before cooking, and always rest meat after cooking; 5–10 minutes for small cuts and chops to 20–25 minutes for large roasts.

A reading of 115–120° is rare; 125–130° is medium-rare; 135–140° is medium; 150–160° is well-done and often dry. Reheat food at 325°. Hold food at 140°. Cook fish, any method, for ten minutes per measured inch of thickness, measured at the thickest part of the fish.

Universal is the term for good manners. Treat every guest in your home with respect and thoughtfulness. You as host set the example for your guests.

Vary the level of background music to set the appropriate tone; softly lilting for cocktails and dinner, a bit louder with after dinner coffee, then turned slowly down or even off when you want the party to end.

Wine and food compatibility is no longer dogma. Just about anything goes because the word today is that if you like the wine and you like the meal, the two will make a lovely marriage with few exceptions. One flavor that's an exception to this rule is horseradish—it can kill any wine. Consider the style of the food you are serving when choosing wines; serve robust wines with hearty dishes; food with a hint of sweetness calls for a little sweetness in the wine.

Xenium is the word for the ancient Greek custom of giving a gift to an honored guest or stranger. Small party favors are a charming gesture at a special party.

Yellow flowers never fail to brighten any space. They add a note of cheer and sparkle on dreary days.

Zero in on the important details of party planning and party design and decorations. Focus your energies on the essential elements and making a few special details top-notch. When you overdo, quality is sacrificed. Likewise, zero in on all your senses when you cook for a party. How does the food look, feel, smell, taste? People who are afraid of cooking simply haven't developed a relationship with food.

Index

D

291

299

S

301

When You're _____ _____ _____ o Know,
You _____ _____ _____ !

For all the ups and downs you're _____ _____ _____ e Complete Idiot's Guides give you down-to-earth answers and practical solutions.

The Complete Idiot's Guide to
Learning French on Your Own
ISBN: 0-02-861043-1 ▪ $16.95

The Complete Idiot's Guide to
Learning Spanish on Your Own
ISBN: 0-02-861040-7 ▪ $16.95

The Complete Idiot's Guide to
Gambling Like a Pro
ISBN: 0-02-861102-0 ▪ $16.95

The Complete Idiot's Guide to
Hiking and Camping
ISBN: 0-02-861100-4 ▪ $16.95

The Complete Idiot'
Choosing, Training,
ing a Dog
ISBN: 0-02-861098-

The Complete Idiot'
Trouble-Free Car C
ISBN: 0-02-861041-

The Complete Idiot'
Trouble-Free Home
ISBN: 0-02-861042-

The Complete Idiot'
Dating
ISBN: 0-02-861052-

The Complete Idiot
Cooking Basics
ISBN: 1-56761-523-6

The Complete Idiot'
the Perfect Weddin
ISBN: 1-56761-532-5

The Complete Idiot's Guide to
the Perfect Vacation
ISBN: 1-56761-531-7 ▪ $14.99

The Complete Idiot's Guide to
Getting and Keeping Your Perfect Body
ISBN: 0-02-861051-2 ▪ $14.95

The Complete Idiot's Guide to
First Aid Basics
ISBN: 0-02-861099-7 ▪ $16.95

The Complete Idiot's Guide to
Starting Your Own Business
ISBN: 1-56761-529-5 ▪ $16.99

The Complete Idiot's Guide to
A Great Retirement
ISBN: 1-56761-601-1 ▪ $16.95

The Complete Idiot's Guide to
Protecting Yourself From Everyday Legal Hassles
ISBN: 1-56761-602-X ▪ $16.99

The Complete Idiot's Guide to
_____ Job You Want
_____ 61-608-9 ▪ $24.95